The Secrets of Masonic Washington

"This is the best book to date on the Masonic influences on the formation and growth of the early American republic. Destined to be a classic, it seamlessly weaves the exotic and esoteric aspects of history together into a guided walking tour of America's occult greatness, showing that 'holy land' is not something that is found somewhere else but is right here beneath our feet. More than just a look at the past, it is a veritable tour of the future and of what America can be again."

MARK STAVISH, DIRECTOR OF STUDIES AT THE
INSTITUTE FOR HERMETIC STUDIES AND
AUTHOR OF *FREEMASONRY: RITUALS,
SYMBOLS & HISTORY OF THE SECRET SOCIETY*

"James Wasserman has an unparalleled track record prospecting in the Solomonic mines of occult worlds and emerging with 24-karat nuggets of secret history. He then subjects these to the assays of rational logic and analysis. From the Hashishim and Knights Templar of medieval times, to America's Founding Fathers of three centuries ago, Wasserman knows how to decode the symbols, unravel the secrets, and find historical gold."

DAN BURSTEIN, EDITOR OF
SECRETS OF THE CODE AND
SECRETS OF ANGELS & DEMONS

"James Wasserman provides us with an informative guidebook to the wondrous neoclassical monuments of Washington, D.C. Use it when you visit the nation's capital and become enlightened and one with its Founding Fathers."

ROBERT R. HIERONIMUS, AUTHOR OF
FOUNDING FATHERS, SECRET SOCIETIES AND
UNITED SYMBOLISM OF AMERICA

Minerva, Goddess of Wisdom, instructing famous inventors (including Freemasons Benjamin Franklin and Robert Fulton) in science, art, and geometry. Note the Mason holding a pair of compasses at left. Detail from *The Apotheosis of Washington* by Constantino Brumidi in the Capitol Rotunda. (Architect of the Capitol.)

THE SECRETS OF
MASONIC
WASHINGTON

A Guidebook to the Signs,
Symbols, and Ceremonies at
the Origin of America's Capital

JAMES WASSERMAN

DESTINY BOOKS
Rochester, Vermont

Destiny Books
One Park Street
Rochester, Vermont 05767
www.DestinyBooks.com

Destiny Books is a division of Inner Traditions International

Library of Congress Cataloging-in-Publication Data
Wasserman, James, 1948–
 The secrets of Masonic Washington : a guidebook to signs, symbols, and ceremonies at the origin of America's capital / James Wasserman.
  p. cm.
 Includes bibliographical references and index.
 ISBN 978-1-59477-266-5 (pbk.)
 1. Freemasonry—Washington (D.C.)—History. 2. Freemasonry—Symbolism—Washington (D.C.) 3. Freemasonry—Rituals—Washington (D.C.) 4. Symbolism in architecture—Washington (D.C.) 5. Washington (D.C.)—Guidebooks. I. Title.
 HS537.D52W37 2008
 366'.109753—dc22
                                                                2008032011

Printed and bound in India by Replika Press Pvt. Ltd.

10 9 8 7 6 5 4 3 2 1

Book design and typography by STUDIO 31 (www.studio31.com) and
 Jon Desautels/Destiny Books
This book was typeset in Sabon and Gill Sans

Photos are by James Wasserman unless otherwise noted.

The maps are reproduced courtesy of American Map Corporation and are copyright © 2007 Alexandria Drafting Company. They have been modified with permission for this publication.

AMERICA

May God continue

to shed His Grace on Thee

George Washington as Master of his lodge by Hattie Burdette. (Copyright the George Washington Masonic National Memorial Association. All Rights Reserved. Photography by Arthur W. Pierson, Falls Church, Virginia.)

CONTENTS

INTRODUCTION

HIDDEN IN PLAIN SIGHT

HIDDEN IN PLAIN SIGHT: thus would I describe the esoteric and occult symbolism of the sacred space of Washington, D.C. Sit down with a map of the city, pencil, ruler, protractor, and pair of compasses. You can draw pentagrams and hexagrams, triangles, crosses, circles, and other multiangled geometrical constructs that will fill the pages of books and websites with potentially erudite speculation and amazing detail. Many people have and many more undoubtedly will.

On the other hand, as we walk through the streets of Washington, D.C., in the course of this book, we will enter an eternal world populated by archetypes in stone—carvings, monuments, statues, buildings, and inscriptions. Like hierophants of the Mystery schools of antiquity, they silently communicate a curriculum designed to inspire, elevate, and teach eternal Truth. Washington, D.C., like Jerusalem or Mecca, offers a pilgrimage for those who seek a greater understanding of the miracle of their homeland and for visitors from other shores come to glimpse the hope of the first great free nation on earth.

Washington, D.C., is the central shrine of America's national religion. This is a nondenominational faith, in line with the Masonic ideal, capable of being shared by all who recognize God as that which has created and sustains the universe. Such is the primal deity worshipped by Christians, Jews, and Muslims, yet it is also the basis of Hinduism,

opposite. Sculpture of *Art* by Francois M. L. Tonetti-Dozzi in the Main Reading Room of the Library of Congress. The other figures in the series include Science, Religion, Law, Poetry, Commerce, Philosophy, and History. Also see pages 21–23. (Photo by Carol M. Highsmith.)

Buddhism, Confucianism, Paganism, and the New Age faiths—in fact every religion and spiritual path. We glance at a sunrise or sunset, a flower, the night sky, a sculpture or painting, the eyes of a baby or a beautiful woman, and find therein God—in whose Name we live and breathe and have our being.

The sacred interaction between heaven and earth is continually mirrored in the iconography of Washington, D.C. The most prominent is the Washington Monument, symbol of the human will aspiring to the heavens while remaining firmly rooted on earth. Washington was the first president, the victorious general who led us in the battle to win our freedom, the model against whom all leaders are judged. Yet, his monument offers a profound statement of impersonality, an expression of both the most austere severity and elegant symmetry—a far cry from the cult of personality dominating modern politics.

The Lincoln Memorial is a temple erected to the dream of equality before the law for all people, and of the indivisible nature of the American union. Lincoln is a modern sacrifice, an offering upon the altar of justice. It is ironic that the nation that dared to aspire to freedom was mired in the ancient institution of slavery. This stubborn holdover from the Colonial era ultimately resulted in the greatest loss of American blood in our history. Its unholy remnants still stain our national self-image. Lincoln sits in mute contemplation to remind us that evil will not be tolerated by the Forces that direct and sustain this country, that our duty is to rise above the errors and sins of our nature.

On the steps of the Jefferson Memorial, we begin our ascent to the world of pure thought, the elegant abode of intellectual clarity and moral rectitude. Standing proud and tall among some of history's most inspiring words, Jefferson gazes upon the city he helped design. His eyes are filled with understanding of the vicissitudes of fashion and the temptations of the moment. His will held firm, he counsels us to persevere with resoluteness on the course of Liberty. In his open rotunda, whose dome resembles an astronomical observatory seeking intimacy with heaven, he advises us to take the long view, that of the eternity in which he now resides.

Continuing on to the Capitol, the Temple of Liberty, we are surrounded by a magical pantheon of those who created a free nation. If we look up, we see the painting of the *Apotheosis of Washington* 180 feet above. Its outer rim proclaims that the gods of antiquity still walk among us. Minerva leads the way in science, rejecting superstition and "consensus," insisting on penetrating to the heart of reality with objective experimentation. Ever-active Mercury continues to inspire commerce as he did in Rome more than two thousand years ago. For he knows that those who close their minds to the benefits of trade have little reason to maintain peace when conflict arises between them, as it inevitably will. Neptune rules his watery realm, raising his trident of power to remind America that he controls some 70 percent of the surface of the earth, that the nation that does not sail mighty upon the sea will fall to the one who does, and that free access to shipping and fishing are as important today as ever. Ceres speaks similar words, pointing out that cultivation of the earth is the lot of human beings. Those who are successful in learning her secrets and pursuing her disciplines will prosper. Those who do not will wither and die. Vulcan leads his workers to the realization that we are put on this earth to build and fashion and construct. Humanity is made up of tool-wielding beings designed to imitate the creativity of their Maker. Finally, Columbia, the female personification of America, wields her sword in fiery demonstration that Freedom is not free. It must ever be defended, protected, and earned—sometimes through the age-old ordeal of trial by combat.

Washington, D.C., is simultaneously a hymnal and a history book, a shrine and a university, a prayer and a symphony. It is a memorial to truth in a culture of lies, a beacon of freedom in a world of tyranny, a ray of hope in the darkness of despair. Let us explore together its invigorating vision of courage and liberty, morality and lucidity, creativity and joy.

Freemasonry and the Cause of Human Liberty

The great object of Masonry is to promote the happiness of the human race.

—George Washington

T he unity between the philosophy of Freemasonry and the
founding ideology of America is well documented. The leadership
of Freemasons in the ceremonies establishing the nation and the capital
city will be recounted in the following pages, as will the artistic contribution
made by Masonic architects and designers. The Masonic membership
of some of the signers of the Declaration of Independence and the
Constitution will be highlighted, as will that of many other legendary
heroes of the Revolution.

There have also been a great many fallacies and urban legends about
Masonry and America, including a host of conspiracy theories that date
back to 1798, when two important but inflammatory books were published
on the Illuminati. If you look on the Internet today, you'll see that
the same alarmist nonsense about satanic influences and hidden agendas
remains alive and well.

Freemasons have been particularly reluctant to accept the membership
of those they cannot fully document with surviving lodge records.
This is commendable, but it may underrepresent certain individuals. Furthermore,
even if someone like Thomas Jefferson was not a Mason—or if
his membership records were destroyed by war, poor record-keeping, fire,

opposite. Medieval Freemasons at work, from Albert Mackey's *History of Freemasonry.*

or other natural occurrences—his spiritual and emotional sympathy with Masonry, his friendship with demonstrable Freemasons whose affiliation records have survived, and the ideals he expressed in his life and writings, all show a remarkable degree of consonance with Masonry.

On the other hand, attributing membership to people who were not Freemasons is intellectually dishonest. The Enlightenment ideals represented in the founding of America were "in the air." The fact that Masonry was a well-organized and representative channel of those ideas made it a wildly popular and successful part of Colonial and post-Revolutionary America. The beauty and integrity of the message of Masonry continues to resonate within America and throughout the world—and, hopefully, will continue to do so for a very long time.

In this book, I will attempt to be as accurate as possible regarding any statements of membership by following the restrictions of accepted modern Masonic scholarship as best as I understand it. However, the broader theme of the permeation of eighteenth-century and later American thought by Masonic and Enlightenment ideology will be obvious in the photographic record of the iconography of the capital.

OPERATIVE FREEMASONRY

Masonry's roots are generally acknowledged to extend to the medieval guilds and trade associations among European stonemasons, men who traveled well beyond their known boundaries to participate in the enormous efforts of church and castle construction. The near-miraculous ability to erect those vast architectural monuments reaching from earth to heaven, raising massive pre-fitted stones hundreds of feet in the air, supporting unimaginable weight with seemingly effortless elegance on completion, decorating these edifices with stained-glass windows that diffused light like the radiant luminosity of direct contact with the Holy Spirit—all imbued Masonry with an aura of mystery, religious significance, and mastery of the secrets of nature.

Medieval guilds of stonemasons were also legally able to establish unique sets of rules and procedures for themselves that included setting criteria and standards for trade practices, establishing qualifications for various levels of workmen, resolving disputes, and electing officers to administer guild activities. The freedom to pursue limited self-government was exceptionally rare during the Middle Ages. Members looked out for their own interests financially and fraternally, establishing charitable funds and other forms of mutual aid to sustain one another. Freemasonry functioned as an early proper form of trade union.

Since they were able to travel to various construction sites throughout western Europe, masons were considered "free of any city," and thus became known as "Freemasons."[1] As strangers with no local roots, they tended to gather themselves together at various worksites. They would erect temporary quarters or lodges where they might live, conduct business, and socialize. They were an itinerant group with widely divergent levels of skill. Builders would range from laborers and unskilled workers, to fine craftsmen, architects, and designers.

Standing somewhat apart from the rigidly enforced power structure of the crumbling feudal system during the later Middle Ages—along with professionals such as lawyers and doctors, merchants, and skilled artisans—Freemasons were part of the dawn of the middle class. The rise of middle class interests would be at the forefront of the call to arms for civil and religious liberty.

Stonemasons developed secret signs and words to allow them to identify their various levels of skill and knowledge. Differing knowledge brought differing rates of responsibility, pay, and prestige. The very lives of fellow workers and many others depended on the integrity of the process of determining competence. If a cathedral collapsed because of flawed design, hundreds might die. Those of higher skill would share their learning with those they deemed worthy of the effort. Upon successful completion of an apprenticeship and examination, such a student would be entrusted with the signs and words of the new level he had attained. Absent modern communication methods, the best way such men could identify themselves was through such mutually agreed upon trademark secrets. This stage of Masonry is called "operative Masonry."

SPECULATIVE FREEMASONRY

In the mid-seventeenth and early-eighteenth centuries, British Masonic lodges expanded to include those educated and philosophic souls attracted to what they believed to be the spiritual wisdom of sacred architecture. The entrance of non-craftsmen into Masonry is known as "speculative Masonry." It has been the trend of membership ever since.

Masonry developed a resonance among the educated elite. This closed society of geometricians, whose skilled work increasingly decorated the landscapes of Europe, stimulated the imagination of many in the nobility, whose interests as a class may heretofore have been limited to the mastery of martial skills. Elias Ashmole, a founding member of the Royal Society, antiquarian, alchemist, and reputed Rosicrucian, is the first known speculative Mason to be initiated when he joined an operative lodge in 1646.[2]

The Grand Lodge of England was formed in 1717 from four London lodges including both craftsmen and non-craftsmen. It was led by a non-craftsman. Within ten years, speculative Masonry was the rule. Speculative Masonry envisions the greatest building project as the construction of living cathedrals within the human heart to serve as fit temples for the indwelling of the Lord.

Geometry was elevated as a higher standard of truth. The ability to convert plans drawn on paper to structurally sound edifices was seen as partaking of the divine ordering of the universe. The well-known Masonic "G" stands for both "God" and "Geometry." In the familiar emblem of American Freemasonry, it is set in the center of a hexagram formed by the compassess and square. The compasses speaks to circumscribing desires and actions with reference to the square of exacting principles of morality and self-control. God is known in Masonry as the "Grand Architect of the Universe."

Yet, Freemasonry is not a religion. It incorporates the essence of all religions in its nondenominational belief in a Supreme Being that does not challenge the religious tenets of its members—whether Christian, Jewish, Muslim, or Deist. While a belief in God is a condition of mem-

The Compasses and Square with the letter G in the center is the predominant emblem of American Freemasonry. The oldest known reference in the United States is an ink and watercolor drawing of the Green Dragon Tavern made in 1773. Paul Revere cast a gilded brass piece in 1796. In 1873 a patent application by a flour manufacturer to trademark the Compasses and Square for commerce was rejected by the U.S. Patent Office on the grounds that it was a familiar Masonic symbol.

bership, Masonry is not a replacement for religion. In fact, Freemasons are assured in their earliest ceremonies that nothing in their oaths will be contrary to law, religion, and morality or inconsistent with their civic obligations.

ANCIENT MYSTERIES

Some Freemasons have claimed a mythic derivation for their craft. In Genesis, after Cain received the mark that would protect him from his fellow man, he built the first city and named it Enoch after his son. Some five generations later his descendant Tubal-cain became the first metalworker, "an instructor of every artificer in brass and iron."[3] It is said that the principles of Masonry were carved into a stone pillar and discovered after the Flood. Freemasons include in their spiritual genealogy such widely respected predecessors as the Egyptian Mystery schools, Pythagoreans, Hermetic brotherhoods, Essenes, Jewish Qabalists, and Druids.

The central myth of Freemasonry is derived from the biblical account of Hiram Abiff, the master builder, commissioned by King Hiram of Tyre and King Solomon of Israel to direct the construction of Solomon's

Hiram Abiff in prayer by Allyn Cox. (Copyright the George Washington Masonic National Memorial Association. All Rights Reserved. Photography by Arthur W. Pierson, Falls Church, Virginia.)

Temple in the tenth century B.C. Although this story is not mentioned in the Bible, Freemasons tell of Hiram being accosted by three Fellow Craft workers who illicitly demanded the Master Mason's word and signs. Possession of these secrets implied knowledge of a sacred nature. Hiram refused to betray his oaths and pass on this information to the unworthy. He was murdered by the villains.

Masonry incorporates the basis of Judaeo-Christian culture in its teaching. It is founded on biblical roots, demonstrates respect for ancient wisdom, cultivates charity, and promotes the highest standards of personal ethical behavior. It is concerned with building men of good character and broad tolerance.

INITIATION

The Entered Apprentice, Fellow Craft, and Master Mason degrees derive from the common medieval trade guild structure and its ranks of Apprentice, Journeyman, and Master. The introductory degree stresses a code of honor and Craft practices, as well as conveying secret signs and handshakes of recognition. The Fellow Craft degree reveals the more esoteric significance of sacred geometry. The Master Mason degree emphasizes the candidate's connection with the three archetypal masters of antiquity—Solomon, King Hiram of Tyre, and Hiram Abiff, the Widow's Son—and the legacy of wisdom they bequeathed to sincere seekers after truth.

Masonic rituals share universal themes with esoteric societies the world over. The candidate experiences a dramatic situation of humiliation, danger, and dependence. He is forced to rely on his own courage, integrity, and internal resources. If blindfolded, he learns it is a symbol of his inability to perceive truth; if raised from a moribund state, he is taught this represents the power of the human soul to overcome death. The mystery plays and symbolism of the order are designed to lead him to a higher and more noble state. He becomes aware of the beneficence of lodge members, who allow him to pass through these experiences without causing him undue harm in his vulnerable condition. The bonds formed between the candidate and the lodge are a central part of the initiation experience. Effective ritual penetrates consciousness to effect personality change on a fundamental level. Such transformative experiences are the essence and genius of initiation.

The use of symbol and ritual speaks to a magical aspect of Masonry as does its emphasis on ancient lore, sacred architecture, fraternal secrets, and divine revelation. These have all tended to characterize it as a spiritual and esoteric brotherhood, in addition to its exoteric identity as an association of men of goodwill. Eighteenth-century Freemasons scorned the popular traditions of low magic. Yet, the intellectual classes of Europe had been exposed to the traditions of spiritual or high magic since the translation of a number of Hermetic writings in the latter half of the fifteenth century. The practice of spiritual magic is an integral part of Hermeticism. Although Freemasonry at large has never been interested in magic, the Hermetic disciplines were pursued in depth by such Masonic luminaries as Elias Ashmole. When Albert Pike published *Morals and Dogma* in 1871, he reasserted Masonry's connection with the Mystery schools of antiquity and Hermeticism.

THE ENLIGHTENMENT

> It was not an event but a way of thinking, a desire to reexamine and question received ideas and values and explore new ideas in new ways. Through an empirical methodology, guided by the light of reason, one could arrive at knowledge and universal truths, providing liberation from ignorance and superstition that in turn would lead to the progress, freedom and happiness of mankind . . . "Truth," "freedom," "liberty," and "progress" were words alluded to in nearly every work of art, public speech and publication. [4]

Names like Isaac Newton, Elias Ashmole, John Locke, Voltaire, Diderot, Benjamin Franklin, and Thomas Jefferson resound through the centuries in testament to the Age of Enlightenment, the glorious eighteenth-century leap beyond the confines of ignorance, superstition, and fear. The eighteenth-century world was one whose doors had been opened wide by the power of the printing press and corresponding growth of literacy. The astronomical realm of the heavens had become visible with the seventeenth-century invention of the telescope, revealing an honorable Creation in which humanity was invited to assume its rightful place.

New trends swept through literate circles. Philosophically minded readers were exposed to the prolific ideas of the *philosophes*, who preached a gospel of reason, civil liberty, human dignity, personal responsibility, and the brotherhood of man. Thinking became fashionable, and social gatherings were devoted to the interchange of ideas. In England, and later in America, these gatherings took place at taverns and dining clubs, in France at the salons and parlors of the wealthy and educated, and in Germany in the newly popular reading rooms.

Following the liberating effects of the Renaissance in the fifteenth century and the Protestant Reformation in the sixteenth, the Enlightenment continued to open the gates of European thought and creativity. People became increasingly free of the tyranny of the monarch and priest with which they had been shackled since at least the fourth-century consolidation of church and state under the Roman emperor Constantine.

The eighteenth-century rise of speculative Masonry in Britain was fueled in part by uniting Enlightenment themes of reason, humanism, sociability, gentility, and philosophy. Yet, while freeing people from the chains of superstition and dogma, the Enlightenment's emphasis on reason left a corresponding hunger for direct contact with the divine. Masonry's genius lay in combining the enduring tenets of religion and the quest for the wisdom of eternity. The legendary histories and rituals of initiation hearkened back to a time when the complexities and turbulence of modern life were as yet unknown, and experience with higher wisdom was possible. Some more esoterically inclined speculative Freemasons sought after gnosis—direct personal contact with the very sources of knowledge and religion.

Discussions of religion were forbidden within the Masonic lodge. A man was entitled to privacy of belief, an alien concept in the preceding centuries of European culture. Deism, Christianity, and Judaism were all treated with respect. At a time when the European intelligentsia were becoming increasingly aware of ancient faiths, Masonry was comfortably positioned to act as a broad-based, nonexclusive repository for the universality of spirituality, whose acceptance was not challenged by Enlightenment values of rationality.

A new examination of social and political organization was also taking place. Early visionaries such as the British Lord Chancellor Thomas More (1478–1535) perceived new possibilities for human society. Executed for refusing to acknowledge the right of Henry VIII

overleaf. The Main Reading Room of the Library of Congress is the American shrine to learning, culture, and intelligence. It is a reification of the principles of the Enlightenment. Sculptures appearing between the arches on top of the columns represent Art, Science, Religion, Law, Poetry, Commerce, Philosophy, and History. Also see page 8. (Photo by Carol M. Highsmith.)

left. Sir Francis Bacon in the Main Reading Room of the Library of Congress. (Photo by Carol M. Highsmith.)
above. Sir Isaac Newton at the entrance to the National Academy of Sciences

to establish the Church of England, More was canonized as the patron saint of statesmen. His book *Utopia,* published in 1516, posited a well-ordered island civilization based on principles of reason and religious tolerance.

A century later, author, statesman, occultist, and philosopher Sir Francis Bacon (1561–1626) wrote *New Atlantis,* published posthumously in 1627. The island paradise he described was replete with scientific and architectural marvels, including "Solomon's house," an academy of higher learning that taught the principles of reason, tolerance, charity, healing, and virtue, and the experimental method. Bacon's vision of the New Atlantis was influential in eighteenth-century thought and among the Founders of the American republic.

The scientist and mathematician Sir Isaac Newton (1642–1727) lived during the Enlightenment period proper. He and his fellow scientists were responsible for the growth of the scientific method of experimentation and observation. Yet Newton also studied alchemy and biblical prophecy. In his important scientific work *Principia,* Newton claimed that his understanding of the mathematics of planetary motion had been known by ancient scholars such as Archimedes and Euclid. Fellows of the Royal Society, of whom Newton was one, were quite active in Masonry, making up more than one-quarter of the membership in the 1720s.[5]

The neoclassical style of architecture, stressing simplicity of ornament, reached back to the ancient themes of Greek and Roman building It was widely promoted by members of the Craft. The famed architect in charge of the rebuilding of London after the devastating fire of 1666, Sir Christopher Wren (1632–1723) was another founding member of the Royal Society and was believed to have been an important participant in the growth of Freemasonry.[6]

Early Freemasons embraced the political philosophy of John Locke (1632–1704), whose ideas were also of great importance to America's Founding Fathers. Locke declared that human beings have natural rights and that reason and rational self-interest motivate people to freely establish governments by their own consent and for their own benefit. Conversely, citizens bear the natural duty to respect and cooperate with a properly constituted government to enjoy the purpose for which they have banded themselves together.

> Men being . . . by nature all free, equal, and independent, no one can be put out of this estate and subjected to the political power of another without his own consent, which is done by agreeing with other men, to join and unite into a community for their comfortable, safe, and peaceable living, one amongst another, in a secure enjoyment of their properties, and a greater security against any that are not of it.[7]

However, should rulers usurp the authority granted them by the people, the citizenry has the right and duty to rebel. Locke also advocated that government be divided into executive, legislative, and judicial functions that were independent of one another and subject to written law.

GROWTH OF FREEMASONRY
IN EUROPE

The four original British lodges that joined to form the Grand Lodge of England in 1717 grew to one hundred forty by 1735.[8] Masonry included members of Parliament and other nobility. Its roots in the operative craft of stonemasonry also continued to attract members of the middle class. Thus it tended to increasing social mobility by breaking down the rigidity of the class structure.

The fraternity expanded rapidly on the Continent. By 1735, lodges met regularly in Madrid, Paris, Hamburg, and The Hague. Scotland and Ireland established independent grand lodges. In 1738, the Pope issued an encyclical banning all participation in Masonry under threat of excommunication. This proved largely ineffective in limiting Masonic growth among Catholics and may even have encouraged it among Protestants.

Although Masonry, in theory, rejected the privilege of birth, members naturally enjoyed the status that contact with the higher classes conferred. There was great delight when kings and nobles in Britain, France, and elsewhere began to join. Of course, as other aristocrats, wealthy businessmen, and professionals learned of the membership of such illustrious individuals, they too were attracted. In early American Masonry, this was mirrored by the membership of the Colonial elite.

With the appointment of the first noble British Grand Master in 1721, elaborate public processions of Freemasons became common. Theater outings, parades, and newspaper articles brought Masonry to popular attention. Though a secret society in terms of its lodge activity, rituals, gestures, and words, Masonry was a prominent feature of the eighteenth-century cultural landscape.

COLONIAL AMERICA AND MASONRY

Organized Masonic activity in America officially began in 1730 with the chartering of a provincial Grand Master for Pennsylvania, New

Jersey, and New York by the London Grand Lodge. St. John's Lodge in Philadelphia, which began to meet circa 1730, appears to have been the first lodge organized in the New World. By 1738 lodges had been started in Philadelphia, Boston, Savannah, New York, Charleston, and Cape Fear. By 1765, Freemasonry was firmly established in all thirteen colonies.

Colonial Masonry was at first an activity of the wealthy elite—Anglophiles, who rejoiced in the connection to the aristocratic and royal elements of the British lodges. Masonic public pageantry and processions also took place in America and were elaborate affairs. An account of a 1755 ceremony in Philadelphia at the opening of the first Masonic hall in America describes 127 men decked in full regalia of aprons, badges and jewels, white gloves and stockings, some with swords, and a contingent of musicians and stewards carrying batons, an open Bible and the Masonic Book of Constitutions carried on crimson pillows, all followed by carriages, coaches, and chariots. The son of Benjamin Franklin was joined by the mayor, the provincial chief justice, the governor, the former governor, the provost of the College of Pennsylvania, and Benjamin Franklin himself.[9]

In practice, such lofty interactions were often wedded to conviviality and occasional boisterousness. Lodge meetings were followed by refreshment and the opportunity for socializing—a mainstay of the fraternity. Decorum was generally observed as part of the Enlightenment emphasis on politeness, but occasionally "boys would be boys." While neighbors might complain about such behavior, most lodges and members sought to maintain an air of respectability that separated them from the secular and self-indulgent eating and drinking clubs that also abounded.

Masonic social activities included sponsoring plays, banquets, and balls. These provided opportunities for interaction with the fairer sex for unmarried brethren, and shared entertainment for married couples. Such events encouraged family harmony by allowing husbands and wives to enjoy each other's company in Masonic settings.

MASONRY'S LINK WITH AMERICA'S
REVOLUTIONARY DESTINY

The Masonic philosophy embodied the political movement under way in America to promote individual liberty and establish a broad-based national identity that encouraged fraternity and equality. Masonic ideals helped the young nation to move beyond the familiar model of a hereditary monarchy and stratified aristocracy exemplified by England. It advocated a meritocracy, in which all people were regarded as equal in the eyes of God and under the law, and they were free to develop themselves to the highest degree to which they aspired, and for which they were willing to work.

High moral character was an essential precept of Masonry. A man's word should be considered his bond. *Honor, discipline,* and *mutual respect* were the bywords of the code of conduct designed to make good men better. Proper manners and social skills, respect for education and learning, and refinement of behavior were all highly esteemed and taught in the lodge. In the rough and tumble world of brawls and vulgarity, Freemasons sought a more polished elegance. A middle-class merchant could become familiar with the behavior he needed to learn as the social fabric of the New World loosened and he might achieve upward mobility.

A good-natured social organization looked at a more optimist impulse in man. John Locke suggested that men were capable of self-government and the beneficent ordering of their passions to a positive end. Masonry offered encouragement along these lines. The meritocracy was perceived as the best means of developing a natural aristocracy of ability to the benefit of humanity. Social distinctions were not ignored, but they ceased to be either chains of bondage for the more talented members of the lower classes or badges of privilege for incompetent members of the higher classes. Education, professional standing, good manners, and successful wealth creation allowed for a broadening of the higher class—an expansion of the elite beyond the terms of birth.

The high principles of Masonry were particularly welcome in the uncertain times leading up to the Revolution. American society was struggling with conflicting political loyalties, denominational conflicts among competing sects, cultural and language issues resulting from increased non-English-speaking immigration, and the problems of balancing self-government with being an English Colonial province. Masonry offered itself as a cultivated and ordered society of far-thinking individuals who could help mediate differences.

ANCIENT AND MODERN FORMS

In 1757 a lodge was established in Philadelphia that would change the nature of Freemasonry in America. The new lodge called itself "Ancient." The members designated the established, more elite lodges, as "Modern." The movement began among Irish brothers in London in the 1740s who rejected the authority of the London Grand Lodge, noting its weakening appeal. They claimed the "Moderns" had revised the old rituals and lost their moral right to represent the Craft. An Ancient grand lodge was formed in London in the early 1750s. The Ancient movement bridged class distinction, both in England and America, and it grew rapidly. By 1760, American Ancient lodges succeeded in organizing their first grand lodge in Philadelphia.

Ancient Masonry was instrumental in the Revolution and in post-Revolutionary society. By 1800, most of the Modern lodges had folded into the Ancients. The values of equality and independence hailed by the Revolution were reflected in the more broad-based appeal of the Ancients, who tended to be less loyal to England than the Moderns were. (In 1813, British Ancients and Moderns joined together to form the United Grand Lodge of England.)

As the American population grew and commerce expanded, Ancient lodges sprouted up within the interior of the country instead of just the coastal centers, as had been the trend among the more wealthy and urban Moderns. Expanded membership opportunities also helped stimulate commerce among brothers in the port cities and interior manufacturing regions, and this helped increase international trade.

MASONRY ON THE EVE OF
THE REVOLUTION

Political protest against England, economic boycotts, and widespread dissent were growing throughout the colonies in the latter half of the eighteenth century. The lodges were prohibited from political activity, but members shared these concerns. Masonic oaths acknowledged the legitimacy of the political order and the civic responsibilities of Freemasons. However, the conflict between Masonic ideals of liberty and the increasingly tense situation with England weighed heavily on all Americans.

During this time, lodges were disrupted by internal political divisions. For one thing, England had been the source of all American Masonic activity. Members had a sense of loyalty to those who had chartered them. Colonists in general, and Freemasons in particular, were at odds on the course to adopt regarding England. Opinion ranged from those who supported continuing dependence upon and obedience to the king; those who sought a legal Parliamentary solution to the question of independence; those whose strong family and commercial ties to England overcame any political concerns; and those who supported a complete break with the mother country.

A significant number of important Masonic leaders supported the cause of Revolution. The fact that the Ancients (for the most part) tended to support the patriot position and the Moderns the loyalist cause may have contributed to the decline of the Moderns. The goals of the American patriots were consistent with the goals of the fraternity. The brotherhood was an important organizing center of the Revolution. And despite logistical problems created by the war, the Ancients grew at a brisk rate during the Revolution.

St. Andrew's Lodge in Boston attracted many of the leading lights of Revolutionary opposition including Paul Revere, John Hancock, Dr. Joseph Warren, James Otis, and William Dawes. In 1764 the lodge purchased the Green Dragon Tavern where it had met since 1752, and it rented out meeting space to a number of groups involved in the coming breach with England. One of these was the Sons of Liberty, led by Joseph Warren, then Master of St. Andrews Lodge and later a Revolutionary general who died at the Battle of Bunker Hill. The infamous Boston Massacre of 1770 was provoked, in part, by members of the lodge who ratcheted up the level of violence during the street protest against new British taxes. When British troops fired on the crowd, there was a huge public outcry over the deaths of five civilians and the wounding of six more—amplified by the propaganda campaign emanating from the Green Dragon. The Boston Tea Party of 1773 was organized at the tavern and included members of the lodge.

THE MILITARY

In 1755, the first year of the French and Indian War in America, there were at least twenty-nine military lodges attached to various regiments within the British army, primarily affiliated with Irish and Scottish grand lodges.[10] King George demanded that American colonists share the burden of war and train and fight alongside British soldiers. Thus, Masonry was spread within the Colonial militias. Rank-and-file militia members tended to be of far lower economic status than the elite members of English-chartered Modern lodges.

The more humble social standing of the Ancients led them to actively recruit within the military. The net effect of military Masonry was the dissemination of Masonry's teachings among the working class—bringing Enlightenment philosophy to less literate Americans. These were people who did not study the writings of the philosophes and other thinkers. Yet they, too, were enflamed and inspired by liberty and equal rights.

Masonry was valuable within the military for another reason. When the Continental army was formed during the Revolution, the first group of officers were men of high status. However, the availability of such men was reduced by several factors. The first was that the wealthy elite were often British loyalists. The second was that if wealthy men were patriots, they often served as leaders of their state militias. It was obvious that trained and talented soldiers were available in the wider pool of Colonial American militia members.

But General Washington's Continental army differed from the state militias. He discouraged fraternization among officers and enlisted personnel, demanding a more formal organization. Elevation of common-born Americans in military rank might be accompanied by some social discomfort. Freemasonry offered a natural remedy for those raised above their original station in life. It encouraged training in good manners and decorum, the social graces, a sense of personal dignity and status, and nonthreatening association with the well to do. The natural hierarchical divisions of the lodge also helped new officers adjust to their leadership roles.

For soldiers of all ranks, separated from homes, friends, and families, Masonry provided camaraderie and an antidote to loneliness and isolation. It also offered spiritual comfort for those of differing denominations. There were at least ten military lodges within the Continental army.[11] More than one story exists of fraternal kindness, respect, and compassion extended between British and American brothers on opposite sides of the conflict.

POST-REVOLUTIONARY MASONRY

Escalating tensions with England prior to the Revolution had raised concerns in the American fraternity because of Masonry's claims to an unbroken tradition tracing back to antiquity. Following the break with England, American Freemasons gradually organized a system of grand lodges administering the affairs of each state, beginning with Virginia in 1778.

The fraternity grew by leaps and bounds after the Revolution. Masonry was inextricably entwined with political leadership to the benefit of both the Craft and the nation. The acknowledgment, teaching, and celebration of high-minded spiritual values were important in the grand experiment of self-government. Republics are erected on the virtues of their citizens, and Masonry taught the lessons of duty, self-sacrifice, concern for the good of the many, and individual morality. "[M]any post-Revolutionary Americans came to see Masonry as an archetype of the republican society based on virtue and talent they were attempting to build."[12]

Masonry was more important in the political life of post-Revolutionary America than at any time before or since. Four of the fourteen presidents of the Continental Congress were Freemasons, as were nine of the fifty-six signers of the Declaration of Independence, thirteen of the thirty-nine signers of the Constitution, and thirty-three of the seventy-four generals of the Continental army.

Steven Bullock writes that from 1804 to the late 1820s, every New York governor but one was a Mason; in North Carolina between 1776 and 1836, Freemasons served as governor for forty-eight of sixty-one years; seven of the thirteen cabinet members of James Madison's administration during the War of 1812 were brothers; and more than half of Andrew Jackson's cabinet were members.[13]

To date, fourteen American presidents have been initiated Freemasons, including George Washington, James Monroe, Andrew Jackson, James K. Polk, James Buchanan, Andrew Johnson, James Garfield, William McKinley, Theodore Roosevelt, William Howard Taft, Warren Harding, Franklin D. Roosevelt, Harry Truman, and Gerald Ford.

ECONOMIC TRENDS IN
EARLY AMERICA

In both Colonial and post-Revolutionary American society, Masonry was a force for improvement. On a philosophic level, Masonic values challenged the established Colonial order of New World aristocratic elite inherited from England. Politically, it provided opportunities for an expanding middle class of merchants and artisans to participate in discussions and organizing efforts to effect change in government consistent with Masonic principles of liberty. And in business, Masonry provided opportunities for strangers to meet within the boundaries of mutual trust and fellowship offered by lodge settings.

The majority of new members were in their midtwenties, the period of life when men are engaged in launching careers. Although the guild idea may not have been active in speculative Masonry, it survived in the patronage system by which more established men took younger brothers under their wing in commerce and politics. The lodge was an excellent place to establish and nurture such connections.

Business dealings among brothers were encouraged by lodge culture. Business contacts among merchants and artisans were solidified by bonds of fealty to greater principles. Architects received commissions through the fraternity. Printers met writers and publishers. Performers, sculptors, and painters were able to mingle with wealthy brothers and find potential investors to further their endeavors. The net effect of such mutual self-interest was perceived as bringing improvement to all of society. When the talented were able to rise, they could better contribute to the common good.

For those outside urban centers, Masonry was especially helpful in breaking through social barriers. Members tended to trust the integrity of those met in a lodge while traveling and conducting business. The chance for fellowship and entering a community of mutual interest made travel and extended stays in new environments more pleasant.

Increased commercial travel began to break down the small town, tight-knit communities that were the hallmark of Colonial America. Masonry provided an extended sense of community to growing numbers of those uprooted from the towns and villages of their birth. As the country expanded westward, Masonry was an integral factor. Masonic lodges were among the first institutions established in new settlements, along with the church, local government offices, and schools. As educated people came west, Masonry assured them of a sense of familiarity, stability, and respectability.

RELIGIOUS ROLE

Masonry rejects atheism. A belief in a Higher Power is a condition of membership, but the specifics of that belief are unchallenged. In the broader society, outside the confines of the lodge, the goal is a culture in which spiritual values are widely shared and respected. A variety of religious persuasions and denominations would ideally coexist in harmony. Competition among sects—and dogmatic attempts to restrict others and impose doctrine—would be as unnecessary as they would be unwelcome.

Masonry celebrates an element of spiritual and religious optimism that has been criticized by those of a darker persuasion. The appreciation of man's relationship with the divine has always been an important component of the fraternity. The success of the Revolution and the enthusiasm for self-government proved a fertile ground for such positive ideals. Similarly, such success may have helped to encourage a more openly religious aspect within American Masonry, as prayers of gratitude and a search for guidance inspired many people to seek after God.

DEDICATION AND CORNERSTONE CEREMONIES

The ceremonial laying of important cornerstones in Washington, D.C., is described in greater detail in the next chapter. Masons led the dedication rites of the White House, Capitol, and other public, religious, and even private buildings in post-Revolutionary America. Discussing the cornerstone ceremony of September 18, 1793—when George Washington in Masonic garb presided over the dedication of the U.S. Capitol— Len Travers describes the progress of the march. When it reached the site of the Capitol, the Masonic contingent, which included Washington, moved from the rear of the procession to the front.

> Entering prepared ritual space, the Masons were in their proper element, and their new position at the head of the procession represented the surrender of temporal to mystic authority. . . . For this rarified moment, the nation's supreme magistrate and the self-appointed high priests of republican virtue assumed what no one denied was their rightful place. . . . The Washington ceremony . . . placed them squarely in the national spotlight and helped establish their role as a kind of republican priesthood, who alone possessed the secret knowledge and spiritual authority for endowing architectural rituals with patriotic significance.[14]

On July 4, 1795, Paul Revere laid the cornerstone of the Massachusetts state house. Masonic ceremonies dedicated bridges, boundary stones, the Erie Canal, the Universities of Virginia and North Carolina (the nation's first state university), government buildings, monuments such as that to the Concord Minutemen and the Battle of Bunker Hill, and churches, including Baptist, Methodist, and Episcopalian denominations.

MORALS AND EDUCATION

It has ever been a concern of Masonry to initiate only men of good moral standing. The prestige of the fraternity and the safety of those who regard membership in Masonry as a badge of honor or seal of approval require that care be extended toward investigating prospective members and cultivating high character once members are accepted.

How could good character be taught? Masonry worked to keep

its focus on the national and universal needs of humanity, rather than the sectarian rivalries that afflicted religious schools. Masonry was inspired by the ancient academies of Egypt and Greece, where the idea that small groups of students could be properly taught by well-qualified and spiritually advanced teachers. Masons welcomed the printing press and the widespread dissemination of learning after the Renaissance. It proclaimed itself the friend of philosophy, science, and reason.

America's Founders asserted that only an enlightened, educated, and morally alert citizenry was capable of republican self-government. Education would end the monopoly on intellectual power held by the old aristocratic classes. Enhanced teaching of morality would equip citizens to temper knowledge with wisdom. Post-Revolutionary lodges played an increasingly large part in building and sustaining the educational efforts of the new republic, seeking to equip citizens with the skills needed for the responsibilities of freedom. Support of schools and colleges devoted to the liberal arts and sciences, lending libraries,

Washington presiding over the ceremonial laying of the cornerstone of the Capitol. (Note the men lowering the stone with a winch to the left of the women seated at right.) (By Allyn Cox, 1952. Copyright the George Washington Masonic National Memorial Association. All Rights Reserved. Photography by Arthur W. Pierson, Falls Church, Virginia.)

historical societies, museums, and publishing activities were all part of this effort.

In later years as America expanded, Freemasons made great contributions to education. Lodges donated land for the University of Michigan, Iowa University, and Baylor College. American Freemasons promoted the establishment of land grant colleges and state-sponsored colleges, and they encouraged public education at all levels. Masonic scholarships encouraged widespread liberal arts education among students of lower economic status.

OTHER SOCIAL EFFECTS
OF MASONRY

Masonry helped play a role in dismantling prejudice and social inequities of the day. At the same time, of course, it reflected them.[15]

Prince Hall was the first known "African" Mason. He is believed to have been born a slave in Boston sometime around 1735 and manumitted in 1770. He was a leader in the Boston black community, which received emancipation during the 1780s. Hall became a Mason in 1775 through a British military lodge. Then came the Revolution. When Hall applied to the Massachusetts Modern Grand Lodge for an upgraded charter, he was refused on racial grounds. He applied to the Grand Lodge of England in 1784 and received a charter in 1787 for his African lodge. In 1791 he declared himself Provincial Grand Master of Black Masonry and chartered lodges in Providence, Philadelphia, and elsewhere.

Hall was able to buttress his outreach as an advocate of social justice through his Masonic affiliation and status. Prince Hall's activities brought attention to the contrast between the high tone of Masonic values and the social dynamics of post-Revolutionary America. Hall specifically identified blacks as the descendants of the Queen of Sheba, bride of King Solomon, highlighting an intimate relationship with the founding myths of Freemasonry. He called upon Masonic leaders of the white community to live up to their moral obligations as brothers. While today there still exists a distinction between black and white Masonry, there are white Prince Hall Freemasons and black mainstream Masons. However, the legitimacy of the Prince Hall movement is not recognized by the grand lodges of eleven states.[16]

Mohawk chief Joseph Brant (Thayendanegea; 1742–1807) was another Mason who crossed the barriers of racial separation. He joined the Craft in 1776 in London, and he remained loyal to the British during the Revolution. However, he saved the life of a brother Mason, Revolutionary officer Captain McKinsty, who had been captured by Brant's tribe and was about to be burned alive. McKinsty made Masonic signs in his plea for mercy, and Brant had him released. After the war, Brant moved his tribe to Ontario, Canada, becoming Master of Lodge in 1798.

The question of women in Masonry has been another challenge to the fraternity. Masonry is a male organization. Although women are not allowed to become Freemasons, individual women have been known to be admitted to the fraternity from time to time. This is extremely rare and entirely irregular.

The first (irregular) female lodge in Boston was founded during the 1790s by Hannah Mather Crocker, granddaughter of Cotton Mather. She had investigated and became enthused with Masonry. She founded St. Ann's Lodge, insisting it was based on the true principles of the fraternity. Her short-lived group pursued allied Masonic good works and promoted women's rights to share in Enlightenment values, such as education and full equality. Crocker's lodge may have been a conceptual antecedent of the Masonic-allied Order of the Eastern Star, founded in 1850 by Dr. Rob Morris and Masonic historian Robert Macoy. The Order of the Eastern Star is open to both Master Masons in good standing and their female relatives. Women members of the Eastern Star are not technically Freemasons; however, the presence of a Master Mason is required to convene a chapter. The initiation ceremony of the order conveys a lineage of powerful biblical heroines as female role models.

left. Mohawk chief and Freemason Joseph Brant. **right.** When she was a child, Elizabeth Aldworth, daughter of an Irish brother, was discovered witnessing an initiation from hiding, circa 1710. The startled Masons decided to give her the first two degrees. (Photos from *Encyclopedia of Freemasonry* by Albert Mackey.)

CHARITY

Within operative Masonry, charitable activities originated to care for poor and wounded brothers and their families. With the growth of the speculative side, charitable practices began informally with collections for ad hoc purposes, evolving into more formalized efforts over time.

Masonic support beyond the membership of the fraternity in Colonial America included aid to students, prisoners, the poor, the infirm, and victims of natural disasters or other tragedies. Due to practical limitations, members were often the first recipients of such care—whether these were widows, orphans, travelers, the sick, or others in need. However, the fraternity's concerns were universal, and its charity extended beyond the limits of its membership to alleviate human suffering wherever it might be found.

Today Masonry may be counted among the more active charitable institutions in the world. The Shriners, an allied Masonic organization, have a hospital outreach, founded in the early twentieth century, that now sponsors twenty-three free hospitals for children, of which six specialize in burns and seventeen in orthopedic medicine. The Masonic Services Association (MSA) was formed in 1918 as a national coordinating body for Masonic charities. Masons fund research and treatment for diseases such as diabetes, cancer, arteriolosclerosis, hearing impairment, cerebral palsy, muscular dystrophy, and heart disease. Masons are also active in scholarship funding and providing summer camps and other programs for the poor.

FREEMASONRY TODAY

Masonry has been an integral part of America for three hundred years. Most of that story is well outside the scope of this essay. I believe the best single book on the history of American Masonry is Mark Tabbert's *American Freemasons: Three Centuries of Building Communities*. It is well written and researched, beautifully illustrated, and the author is both a qualified historian and a Freemason.

Here are some closing thoughts. A great scandal hit Masonry and resulted in the Anti-Masonic campaign beginning in 1826. It was a devastating blow to the American "republican priesthood." A kidnapping and presumptive murder were attributed to lodge brothers in upstate New York. The jealousies, suspicions, and resentments swirling below the surface against the Masons erupted with unexpected fury. Anti-Masonry was so virulent it actually gave rise to the first third-party political movement in America. By 1840 Masonry had lost half its membership. When the crisis finally dissipated during the 1840s, Masonry gradually rebuilt itself. Within the next three decades, the American fraternity surpassed its original size but was never to return to the prominence chronicled here. Exoteric groups like the Odd Fellows, founded in 1867, and the later Elks, Rotary, and Kiwanis clubs would offer fellowship and the opportunity to pursue beneficent civic activities on the Masonic pattern.[17]

In 1871 Albert Pike published his important work *Morals and Dogma*. He is immortalized holding a copy in the statue shown on page

111. Pike's work stressed the importance of the Western Mystery tradition to American Freemasons. He promoted the belief that the fraternity's roots are to be found among the wisdom schools of antiquity. His work became a spiritual and intellectual banner for readers who hungered after an esoteric dimension in Freemasonry. Numbering some 850 pages of complex text, the book does not enjoy widespread appeal, but its importance cannot be ignored.

With the dawning of the twentieth century, Masonry reached out to a larger membership base, seeking to expand so that it could pursue great and worthy projects. Masonic charity outreach from 1910 through the 1920s became a major part of Masonry's activities, raising large sums to help many in need. This was also the period of ambitious building projects that saw the construction of lodges in many American cities and large towns. The George Washington Masonic National Memorial is one, as is the House of the Temple (see photos on pages 44 and 171).

After World War II, more blue-collar men were admitted to the fraternity. Men who had fought bravely in the war were hardly to be denied entrance because of lack of a college education or refined social manners. Masonic membership became even more broad based and less elitist. At the same time, the culture of the "greatest generation" made Masonic membership seem an honorable and worthy goal. Men who had fought and won a brutal war together had a bond, and the excessive individualism of postwar American society played no part in it.

During the 1960s, the "baby boomers" came of age. They did not, as a rule, join Masonry. This generation tended to be more self-involved and inherently rebellious—uninterested in conforming to wider social norms or walking in the footsteps of their parents. Many of the "hippie" generation were attracted to romantic variations of Western mysticism like Wicca or the Golden Dawn. Others searched out exotic beliefs and practices like yoga, Sufism, Taoism, and Tibetan Buddhism. Still others pursued solitary spiritual paths of meditation and ritual magic. Finally boomers went down the self-help route of Scientology, Arica, and the dozens of other short-lived unions between age-old spiritual disciplines and pop psychology.

Modern Freemasons see a trend developing among those born in the 1970s and 1980s. People under forty are joining Masonry in record numbers not seen in the past forty years. Many of these new members are looking for the refined and cultured style reminiscent of the eighteenth- and nineteenth-century Masonic experience. Lodges today are likely to organize monthly lectures on spiritual topics, symbolism, mythology, and occultism in polite settings. These are suit-and-tie events, followed by convivial dinners, during which members and their wives enjoy a genteel atmosphere.

While the future of Masonry promises to be bright, several challenges face the modern Craft. How can older members channel and encourage the energy and enthusiasm of new members? Such people tend to be independent, and the modern world offers much competition for their attention. On the other hand, how can Masonry maintain its standards and identity in the face of Harry Potter and the Jedi Knights? While new members might be encouraged to fully participate and contribute their ideas and insights, Masonry must be careful of what some members term "Liberation Freemasonry." In other words, how does the fraternity make its stand to preserve tradition against the demands of undisciplined modernism? For example, co-Masonry (the membership of women) and atheism are both popular ideas in our diversity-obsessed culture. However, acceptance of these would blur the identity of Freemasonry, turning it into something it is not.

Freemasonry is the longest-lived and most successful movement of its kind. We have traced its roots to the earliest days and glimpsed hints of its future. In the iconography of America's capital city, we will discover its timeless message.

The George Washington Masonic National Memorial in Alexandria, Virginia, completed in 1932, was built with contributions from Freemasons throughout the United States. (Copyright the George Washington Masonic National Memorial Association. All Rights Reserved. Photography by Arthur W. Pierson, Falls Church, Virginia.)

THE MASONIC DESIGN
OF WASHINGTON, D.C.
Showcase of American Liberty

ARTICLE I, SECTION 8 OF THE CONSTITUTION calls for a territory not exceeding ten square miles to be set aside as the seat of government for the United States. The District of Columbia was so named by a commission appointed by President Washington in 1791. "Columbia" is the female form of the surname of Christopher Columbus, idealized as a founding hero by mid-eighteenth-century Americans.[1] On October 12, 1792, the 300th anniversary of the arrival of Columbus in the New World, the first Columbus Day was celebrated. The next day— October 13, 1792—the Masonic cornerstone laying ceremony for the White House took place. (Coincidentally, this was the 485th anniversary of the arrest of the Knights Templar in France.)

Washington, D.C., provided the opportunity to build a capital from the ground up. It was unlike the thriving capitals of Europe, such as London or Paris, which had evolved over many centuries from villages to cities to seats of government and were thus home to a cacophony of winding streets, alleys, slums, and the baggage of the past. Washington was envisaged as a newly planned virgin edifice that could stand up to the world as the showpiece of the American experiment—a proud monument to all that was new and fresh, filled with classical beauty and bold modern technology, honoring both history and innovation, a proof to the world of the ability of this nation to survive its threatened infancy, with a hint of intimidation to keep enemies at bay.

The capital was also to be a testament to the Enlightenment ideals that motivated the Founders and the city's designers, many of whom were Freemasons, and all of whom were in sympathy with the Masonic values of liberty, fraternity, and equality. The classic architectural forms were intended to bring perfection and stability to the modern dream of a new and revolutionary political development called America, the realization of ancient hopes and aspirations.

Since 1774, the Continental Congress had been meeting in various locations: Philadelphia, Baltimore, Lancaster, York, Princeton, Annapolis, Trenton, and New York City. Some people felt a moving center was more representative for a government of the "several states." However, with the ratification of the Constitution in 1787, this changed.

The District of Columbia, donated by Maryland and Virginia, was mostly swampland cradled between the two forks of the Potomac River. It was an inhospitable area that may have been used as a meeting ground by councils of the Algonquian Indians and certainly had a long history of use by numerous Indian tribes.[2] The District was chosen as a compromise between the states of the North and South, lying approximately midway between the then-existing northern and southern borders of the nation. The centrality of Washington, D.C., is an important part of its overall design and message. It is conceived as the radiant heart of the American republic.

The capital is a perfect ten-mile square whose diamond points mark the four directions. Andrew Ellicott and Benjamin Banneker did the surveying work. The cornerstone of the Federal District was laid on April 15, 1791, at Jones Point on the Potomac by Alexandria Lodge No. 22, of which George Washington was a member.

The square in Masonry refers to moral integrity—equality, fair dealing, and honesty—from whence came the expression "square deal." The geometry of the capital may have been intended as a symbolic statement that America will live up to its obligations. The square is also a symbol of physical existence as defined by the interplay of the four elements: Fire, Air, Earth, and Water. These elements are not considered to be the literal qualities of their physical representatives but

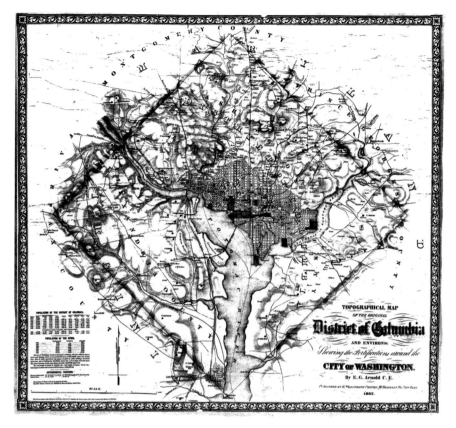

The calculations for the perfect square George Washington sought for the capital city were performed by surveyor Major Andrew Ellicott and free-black mathematician Benjamin Banneker. Placing the forty markers at one-mile intervals took the team nearly two years. (Courtesy of the U.S. Commission of Fine Arts.)

the ideal components of God's creation. Thus Fire represents the intention and will, Water the creative emotions, Air the power of thought and communication, and Earth the principle of solidity, or mass. The animating Spirit is the fifth element, or quintessence. In the case of the capital, the quintessence is the spirit of Liberty that runs so powerfully through the archetypal images we will see in the walking tour and is so eloquently expressed in the Declaration of Independence, the Constitution, and the Bill of Rights. These three documents communicate the living spirit of America.

THE L'ENFANT PLAN

Pierre Charles L'Enfant was the primary designer of the city, chosen and assisted by George Washington, with many suggestions from Thomas Jefferson. L'Enfant had designed the Federal Hall in New York City, the nation's first capital. He recognized the historic opportunity the project offered. He created the familiar pattern of the city with its grid of streets and avenues and its broad diagonal avenues with their fifteen associated traffic circles, symbols of the fifteen states then part of the union. His was a grand vision. He served for a year until his arrogance alienated other participants beyond Washington's ability to mediate. He was fired in January of 1792. However, in large part, his overall design survived.

L'Enfant and Jefferson agreed upon the classical style favored by humankind for thousands of years. Its natural shapes, simplicity, elegance, and utility best conveyed the moral values at the heart of the American ideal. By studying and continuing to develop the best from the past, America was able to pursue perfection while standing on the shoulders of those who had done so before. The classical style forswears the showy excesses of other architectural styles whose messages of opulence and egotism were rejected by this hardier group of patriots.

The Founders were schooled in the Bible and other classical literature. They understood the ancient archetypal pattern for the proclamation of a nation. They had read descriptions of Solomon's Temple built circa 900 B.C. and studied the great edifices of Egypt, Rome, Mesopotamia, India, and elsewhere. The establishment of the republic was to be memorialized in grandeur and executed with ambition worthy of its unique place in history. The architecture of Washington, D.C., unabashedly celebrates power, pomp, and circumstance. It is meant to inspire. Its impressive scale unequivocally states that it is a lasting and serious enterprise. While its magnificent scale may suggest the palaces of European monarchies, it is tempered by a desire to celebrate the democratic republic. The aesthetic challenge that has faced America's artists and architects during the past two hundred years is how to keep such magnificence in scale with the ideal of individual liberty.

The National Archives stands on the site originally chosen by L'Enfant for a national church. The archives house the original sacred scriptures of American liberty: the Declaration of Independence and the Constitution. (Photo courtesy of the National

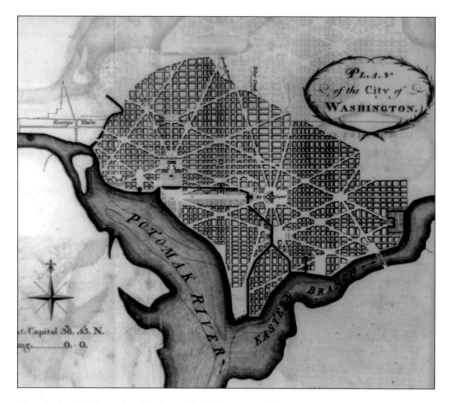

Here is the L'Enfant plan for the capital city, as modified by surveyor Andrew Ellicott in 1792. (Courtesy of the Library of Congress.)

The L'Enfant plan connected the White House and Congress by the main thoroughfare of Pennsylvania Avenue. This was originally intended to be a direct connection with an unobstructed view of the two centers of power separated by nearly a mile. It is said that this symbolically rich opportunity for the executive and legislative branches to "keep an eye on each other" was interrupted by a temper tantrum of Andrew Jackson. His disgust with the antics of the Congress of his day caused him to jam his cane into the ground to the southeast of the White House and declare it the site of the new Department of Treasury Building. See pages 134–37 of the walking tour for photos.

Another interesting part of the story of the development of the capital city is the chronic lack of funds that delayed its full implementation for well over a century. Building spurts would be followed by periods of inactivity due to scarce financial resources. From 1793 to 1800, George Washington and others scrambled to raise money through property sales, donations, lotteries, stock options, and the like with little success. In 1800, the federal government committed itself to the costs. But there were still constant delays and shortages.

During the first decades of the nineteenth century, the Capitol and the White House were separated by swampland, muddy paths, and a few houses. Livestock grazed, open sewers added to the fetid air quality especially during the summer months, and mud was everywhere. A hundred years passed before the city was fleshed out to anything like its proper form. In 1902, the McMillan Commission plan was the first serious attempt to finally realize the dreams of Washington, Jefferson, L'Enfant, Ellicott, Banneker, and the many others who had struggled for a century with limited resources to build the capital city.

THE POLITICS

The slow growth of the capital was mirrored by the development of the American form of government. While the Constitution laid out a framework upon which to build, the practical details of its operation were left to experience and experimentation, trial and error. The inefficiency of the institutions set up by the Constitution is well illustrated by the delays and frustrations that attended the growth of Washington, D.C. But, such opposition, even antagonism, within the Constitutional design is at the heart of American liberty. How does one structure a government, whose nature is to expand and dominate, from threatening the rights of the individual?

The Founders answered that question with their famous system of checks and balances. They divided the national government into three competing branches, each tasked with separate responsibilities: legislative (the Congress), executive (the president), and judicial (the Supreme Court). Jefferson wrote, "My construction of the constitution is . . . that each department is truly independent of the others, and has an equal right to decide for itself what is the meaning of the constitution in the cases submitted to its action; and especially, where it is to act ultimately and without appeal."[3]

The executive branch—the president and his appointed assistants— is in charge of administering and enforcing the laws of the land. The Founders rightly perceived that the executive branch tends to usurp more of the functions of government than it is entitled to. This had been the case of virtually every executive branch in history.

So they opposed the executive by a powerfully constituted legislature. To help keep it in check, the legislative branch was divided into two houses (making it bicameral). A popular House of Representatives was elected to represent the interests of the people. A more reflective body, the Senate, was elected by the states, and it was intended to represent their interests.[4]

Both the executive and legislative branches were balanced by the judiciary. This is ideally an apolitical force, weighing its decisions from a more rarified perspective, interpreting the federal laws and the Constitution in cases of actual dispute. Like a secular priesthood, the Court should focus its attention on the national scriptures it is charged with apprehending. These include the Declaration of Independence, Constitution, Bill of Rights, Federalist Papers, and Anti-Federalist Papers. (The Federalist and Anti-Federalist Papers were written arguments made during the Constitutional Convention and subsequent year-long period of ratification.) The ratification debates forced the Founders to explain exactly what they intended to create to convince the nation to approve the Constitution. The arguments contained in these documents successfully won over the people and the states, and America was set on its course.

The national government is balanced or opposed by the states. In the initial design, the states were relatively autonomous within certain limitations imposed by the Constitution. In the interest of unity, states agreed not to erect tariffs on other states, or coin money, or declare war, or enter into treaties with foreign governments. They agreed to provide a republican form of government for their citizens, and to accept the powers of the national government as enumerated in the Constitution.

A rendering of the plan for Washington, D.C., from 4,000 feet above Arlington, painted by Francis L. V. Hoppin for the McMillan Senate Commission in 1902. It clearly shows the cruciform geometry of the capital city—the Capitol and Lincoln Memorial on the east/west axis, and the White House and Jefferson Memorial on north/south axis. Several people have noted the possibility of overlaying the Masonic Compasses and Square emblem upon this plan. The Washington Monument would be the location of the letter G. (Courtesy of the U.S. Commission of Fine Arts.)

State governments were generally also organized on the pattern of executive, legislative, and judicial branches. They faced competition from local governments such as county, city, and towns. Interestingly enough, the U.S. Constitution says nothing about the structure of state governments. The Founders understood that anything beyond the limited guarantees made by and to the national government was none of their business. (Imagine that!)

In the American design, the people balance all aspects of government from the national, to the state, to the local. The Founders expected the people to be a group of fiercely independent souls, resentful of intrusion by outside entities in their personal lives. The goal of the people should be autonomy. However, to best promote liberty and maintain order, they must agree to be restrained from the excesses of mob rule—the inflamed passions of the "will of the majority." This restraint is provided by a written Constitution and a Bill of Rights, which protect the primary constituent of a democratic republic: the individual. For it is the individual who balances or opposes the people. In modern terms,

The *Signing of the Declaration of Independence* hangs in the Capitol Rotunda. It was painted in 1819 by John Trumbull. The committee, led by Jefferson and including Benjamin Franklin and John Adams, presents the Declaration to John Hancock, president of the Continental Congress. Jefferson, as a gag, reportedly paid the artist to show him stepping on Adams's foot!

the ultimate minority is the individual whose rights must be respected as a condition of liberty.

All in all, it is a remarkably diverse and diffuse arrangement of power, purposely designed to be inefficient so that it can protect liberty against the encroachment of power but be efficient enough to protect order from the encroachment of chaos.

We tend to take for granted the agreement between the disparate elements and personalities that resulted in the Constitution and its subsequent ratification by the states. However, it was an unprecedented step

in all of human political history. That people would come together; willingly accept limitations on their behavior; hand power to others, while retaining a measure of control over those they so chose with the powers reserved by the Bill of Rights; balance the interests of national, state, regional, and local interests—this was a nearly miraculous formulation that has resulted in the longest-lived Constitution on earth, and "indeed, the first written Constitution in the history of the world."[5]

A SYMBOLIC INTERLUDE

American government is designed to be a tug-of-war between competing interests and opposing centers of power. The task of the Founders was to balance the selfish interests of all participants and attempt to inspire cooperation. The balance point between these interests is the sole moment of action for government. Think of the Masonic plumb line swaying back and forth as it seeks to find the true vertical, or the balance scales in motion while they try to reach the point of equality between disparate elements. The Constitutional system of checks and balances reflects Masonic principles.

We discussed above the division of the national government into three branches, and the more important division into a national government, a series of independent state governments, and the people. This tripartite separation of powers recalls the principle of the Masonic triangle. Renowned Masonic historian Albert Mackey writes, "There is no symbol more important . . . throughout the whole system of Freemasonry, than the triangle. [It] represents the Great First Cause, the creator and container of all things as one and indivisible, manifesting himself in an infinity of forms and attributes in this visible universe."[6]

Let us contemplate this symbol. The infinite seeks manifestation. It projects itself as the point, defined by its position, one coordinate. Further seeking fulfillment, the point extends outward to become the line, now adding the concept of reference to another, creating length, reaching to infinity. But by manifesting a third point, and forming the triangle, the point has defined itself in relation to two others, and it has

A symbol dating back to at least ancient Egypt, the all-seeing Eye of God peers out from within the Triangle of the Ideal Plane. The Egyptians conceived of the Eye of Providence as both solar (right eye of Ra), and lunar (left eye of Thoth). The single eye also represents an awakened Ajna chakra, the "third eye" of spiritual enlightenment.

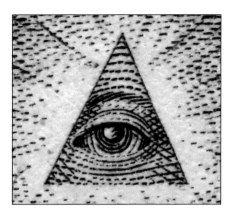

become a self-contained unit, the plane, fully independent in two dimensions, at rest in perfect harmony.[7]

The Founders added an eye in the middle of the triangle, which you can find on the back of the U.S. one dollar bill. The eye represents the central illuminating intelligence of the universe. It is the infinite, that which started the entire process by manifesting itself as the point. It is the All-Seeing Eye of God.

One way to interpret this symbol in the context of the American government is the following: The Eye in the Triangle is manifest in the tripartite division of the branches of the national government—legislative, executive, judicial. All are sprung into existence by the Holy Spirit of Liberty seeking to manifest itself on earth within a formal political structure. The eye might represent the spirit of the Declaration of Independence, the nation's great proclamation of liberty.

Another provocative interpretation is to see one point of the triangle as the national government, the second as the states, and the third as "we the people."[8] What then is the eye within this particular triangle? The individual is the "I" in the triangle. The individual stands alone as the living spirit and motivation of the whole enterprise. Lest we forget, every president, congressperson, and judge, every member of "the people" is, first and foremost, an individual. If government is not designed to protect and respect the individual—the cornerstone of humanity—there is no liberty.

THE WHITE HOUSE: THE EXECUTIVE BRANCH

The White House was the first building in Washington, D.C., to receive the Masonic cornerstone ceremony. In his original plan, L'Enfant called it the "Presidential Palace." Washington and Jefferson quickly changed the name to the "President's House." L'Enfant was fired before he came up with the architectural plans for the building. A contest was announced and won by Master Mason James Hoban on July 16, 1792. Construction began immediately with digging the foundation. On October 13, 1792, work was sufficiently advanced that a cornerstone was ceremonially laid.

The ceremony was led by Master of Maryland Lodge No. 9, Peter Casanave. Afterward the participants gathered at the Fountain Inn to enjoy an "elegant dinner" and at least sixteen recorded toasts: to the United States, President Washington, Freemasonry, the District of Columbia, the Constitutional liberties of the people, and Thomas Paine among others. The exuberance of the festivities may help explain the inability of the revelers to subsequently pinpoint the exact location of the cornerstone.

Construction of the President's House took ten years. John and Abigail Adams were the first family to live there near the very end of Adams's presidency. When Thomas Jefferson moved in, he hired Freemason and architect Benjamin H. Latrobe to redesign the interior and add the north and south porticos.

The President's House was burned by British troops on August 24, 1814. In March 1815, James Hoban returned to rebuild it. It has since been called the White House, because it was painted white to hide the stains of the smoke and flames. The restoration was finished in just under three years.

In 1948, during the presidency of Freemason Harry Truman, a massive rebuilding of the White House was undertaken because of cracked walls in both the interior and exterior, sagging floors, and other structural problems in the 150-year-old building. A search was made for the cornerstone, in part using a mine detector, because it was known that a brass plate had been affixed announcing the date, naming the partici-

Mason marks shown on a stone found during the Truman renovation of the White House. It is now part of the great fireplace of the old kitchen on the ground floor. (Photo by George F. Mobley, courtesy of the White House Historic Association, 2814.)

pants, and invoking a blessing. The strongest readings were recorded in the southwest corner of the White House, but Truman refused to allow any more digging than was necessary. If the construction uncovered the stone, so be it. If not, he would not sanction exploration for curiosity. The cornerstone was never found.

However, several stones were uncovered that had Masonic markings. Truman had them set aside. Some were used to build a decorative fireplace on the ground floor of the White House. The others were distributed to each of America's grand lodges.

THE CAPITOL: THE LEGISLATIVE BRANCH

Thomas Jefferson, writing to Benjamin Latrobe in 1812, described the Capitol as the "first temple dedicated to the sovereignty of the people."[9] The Capitol was originally intended to be erected at the precise center of the diamond-shaped district, but practical considerations led to it being placed slightly eastward. However, it is the center of the district street

The Star in the Crypt is the directional center of the street plan of Washington, D.C., the origin of the four quadrants. The Crypt was originally intended as the burial place of George Washington. It is one floor below the Rotunda. His family honored his request not to allow his body to be removed from his beloved Mount Vernon.

plan and is oriented to the four cardinal directions. In the Crypt under the Dome is the Star marking the origin of the four quadrants of northeast, northwest, southeast, and southwest. The Capitol is also the origin of the numbered and lettered street names of the city.[10]

The cornerstone-laying ceremony at the Capitol was an elaborate Masonic affair presided over by President Washington on September 18, 1793. Prayers, chanting, and volleys of artillery accompanied the dedication address. Four lodges were present. A large engraved silver plate commemorating the event and the participants was placed into the foundation. The three-foot square cornerstone was set down, and Washington trued it by the square, level, and plumb line. He then made the ceremonial offering of corn, wine, and oil (Masonic symbols of health, peace, and plenty). He wore the white gloves and apron of the brotherhood.

The Capitol cornerstone has also not been located. The newspaper article describing the ceremony makes it clear that it was placed below ground level. The lack of detailed construction records and numerous variables regarding the exact location have left a mystery. The centennial plaque placed in 1893 in the southeast corner of the north wing of the Senate announces that somewhere "beneath this tablet" the cornerstone

opposite. Washington laying the cornerstone of the Capitol is depicted on the upper left panel of the left valve of the bronze Senate doors by Thomas Crawford and William Rinehart, 1868. (Architect of the Capitol.)

was laid. Various testing methods including soil sampling and metal detectors have thus far failed to find the original cornerstone.

The Capitol building was designed by the winner of a competition to pick the architect, an amateur named William Thornton. The construction had to be supervised by trained architects. In 1803 Benjamin Latrobe teamed up with Thomas Jefferson and construction got on to a proper footing. However, during the War of 1812 much of the Capitol was also burned by British troops. Latrobe took on the reconstruction. Freemason Charles Bulfinch completed the task in 1826. The current dome of the Capitol was added by Freemason Thomas U. Walter, then Architect of the Capitol, when Congress authorized the expansion of the Capitol in 1855. It was a ten-year construction project that spanned the difficult period before and during the Civil War. The Rotunda beneath the Dome is the place of convergence for members of the Senate and House, citizens in interaction with their representatives, and the three separate branches of government during ceremonial occasions.

The decision to locate the Capitol, the People's House, on the highest most prominent location of the city, Jenkins Hill, is significant. Almost any other government on earth would have chosen this site to honor the executive. Putting the legislature in the center of the capital city echoes the genius of the American Constitutional system.

SUPREME COURT: THE JUDICIAL BRANCH

The Supreme Court did not have an official site assigned it as did the legislative and executive branches. It is a reasonable assumption that L'Enfant planned for the Court to be located in Judiciary Square, along Pennsylvania Avenue between the White House and the Capitol. However it was not drawn on his plan, and it was never built there. The present location of the Court even higher atop Jenkins Hill than the Capitol may be ironic testimony to the unanticipated prominence it has achieved. The cornerstone for the present building was laid on October 13, 1932, the 140th anniversary of the White House ceremony. Construction was completed in 1935.

Freemason John Marshall served as Chief Justice from 1801 to 1835. He largely defined the role of the Supreme Court. The Constitution is somewhat vague about the Court being a co-equal branch of government. Marshall, however, radically enhanced the power of the federal judiciary. In Marbury vs. Madison, 1803, he asserted the doctrine of "judicial review," declaring a law passed by Congress unconstitutional. This angered his cousin President Thomas Jefferson, who lamented it made the Constitution "a mere thing of wax in the hands of the judiciary, which they may twist and shape into any form they please."

The very first bill introduced in the United States Senate was the Judiciary Act of 1789, which divided the country into thirteen judicial districts of three circuits. For the first 101 years, Supreme Court justices were required to "ride circuit," holding court twice a year in each of the thirteen judicial districts. The Supreme Court was first called to assemble in 1790 in New York City. They heard and decided their first case in 1792. Next, they moved to Philadelphia. When the federal government was established in Washington, the court was housed in a basement room in the United States Capitol in 1801. The Old Supreme Court, designed by Benjamin Latrobe, is open for visitors during the U.S. Capitol tour and is beautiful.

AMERICAN CULTURAL VALUES

Washington, D.C., is a history book for generations of Americans, meant to inspire and offer moral instruction in commonly held values. It annually hosts millions of visitors including families seeking to educate themselves and their children, school kids on class trips, Americans seeking to understand their national roots, and visitors from countries worldwide.

Images of courage, honor, heroism, integrity, self-discipline, self-sacrifice, intellectual inquiry, creativity, and industry are regularly encountered in the statues, paintings, architecture, and inscriptions of the city. We are led to understand certain truths that have helped build the freest, most widely prosperous, and healthiest nation in history.

Among these are the economic requirements of work, trade, exchange, specialization of tasks, research, land cultivation, and animal husbandry. On matters of military significance and national survival, we are reminded of the importance of preparedness. We are witness to the virtues of our citizen-soldiers who have fought with ferocity against enemies, and, when necessary, been willing to sacrifice their lives for the good of the whole. We learn that the union of science, industry, and ethics allows for an enlightened approach to meet the demands of any situation; that honest empirical research and the scientific method have successfully advanced civilization since the first caveman discovered fire. Moreover, we realize that our survival, prosperity, and progress are all made possible by the rule of law and equality before the law.

We are summoned to our moral and ethical obligations as individuals and as a nation by exposure to the biblical roots of Western culture. We note in the inscriptions and monuments that this republic was erected by people of great erudition, immersed in the classics and scripture. The words of the prophet Samuel, warning the Israelites of specific abuses to be expected from the kings they desired, could not have been far from the minds of those who wrote and signed the Declaration of Independence and its itemized list of royal violations.

And Samuel told all the words of the LORD unto the people that asked of him a king. . . . This will be the manner of the king that

left. Themis, the goddess of freedom and justice, prepared to offer the olive branch of peace with her right hand, while she holds the sword of defense at the ready in her left. A clear-eyed perception of human nature is an absolute necessity for the survival and success of liberty.

right. Nathan Hale, Freemason and American hero, was but twenty-one years old when he was arrested as a spy by the British. About to be hanged, he uttered the immortal words, "My only regret is that I have but one life to give for my country."

The Second Division Memorial in the Ellipse honors the soldiers of WW I. Two wings were later added for WW II and the Korean conflict. The central design is identical to the Ace of Swords card in many tarot decks.

shall reign over you: He will take your sons, and appoint them for himself, for his chariots, and to be his horsemen; and some shall run before his chariots. . . . And he will take your daughters to be confectionaries, and to be cooks, and to be bakers. And he will take your fields, and your vineyards . . . and give them to his servants.[11]

Perhaps the most important lesson of the capital city is that we are capable of finding solutions to the problems of life. We are heir to an optimistic self-confidence and integrity of purpose that will triumph over adversity as we have countless times in the past. The city is filled with heroic images of men and women who stood proud and tall before oppression, violence, and evil and refused to compromise—were it at the cost of their lives. America has erected shrines to science (the National Academy of Sciences), monuments to learning (the Library of Congress), archives to history (the Smithsonian Museums), and temples to freedom (the Capitol). Washington, D.C., proclaims that humanity is a successful species. We just need to keep learning how to keep getting it right.

THE NATIONAL RELIGION

Masonic philosopher Albert Pike wrote, "A nation cannot renounce the executorship of the Divine decrees. As little can Masonry."[12] One of the conditions of membership in the Craft is a belief in God. And one of the most important traditions is that such belief is a private matter, not to be the subject of further inquiry by the brothers. This is a prime example of the all-important Masonic virtues of tolerance and religious liberty.

The Founders were deeply aware that their ability to create a free nation was the result of the alignment of their actions with the natural order of the universe and the will of God: "We hold these truths to be self-evident, that all men are created equal, that they are endowed by their Creator with certain unalienable rights, that among these are life, liberty and the pursuit of happiness. That to secure these rights, governments are instituted among men, deriving their just powers from the consent of the governed."[13] Reading the arguments and discussions, letters and speeches, articles, essays, and books of the Founding Fathers, we repeatedly encounter their acknowledgment of an actively involved Higher Power.

The recognition/invocation of the union between the secular and the sacred extends from the most ancient civilizations to the modern world. Jeffrey Meyer states, "There is a religious message implicit in most of the buildings, memorials, art, and iconography of Washington that recalls the original conviction so often stated by the Founding Fathers, that the Almighty stood behind the American experiment."[14] Political rulers have ever sought to proclaim their alliance with the invisible forces sustaining the universe. Washington, D.C., is planned as the national point of intersection between heaven and earth.

Freemasonry is based on the spiritual model of sacred architecture. As the initiate builds his sacred space with the tools of the Craft, his self and soul unite into an engine of divine unity and moral purpose. Similarly, as the structure of Washington, D.C., was planned and erected by many—a significant percentage of whom were Freemasons—the national character was both displayed and formed. This process continues today with ritual invocations and ceremonies that repeat the themes of self-dedication and the seeking of divine favor.

The metaphor of divine kingship resonates at a very basic level of the human psyche, engendering the continuous archetypal and anthropomorphic symbolism of deity and political rulership. Whether it be through Christ or Horus, Solomon or Louis XIV, human beings naturally believe that heaven will favor the nation whose leadership acts in harmony with the Holy Spirit. The Prayer Room in the U.S. Capitol, located near the Rotunda and open to members of the House and Senate since 1955, is modern testimony to the age-old custom of a nation's leaders acknowledging an even higher Authority. The open Bible reminds us of the centrality of that book in Western culture, America, and Freemasonry.[15]

Jeffrey Meyer discusses an important spiritual shift that is apparent in the American vision of politics. While the Founders recognized and cultivated the guidance of the divine, "instead of channeling power through the ruler to the people, they believed that the Almighty had done the reverse, vested the power primarily in the people. The new republican form of government was not a rejection of the religious source of political power but a reinterpretation of how it operated."[16]

Religion has also had a negative context, which America's Founding Fathers sought to avoid. By foregoing the identification of state power with one religion, long a characteristic of Europe, they encouraged competition between religions. None was able to grow to the extent that it could enlist military power against nonadherents. Nor could the edicts of one faith trump the beliefs of another. The "marketplace" of ideas and faith was an open forum in which people were free to believe or not believe. This has protected Americans from the domination of a broad-based alliance of religion with the power of the state, and it will hopefully offer the same protection against the domination of a broad-based alliance of secularism with state power.

As any visit to Washington, D.C., will make abundantly clear, and as the pages of the walking tour demonstrate, a belief in God is an integral part of America's political and cultural heritage. The design of the Founders allowed people to worship in the language most compatible with their inner striving. Were America to eliminate every reference to God in a public building in Washington, D.C., precious few buildings would be left standing!

Perhaps the best example of America's national religion is Thanksgiving. People of all faiths (and those of no faith) gather together in their homes—some to offer thanks to the God of their understanding, others to simply enjoy the company of family and friends on the national harvest holiday. The language of President Washington's proclamation of the first Thanksgiving (shown on the following page) may help us to understand the proper role of faith and government in the American tradition as understood by this Freemason and Founding Father.

General George Washington praying at Valley Forge, Pennsylvania, in June of 1778. The Continental army had survived a miserable winter after making camp here in December of 1777. Their stay was characterized by near starvation, rampant disease, and a terrible lack of provisions such as blankets, clothing, and shoes. The army also suffered from a lack of consistent training. The Revolution hovered on the edge of disaster. Yet, at the end of February the brutal winter weather began to improve. Freemason Baron Friederich von Steuben (see page 140) arrived to oversee the military training program. In March, General Nathanael Greene was appointed head of the Commissary Department, and supplies and food slowly started to arrive. By May, the French began to furnish military and financial support. On June 19, 1778, a revived Continental army marched out to continue the battle against the British. (Painting by Lambert Sachs. Copyright the George Washington Masonic National Memorial Association. All Rights Reserved. Photography by Arthur W. Pierson, Falls Church, Virginia.)

By the President of the United States of America— A Proclamation

WHEREAS IT IS THE DUTY of all Nations to acknowledge the providence of Almighty God, to obey his will, to be grateful for his benefits, and humbly to implore his protection and favor—and Whereas both Houses of Congress have by their Joint Committee requested me "to recommend to the People of the United States a day of public thanksgiving and prayer to be observed by acknowledging with grateful hearts the many signal favors of Almighty God, especially by affording them an opportunity peaceably to establish a form of government for their safety and happiness."

Now therefore I do recommend and assign Thursday the 26th day of November next to be devoted by the People of these States to the service of that great and glorious Being, who is the beneficent Author of all the good that was, that is, or that will be—That we may then all unite in rendering unto him our sincere and humble thanks—for his kind care and protection of the People of this country previous to their becoming a Nation—for the signal and manifold mercies, and the favorable interpositions of his providence, which we experienced in the course and conclusion of the late war—for the great degree of tranquility, union, and plenty, which we have since enjoyed—for the peaceable and rational manner in which we have been enabled to establish constitutions of government for our safety and happiness, and particularly the national One now lately instituted, for the civil and religious liberty with which we are blessed, and the means we have of acquiring and diffusing useful knowledge; and in general for all the great and various favors which he hath been pleased to confer upon us.

And also that we may then unite in most humbly offering our prayers and supplications to the great Lord and Ruler of Nations and beseech him to pardon our national and other transgressions—to enable us all, whether in public or private stations, to perform our several and relative duties properly and punctually—to render our national government a blessing to all the People, by constantly being a government of wise, just, and constitutional laws, discreetly and faithfully executed and obeyed—to protect and guide all Sovereigns and Nations (especially such as have shown kindness unto us) and to bless them with good government, peace, and concord—To promote the knowledge and practice of true religion and virtue, and the increase of science among them and Us—and generally to grant unto all mankind such a degree of temporal prosperity as he alone knows to be best.

Given under my hand at the City of New York the third day of October in the year of our Lord 1789.

—Go. Washington[17]

A
WALKING TOUR
OF THE
CAPITAL

The Walking Tour of the Capital is divided into eight sections surrounding the National Mall area. We will move from the Capitol
building in the east, starting at 1st Street and Maryland Avenue,
proceed north to Union Square, and then west to Judiciary Square,
Federal Triangle, the White House, and National Academy of Sciences. We next turn south to the Lincoln Memorial and Washington Monument and proceed on to the Jefferson Memorial. We
conclude the tour by returning northeast to the National Mall and
its Smithsonian Institutions.

To find the street addresses of these images, sculptures, and
paintings, please see the Directory of Sites on pages 172–76. This
directory is organized by book page number for easy reference and
includes the name of the image, its date, location, and the name of
the artist, when available.

The colored bands at the top indicate the subsections within
the tour area for easy reference. The street map of Washington,
D.C., that follows presents an overview of the areas covered by the
walking tour and their position in the city.

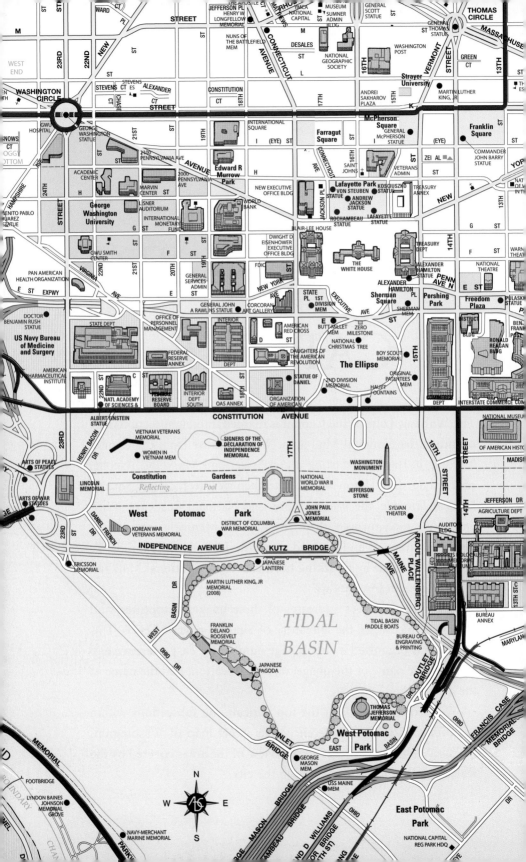

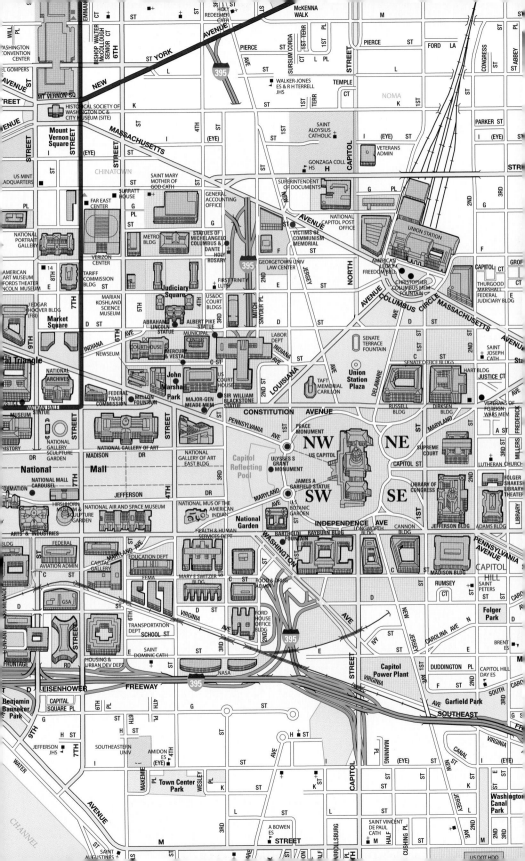

The east entrance of the Capitol in happier times (1997) before the extraordinary security measures post-September 11, 2001. Today a visitor center is under construction here. The east entrance was the standard access point to the Capitol for the first hundred years, until the western entrance was fashioned into its present form by the landscaping genius of Frederick Law Olmstead after 1874. The Washington Monument and Lincoln Memorial may be seen to the west, at left. (Architect of the Capitol.)

THE CAPITOL AREA

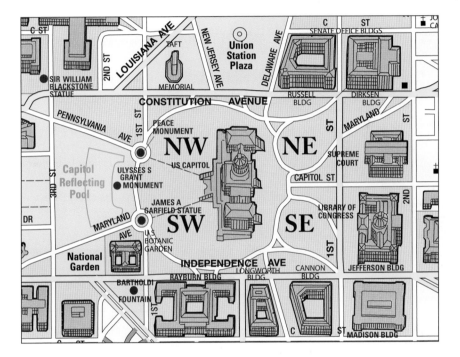

Y OU MIGHT START OUT by getting your ticket for the Capitol tour. While waiting, visit the Capitol grounds shown on the following pages. They are a treasure trove of esoteric and Masonic symbolism. They include the Reflecting Pool, Garfield statue, Peace Monument, General Ulysses S. Grant Memorial, Botanical Gardens, and more.

opposite. The statue of President Garfield is filled with esoteric symbolism. Garfield was a Mason, soldier, congressman, and president, assassinated in 1881 after only six months in office. Details on the following pages illustrate various aspects of his life and the Masonic principles of good citizenship and service they embody. Lady Freedom atop the Capitol is visible at right.

Figures on the Garfield statue:

left: Mythic warrior grasps the hilt of his sword in a vigilant, but calm, attitude.

lower left: Legislator holds a tablet that reads "Law, Justice, Prosperity." These three concepts are both the requirements for, and the fruits of, a well-governed society.

lower right: The young scholar, deep in study, prepares himself to temper the world of politics and the arts of war with wisdom.

above. The mourning woman standing atop the Peace Monument (left) bears a resemblance to the famed Weeping Virgin of Freemasonry (right) mourning the unfinished Temple and the death of Master Mason Hiram Abiff.

left. Victory, holding the wreath of peace, is surrounded by two cherubs. The infant Mars is wearing a battle helmet and holding a sword. Baby Neptune grasps a trident. A seashell is centered between them. The interplay of the forces of the unconscious with three-dimensional reality demand military awareness—even in a monument dedicated to peace.

The *Bartholdi Fountain* is part of the U.S. Botanical Gardens. The Three Graces of Greek mythology are Beauty, Charm, and Joy, daughters of Zeus, the creator god of Olympus. Frédéric Auguste Bartholdi was a Freemason whose most famous work is

above. View of the Capitol facing east from the Reflecting Pool. The Senate is to the left, the House to the right. The famed Capitol dome is in the center, with the Statue of Freedom atop. General Grant stands guard with soldiers of the Union army and four lions, protecting the seat of government from the forces of invasion and rebellion.

opposite. The Statue of Freedom by Freemason Thomas Crawford has stood atop the Capitol dome since 1863, when the present dome was erected. She faces east, greeting the rising sun. The shield in her left hand displays thirteen stripes. The laurel wreath, also in her left hand, is the symbol of victory. Her sword is sheathed. Her gown is drawn together by a brooch inscribed "U.S." She is officially known as *Freedom Triumphant in War and Peace*. She stands nineteen and a half feet high. All statues in Washington, D.C., have since been limited to a height of nineteen feet that Freedom may reign supreme. (Architect of the Capitol.)

above. *Justice and History,* sculpted by Freemason Thomas Crawford in 1860, is located above the Senate entrance on the east front of the Capitol. Justice, at right, holds a book entitled *Justice, Law, Order* in her left hand, and a pair of scales in her right. History holds a scroll reading "History July 1776." They both recline against a globe. Holding true to these principles, America can maintain its integrity. By understanding and teaching the history and design of this great experiment in human liberty, future generations can continue the progress of our past. Justice, Law, and Order are the foundations of American prosperity. Equality before the Law is the antidote to tyranny. Liberty begins with Justice, a common thread through Masonic teachings and the symbolism of Washington, D.C. (Architect of the Capitol.)

opposite above. *The Apotheosis of Washington,* painted by Constantino Brumidi in 1865, appears on the ceiling of the Capitol dome. It shows the Father of America ascending to Heaven and his place among the gods, accompanied by two figures representing Liberty (to his right) and Victory (to his left). Completing the triangle are thirteen maidens representing the original thirteen states. On the circular outer rim are the archetypes that constitute a vibrant nation including (clockwise beginning below Washington): War, represented by Columbia or *Armed Freedom;* Science, by Minerva; Marine, by Neptune; Commerce, by Mercury; Mechanics, by Vulcan; and Agriculture, by Ceres. The immense fresco is set 180 feet above the ground and covers 4,664 square feet. (Architect of the Capitol.)

opposite below. Detail of Washington's ascent. Washington has ever been accorded mythic status in America. Thomas Jefferson, his friend for three decades, wrote, "[N]ever did nature and fortune combine more perfectly to make a man great, and to place him in the same constellation with whatever worthies have merited from man an everlasting remembrance." (Architect of the Capitol.)

These two profoundly esoteric images face each other in the National Statuary Hall, the meeting place of the House of Representatives between 1807 and 1857. (Both photos, Architect of the Capitol.)

above: *Liberty and the Eagle,* sculpted by Enrico Causici, was placed in the Capitol circa 1817. It was located above the desk of the Speaker of the House. The scroll in her right hand is the Constitution. The eagle, far-seeing symbol of American power, is at her right. At her left is the *fasces,* the Roman symbol of power, a bound bundle of wheat. While each stem is weak by itself, when wrapped together, all stand firm in unity, *E Pluribus Unum,* "Out of Many, One." The fasces is bound even tighter in this sculpture by the Serpent of Wisdom wrapped around it. The unity remains eternally triumphant.

opposite: *The Car of History* fashioned by Carlo Franzoni in 1810, is the oldest sculpture in any government building in the country. It depicts Clio, Muse of History, daughter of Zeus and Mnemosyne (Goddess of Memory). She stands gracefully in her winged chariot, recording the proceedings of the House in her book. The chariot wheel, housing the clock, rests on a segment of the zodiac comprising Sagittarius, Capricorn, and Aquarius. Sagittarius is ruled by Jupiter, the Roman Zeus, and Capricorn and Aquarius by Saturn, Lord of Time. She is thus a source of good fortune and provides an abiding sense of eternity as she watches over the daily deliberations of the young nation.

above. *America and History* by Allyn Cox, ca. 1951, from the first panel of the Capitol frieze in the Rotunda. America, wearing a liberty cap, stands in the center with spear and shield. To her right sits an Indian maiden with a bow and arrows, representing the untamed American continent. At her left is a female figure representing History. She holds a stone tablet to record events as they occur. An American eagle perches on a fasces, symbol of the authority of government. (Architect of the Capitol.)

opposite. On the south side of the Capitol stands the Rayburn House Office Building. These figures face each other at the entrance. The female resembles Pallas Athena, civic goddess wise in the ways of Peace. She is identified as the *Spirit of Justice*. She holds the lamp of illumination and truth in her right hand, while her left hand, resting on the shoulder of a young child, indicates justice tinged with mercy. The severity of her male counterpart, the *Majesty of Law*, is indicated by the sword held unsheathed before him. Yet he also holds a book of federal laws in his left hand, embossed with the seal of the United States. Law tempers his severity with a written code of conduct. There are limitations upon his power, the "chains of the Constitution," that bind him from the arbitrary exercise of dominion. Together these yin and yang figures recall the Masonic principles enshrined in *Liber Librae:* "Remember that unbalanced force is evil; that unbalanced severity is but cruelty and oppression; but that also unbalanced mercy is but weakness which would allow and abet Evil."

above. We continue east up the hill on Independence Avenue, making a left on SE 1st Street to discover the American Temple of the Enlightenment, the Jefferson Building of the Library of Congress. Shown here is the west entrance, its steps worn smooth by those countless Americans and others who have sought after human understanding. The library was established by an act of Congress and signed into law by President John Adams in 1800. When the original library was burned by the British in the War of 1812, Thomas Jefferson offered to sell his own books in 1814. He passed along 6,487 books that he had collected over fifty years. The present building opened its doors in 1897. Today it houses more than 29 million books and 58 million manuscripts.

opposite. Outside the entrance to the library along the street stands this fountain, a collection of statues depicting the *Court of Neptune,* sculpted by Roland Hinton Perry in 1897. This mythic tribute to the King of the Unconscious and Lord of the Gateway to the Magical realm is a bold demonstration of the artistic celebration of America's mythic unity with antiquity.

There are three main doors at the west entrance of the Library of Congress, now used for special events. (During your visit to the library you'll note the standard entrance is clearly marked at ground level.) Pictured here are details of the rightmost door of Writing. The doors on the left symbolize Tradition, while those in the center represent Science. (For reference, please note photo on page 90.)

above. Writing doors in bronze by Olin L. Warner and Herbert Adams, ca. 1895. The figure at left holds the Mirror of Reflection and the Serpent of Wisdom. The figure at right, the Torch of Illumination and Vine of Creativity. (Photo by Carol M. Highsmith.)

opposite above. Art spandrels by Bela Lyon Pratt, ca. 1895, convey a dreamy quality. The sculptress at left is working on a bust of Dante. She and her companion, the painter on the right, exude a sense of timeless ease and creativity.

opposite below. Bronze tympanum by Olin L. Warner, ca. 1895, is also titled *Writing*. The students include an Egyptian, a Jew, a Greek, and a Christian, all seated at the feet of a veiled teacher. These figures depict the four most literate Western cultures.

above. Busts of Thomas Jefferson and George Washington on opposite sides of the Great Hall were copied from the works of sculptor Jean-Antoine Houdon (1741–1828). (Both photos by Carol M. Highsmith.)

left. James Madison, the father of the Constitution and fourth president of the United States, in the Madison Building of the Library of Congress, a block south of the Jefferson Building. The cornerstone was laid in 1974, and the building opened in 1980. This statue of the young Madison is by Walter K. Hancock.

opposite. The Great Hall of the Library of Congress, whose opulence must be appreciated in person. On the floor is a great zodiac (see also next spread). The entrance to the Reading Room is along the central corridor. (Photo by Carol M. Highsmith.)

above and opposite above. Zodiacal signs on the floor of the Great Hall of the Library of Congress. These surround a great central sun with markers of the four directions, shown on the opposite page. (The sun is a detail of a photo by Carol M. Highsmith.)

The large number of zodiacs throughout Washington, D.C., suggest a spiritual dimension to the understanding of America's role in the world, as if it were perceived to be an ornament of the starry heavens.

The extraordinarily ornate and detailed ceiling of the Great Hall includes angels holding a shield on which is shown the Book of Wisdom and Lamp of Truth. (Photo by Carol M. Highsmith.)

above. The Saturn Clock shows the Lord of Time soaring aloft accompanied by two angelic beings nurturing young cherubs at their sides. They move against a background of astrological signs, while two youths beside the clock are engaged in study and contemplation. The themes of age and youth, time and eternity, and the mythic identification of Saturn with concentration and self-discipline are all evident in this design. (Photo by Carol M. Highsmith.)

opposite. One of a pair of grand staircases leading to the second floor, each graced with bronze statues of a female holding an electric lamp, in celebration of the taming of that force by American scientist Thomas Edison. (Photo by Carol M. Highsmith.)

The Supreme Court stands north of the Library of Congress. This is the pediment at the east entranceway, depicting the great lawgivers who contributed to the Western system of justice. Moses sits in the center, holding the two tablets on which God inscribed the Ten Commandments, the basis of the American legal system. On the left is the great fifth-century B.C. lawgiver of China, Confucius. On the right is the Athenian Solon, who codified Greek law in the sixth century B.C. Thus we acknowledge the great civilizations of the past in our own quest for Justice.

The inscription on the pediment reads "Justice, the Guardian of Liberty." It gives voice to a sublime Masonic principle that no one is above the law, and no one is below it. This does not mean that everyone shares the same talents, or that life or law will provide equal outcomes. It does mean that no matter how talented, educated, wealthy—or common, ignorant, and poor—each individual is equal before the blindfolded Lady of Justice.

The Supreme Court is charged with interpreting the scriptures of American Law: the Constitution, Bill of Rights, Federalist Papers, and other writings of the Founders. For it is upon history that law must rest. The west front pediment carries the inscription "Equal Justice under the Law." Remove Law, and you have the unchecked excess of either the dictator, party, or mob.

Flagpole at west entrance to the Court. Clockwise from top left: Cherub holds the Wand of Dominance, a globe topped by an American eagle in his left hand, and a pen in his right. The next holds the Book of the Law—whether the Bible, Constitution, or codified laws. The cherub at lower right carries the Torch of Illumination and balances a head on his knee, brightening the minds of those in his domain. The fourth cherub holds the Scales of Justice and Sword of Discernment, like the Justice card of the tarot.

The Contemplation of Justice on the north side of the west entrance staircase to the Supreme Court features a cloaked woman in deep thought, her left hand resting on a book, while, in her right hand, she holds the figure of a woman. This speaks to the enormous power exercised by the Law and thus to the true importance of Justice.

The Authority of Law on the south side of the west entrance staircase holds a tablet that reads "Lex" or Law. He also cradles an upright sword with his left arm. These two figures should be compared with those in front of the Rayburn Building shown on page 89. It is interesting to note that the sword of this figure is sheathed.

UNION STATION

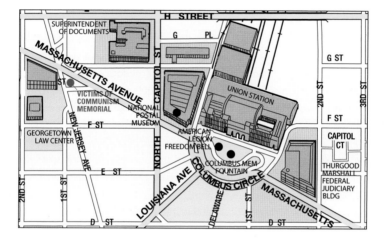

U NION STATION is the central hub of the Capitol area rail, bus, and subway transportation system. It is also the site of a large statuary group honoring Christopher Columbus and the discovery of America in 1492.

The main facade of Union Station is home to six massive mythic figures by master sculptor Louis Saint-Gaudens. Archimedes (Mechanics) is shown opposite. The others are Prometheus (Fire), Thales (Electricity), Themis (Freedom) (see page 65), Apollo (Inspiration), and Ceres (Agriculture). An impressive group of three American eagles stands to the west of these, two in the facade and one atop a metal column.

Union Station is a simple walk north on 1st Street after you visit the Capitol, Library of Congress, and Supreme Court. It is well worth it.

opposite. Recalling the image of the Medieval Operative Stonemason, the statue of Archimedes, with a pair of compasses and gavel, stands watch at Union Station. He displays an intensity of focused concentration that bespeaks the grandeur of his creations to follow.

opposite. One of the capital's newest and, as yet, most unfamiliar monuments, this is the *Victims of Communism Memorial.* It was dedicated by President George W. Bush on June 12, 2007, the twentieth anniversary of President Reagan's historic speech at the Berlin Wall in which he declared, "Tear down this wall." The authorizing legislation was passed by Congress in 1993 and signed by President Clinton.

The figure of the Goddess of Democracy is a ten-foot-high bronze replica of that erected by students during the Tiananmen Square protests of 1989. The original, inspired by the Statue of Liberty, was constructed by students of the Central Academy of Fine Arts in only four days, using styrofoam and papier-mâché over a metal armature. It stood thirty-three feet high.

The statue lasted only five days before being crushed by tanks of the Communist Chinese troops. The students, acknowledging the likelihood that it would not long sur- vive, wrote, "On the day when real democracy and freedom come to China, we must erect another Goddess of Democracy here in the Square—monumental, towering, and permanent. We have strong faith that that day will come at last. We have still another hope: Chinese people, arise! Erect the statue of the Goddess of Democracy in your mil- lions of hearts! Long live the people! Long live freedom! Long live democracy!"

There is perhaps no stronger statement of the true Masonic principles of Liberty, Equality, Consent of the Governed, the Spirit of Free and Open Inquiry, and the Inherent Dignity of the Individual.

The purpose of the Congressionally authorized monument is "to commemorate the more than 100 million victims of Communism." President Bush named some of those in his dedication address: "They include innocent Ukrainians starved to death in Stalin's Great Famine; or Russians killed in Stalin's purges; Lithuanians and Latvians and Estonians loaded onto cattle cars and deported to Arctic death camps of Soviet Communism. They include Chinese killed in the Great Leap Forward and the Cultural Revolution; Cambodians slain in Pol Pot's Killing Fields; East Germans shot attempting to scale the Berlin Wall in order to make it to freedom; Poles massacred in the Katyn Forest; and Ethiopians slaughtered in the 'Red Terror'; Miskito Indians murdered by Nicaragua's Sandinista dictatorship; and Cuban *balseros* who drowned escaping tyranny."

Such tyranny may be considered the exact antithesis of the values promulgated by Freemasonry and the political system designed by America's Founders.

JUDICIARY SQUARE

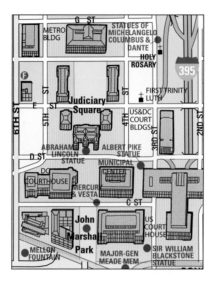

CONTINUING ON to Judiciary Square will reveal a particularly rich vein of esoteric symbolism and Masonic history. Nestled among the Municipal offices of the District of Columbia we find the statue of Albert Pike at Police Headquarters, a lesser-known statue of Abraham Lincoln, a rich grouping of medieval and Renaissance luminaries, and statues honoring two great legal minds, John Marshall and Sir William Blackstone. The Municipal Center high-reliefs (pages 112–13) are among the most occult on the route.

opposite. Statue of Albert Pike (detail). A goddess in Greek dress holds the banner of the Scottish Rite. The symbol of the Masonic double-headed eagle traces back to the ancient Sumerian city of Lagash. It was used by Charlemagne when he became Holy Roman Emperor, ca. 800. It was adopted by Freemasonry in the mid-eighteenth century. The eagle is surmounted by a Prussian crown and perched on a sword from which hangs a scroll bearing the motto: *Deus Meumque Jus,* or "God and my Right." The Supreme Council of the Scottish Rite, Southern Jurisdiction, sponsored and paid for the statue. See page 111.

above and left. Three classical Renaissance figures long identified with the esoteric movement include Dante, Michelangelo, and Columbus.

opposite. Sovereign Grand Commander of the Ancient and Accepted Scottish Rite of Freemasonry of the Southern Jurisdiction of the U.S.A., General Albert Pike (1809–1891) was one of the foremost Masonic scholars and doctrinal innovators in the history of the American Craft. Lawyer, statesman, soldier, writer, and poet, he is mentioned throughout the text. Note he holds a copy of his clasic text *Morals and Dogma of the Ancient and Accepted Scottish Rite of Freemasonry.*

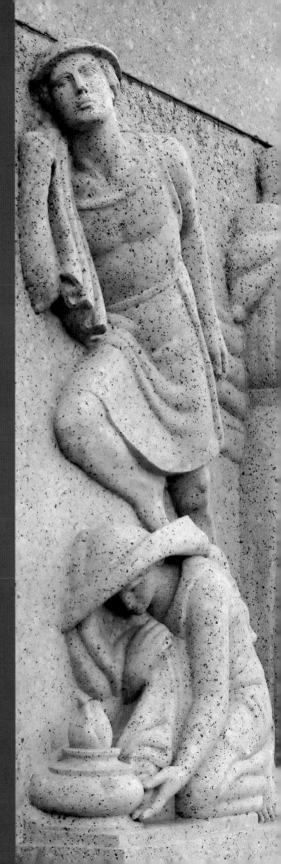

opposite above. *Urban Life* (east panel). Mercury rules thought, writing, commerce, travelers, and thieves. He is the guardian of the Mysteries. Flying heavenward, his cloak streams behind him. Vesta, the virgin goddess of the hearth, tends the sacred flame of her altar. Aesculapius, god of healing, son of Apollo, holds his staff wrapped with a serpent before the seated Maia. She is one of the seven sisters of the Pleiades, daughter of Atlas, and mother of Mercury by Zeus. David Ovason presents a fascinating astrological interpretation of this panel. On the other hand, the official explanation is interesting in that it personifies such archetypes as mundane necessities. Thus Maia represents the courts; Aesculapius, hospitals; Mercury, commerce; and Vesta, the sanitation department (the purifying nature of her flame, no doubt!). The confluence of myth and reality, sacred and profane is instructive. As in a magical invocation, heaven is brought to earth and the Gods truly walk among us.

opposite below. *Light, Water, and Thoroughfare* (west panel). Here the goddess Columbia pours water into the basin for the mother and child at her right. In her left hand, she holds a lamp to light the way for the traveler walking east. While the official interpretation again places all this within a mundane context of various necessary urban functions, I was immediately struck by the resemblance of these figures to the Star and Hermit cards of the tarot.

right. Figures shown in high-relief.

FEDERAL TRIANGLE

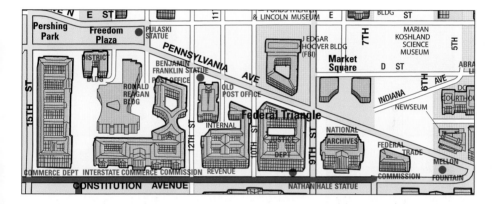

FEDERAL TRIANGLE is the central hub of the national bureau-cracy and home to the National Archives, treasure-house of the American soul. The Mellon Fountain at the eastern tip resonates with esoteric imagery in its beautiful zodiac. Such symbolism is amplified by several depictions of the four hermetic elements of the Mystery traditions (122–25). Mythic and heroic figures continue their instruction in America's national values. Even the Internal Revenue Service building is inscribed with the perhaps unpleasant truth noted by Supreme Court Justice Oliver Wendell Holmes, "Taxes are what we pay for a civilized society."

opposite. These two figures sit outside the Pennsylvania Avenue entrance to the National Archives. The female holding the open book is known as Future. On her base is the inscription "What is Past is Prologue," a quote from Shakespeare's *The Tempest.* The male figure is called Past. The inscription on his base reads "Study the Past," part of Confucius's quote, "Study the past if you would divine the future." This couple should be compared with their counterparts at the Constitution Avenue entrance shown on page 119.

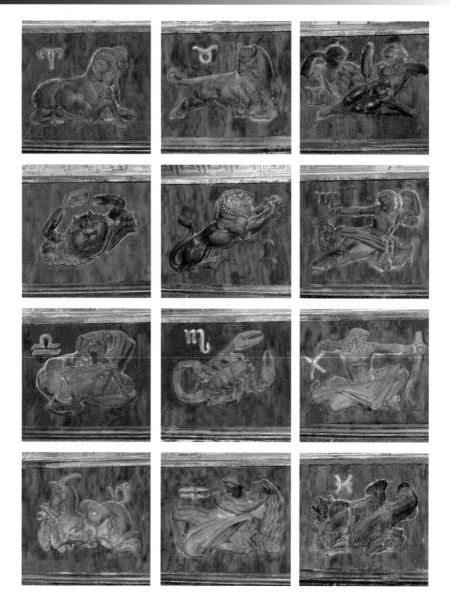

These astrological signs decorate the Andrew W. Mellon Memorial Fountain, at the apex of Federal Triangle where Constitution and Pennsylvania Avenues intersect. They were sculpted by Sidney Waugh, also responsible for the Steuben Zodiac shown on pages 146 and 147. James M. Goode in his invaluable guide *The Outdoor Sculpture of Washington D.C.* says that the signs are positioned on the Mellon Fountain so that Aries will be illumined at sunrise of the vernal equinox. Mellon (1855–1937), a Freemason and financier, also served as Secretary of the Treasury and U.S. Ambassador to England.

above. Detail of the Constitution Avenue central pediment of the National Archives shows the seated Recorder of the Archives. Below him are two rams and a band of papyrus plants. On either side are figures holding the Constitution and Declaration of Independence. The winged horses signify aspiration.

below. The Pennsylvania Avenue pediment shows the figure of Destiny seated between two eagles atop fasces pillars. Above the eagles are two winged figures representing Patriotism. At left is a mounted farmer and his wife, symbolizing the "Arts of Peace." At the right is a mounted cavalryman and marching soldier, carrying the swords of vanquished enemies, signifying the "Arts of War."

opposite top. Water. The female reclining on a sea horse with serpent's tail is surrounded by her iconic dolphins. In the tarot, she is Cups.

opposite below. Air. Mercury with his winged headpiece and Caduceus is beside the eagle. He reclines upon a horse that soars swiftly through the clouds. Cherubs of the winds are at either end. In the tarot, he is Swords.

above. Earth. The reclining figure is seated upon stones and rests against the Bull of Taurus. In the right corner of the pediment is a sheaf of wheat. At left is a millstone. In the tarot, he is Disks.

below. Fire. The female is resting between two Rams of Aries. Her vase pours forth the abundant fruits of industry. In the tarot, she is Wands.

above and opposite above. The four pediments of the Department of Commerce Building along 15th Street between Pennsylvania and Constitution Avenues also show the four elements. Mining and Fisheries above are attributed to Earth and Water as shown in details. On the opposite page, Aeronautics above is attributed to Air, and Foreign and Domestic Commerce to Fire (symbolized by the Fire sign of the Ram).

opposite below. This lovely grillwork tops the parking gates of the Department of Commerce. The griffin is a hybrid figure, a solar symbol carrying the message of regeneration. The front half of his body is that of an eagle, the back half a lion with a serpentine tail. The griffin is generally regarded as a beneficent being, sacred to Apollo, and known for his love of gold and sparkling precious stones, particularly the emerald. The griffin is the guardian of tombs but also of the path of salvation and is depicted beside the Tree of Life in Babylonian cylinder seals.

above. The Ronald Reagan Building and International Trade Center was dedicated in 1998. It is located on Pennsylvania Avenue, along which the presidential inauguration procession passes, a tradition started by Thomas Jefferson. The first president sworn in at the Capitol, he walked there from the White House.

opposite above. The Department of the Post Office pediment along Pennsylvania Avenue shows a youth handing the Torch of Enlightenment to his counterpart, both kneeling in front of a globe.

opposite middle. The central figure on the 12th Street pediment of the Post Office building is called the *Spirit of Progress and Civilization.* On the left is the Bearer of the Printed Word. At the right is Mercury, Lord of Commerce and Communication. The horses on the left symbolize mail delivery by land; the sea horses at right, delivery by water.

opposite below. The two figures Law and Justice recline on either side of the seal of the District of Columbia surmounted by an eagle. They are on the Pennsylvania Avenue side of the District of Columbia Executive Office Building.

Freedom Plaza has images of the Great Seal of the United States inset in the sidewalk.

top left: Obverse.
middle left: Reverse.
bottom left: 1841 variant.

The design for the Great Seal was begun by a committee, chosen at the signing of the Declaration of Independence, that included Thomas Jefferson, Benjamin Franklin, John Adams, and antiquarian Eugene Simitiere. They proposed the motto *E Pluribus Unum* (Out of Many, One) and the All-Seeing Eye. The phrases *Novus Ordo Seculorum* (New Order of the Ages) and *Annuit Coeptis* (He Favors Our Undertaking) were added in 1782 when the final design (as modified by Charles Thomson and William Barton of the third committee) was approved.

The Eye in the Triangle was considered such an overtly Masonic symbol that a die of the reverse was not struck until 1935, when Vice President and Freemason Henry Wallace suggested that both sides appear on the dollar bill. The idea was accepted by President Franklin Roosevelt, also a Freemason. (The Eye in the Triangle is, however, not a specifically Masonic symbol, as discussed on page 57.)

The Freedom Plaza version of the reverse has an incorrect number of bricks in the pyramid.

The White House, Ellipse, and Lafayette Park

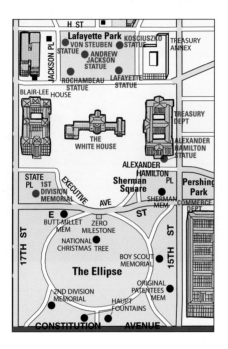

The President's House reminds us of the position of the executive branch in the American design. Compare the beautiful but comparatively modest White House with the opulence of the Capitol. Nearby Lafayette Park immortalizes a group of Masonic Revolutionary heroes from other countries who helped us win our freedom. The Ellipse bears eloquent witness to the human cost of that freedom, memorializing the heroism and courage of the members of America's armed forces, whose devotion to duty and honor has built and sustained this country.

above. The President's House, worldwide symbol of the American executive branch, was painted white after being burned during the War of 1812. It has since been known as the White House. George Washington and Thomas Jefferson both played a role in its design, along with architects and Freemasons James Hoban and Benjamin Latrobe. Despite its opulence, it is modest in comparison to many Old World executive quarters such as Buckingham Palace or Versailles. The Masonic cornerstone laying ceremony took place on October 13, 1792.

opposite below. This photo demonstrates the lack of precise alignment between the White House and the Washington Monument. It is shot facing the center of the north side of the White House with the monument clearly to the east. The Jefferson Pier Stone, determined by a survey ordered by Thomas Jefferson in 1804, marks the proper alignment (see page 135).

above. The Jefferson Pier Stone marks the precise alignment of the east-west and north-south axis between the Capitol, Washington Monument, and White House. It is 390 feet northwest of the monument.

Alexander Hamilton, Freemason, Founding Father, first Secretary of the Treasury, and a coauthor of *The Federalist Papers*. Hamilton, Jefferson, and Madison were initially responsible for crafting the political compromise that established the nation's capital on the banks of the Potomac.

Lafayette Park, across the street on the north side of the White House, displays five major statues honoring Freemasons. Four foreign allies who served as generals during the Revolution stand at each corner of the park, while the legendary American president and general Andrew Jackson guards the center.

above. Andrew Jackson (1767–1845), ramrod straight upon his mighty steed, raises his hat to salute his troops at the Battle of New Orleans during the War of 1812, a decisive victory for the United States.

opposite. The Marquis de Lafayette (1757–1834), a French nobleman, served as a general in the American army. He became an intimate friend of George Washington, who took a paternal interest in the brave young man. Lafayette was a staunch diplomatic proponent for the American cause at the court of the French king Louis XVI.

above. Major General Friederich Wilhelm von Steuben (1730–1794) established the training program for the Continental army. This scene is entitled *Military Instruction.*

opposite. Major General Comte Jean Baptiste de Rochambeau (1725–1807), another French ally and general in the American army, later served as Marshal of France. Female Liberty here grasps two flags symbolizing the unity of France and America during the Revolution. Her sword is drawn in defense of the eagle, the heraldic image of America.

above. Brigadier General Thaddeus Kosciuszko (1746–1817) was a Polish military engineer who volunteered in 1776 and made significant contributions to the American Revolution. He built fortifications at Saratoga and West Point in New York and along the Delaware River. He was commissioned Brigadier General in a show of gratitude by Congress in 1783. He returned to Poland in 1784 to fight against the Russian occupation of his homeland. The eagle is shown crushing the neck of a serpent, here a symbol of the evil of tyranny.

opposite. Mythic scene of nymphs and satyrs on two classical bronze urns, technically called the Navy Yard Urns, by an unknown artist. They were cast in 1872 in the same furnace used to cast brass cannons during the Civil War. They stand at the south entrance to Lafayette Park, in tribute to both the classical orientation and playfulness of our national spirit.

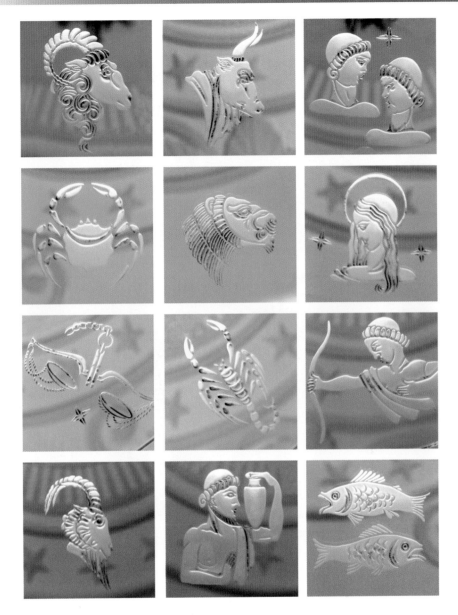

opposite and above. This photo is taken from the Constitution Avenue entranceway of the Federal Reserve Board building. The exterior of the building is a work of understated architectural elegance. The interior is breathtaking. The two lamps hanging from the ceiling at either end of the hall are the work of Sidney Waugh, chief associate designer for Steuben Glass, circa 1937. The beautiful blue dome of the star-filled night sky is encircled by a zodiacal band cut in glass. The twelve figures are shown above in their natural sequence.

Seated Mercury by John Gregory, sculptor of the *Urban Life* scenes in Judiciary Square (see pages 112–13). David Ovason makes a convincing case that this is a rare female form of Mercury. Mercury is an androgynous deity whose sexuality mirrors the environment, ruler of Gemini and Virgo, quicksilver, liquid metal flowing in radiance, embracing all contradictions in mystic splendor. She is holding Mercury's iconic image, the sacred caduceus, symbol of the awakened Kundalini within the spine, the free-flowing energy of the Ida and Pingala nadis entwined around it. Since the caduceus shows the state of perfect health, it has been adopted as the emblem of the medical profession. She rests her hand on a shield, engraved with the seal of the Federal Reserve Board.

right. This classical lamp is on the second floor of the Federal Reserve Building.

below. The griffin's identification with the sun explains his love of gold, and talent for locating hidden hoards of treasure. Griffins were much sought after by alchemists. They were viewed by some as a symbol of Christ, by others of the Devil. Two griffins escorted Alexander the Great on a celestial flight of seven days to the gates of heaven. The claws and feathers of the griffin carry magical healing properties. They can only be received as a freely given gift to one who has cured the griffin of an illness. A poisoned liquid changes colors if served in a cup fashioned from his claw. They were thus much sought after in the halls of power.

This memorial to Albert Einstein on the grounds of the National Academy of Sciences was unveiled on April 22, 1979, the centennial of the great scientist's birth. Einstein is depicted holding a paper with mathematical equations summarizing three of his most important contributions: the photoelectric effect, the theory of general relativity, and the equivalence of energy and matter. The star map at the statue's base is embedded with more than 2,700 metal studs representing the planets, sun, moon, stars, and other celestial objects accurately positioned by astronomers from the U.S. Naval Observatory as they were on the dedication date. It is the world's largest zodiacal map.

above. The ceiling of the Great Hall of the National Academy of Sciences. Chartered by Congress in 1863, the Academy originally met wherever they could find space. During World War I, the importance of science for the survival of the nation became painfully clear, as was the academy's need for a permanent location. This magnificent edifice, erected as a Temple of Science, was dedicated in 1924. The ring around the ceiling hymns the accomplishments of science as the "Eternal Guide to Truth," "Conqueror of Disease," "Multiplier of the Harvest," "Explorer of the Universe," "Pilot of Industry," and "Revealer of Nature's Laws." The figures in the eight diamonds represent (clockwise from noon) Botany, Mathematics, Physics, Astronomy, Chemistry, Geology, Anthropology, and Zoology.

opposite. The four bronze doors inside the entranceway of the National Academy of Sciences each display three signs of the zodiac, shown here in their natural order.

President Abraham Lincoln sits in eternal contemplation. He held the country together at great cost, nationally and personally. America remains one nation under God, with equal justice under the law for all citizens. (Photo by Timothy McCarthy/Art Resources, NY.)

West Potomac Park and the Tidal Basin

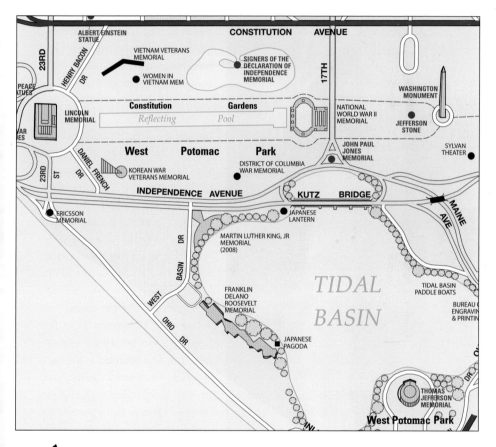

AT LAST WE COME to the heart of America. The Washington Monument, Lincoln Memorial, and Jefferson Memorial are worldwide symbols of the courage, genius, and spiritual aspirations of this nation's leaders and its people. The elegance of the McMillan Plan of 1902, illustrated and discussed on page 53, has come into being, modified of course, in the monumental core of the nation.

left. Freemason John Paul Jones (1747–1792) is America's first naval hero. In 1779, in command of the *Bonhomme Richard*, Jones engaged in a fierce sea battle with the British vessel *Serapis* in the North Sea off the coast of England. After much damage to Jones's vessel, the opposing captain called upon him to surrender. Jones replied, "I have not yet begun to fight!" The contest ended in American victory, but Jones's ship was damaged beyond repair. He is buried at the United States Naval Academy in Annapolis.

opposite. This stunning photo captures the essence of the plan, the beauty, and the philosophy of Washington, D.C. In the foreground is the Temple of Equality and shrine of human dignity, the Lincoln Memorial. Aspiring heavenward is the elegant simplicity of the Washington Monument, whose impersonal Egyptian design speaks to the idealism of the chosen vessel who led this nation as its first president and set a high example for those who followed. In the background is that domed Capitol, home of the United States Congress, designed to serve as the voice of the American Republic. All three archetypal representations sit under the sky, servants to a greater force of whose will they are to be the agents. (Photo by Photopix, courtesy of Getty Images.)

opposite and above. The Thomas Jefferson Memorial.

Thomas Jefferson (1743–1826) was the author of the Declaration of Independence in 1776. It declared the principles of the most successful attempt to establish human liberty in the history of mankind.

> We hold these truths to be self-evident, that all men are created equal, that they are endowed by their Creator with certain unalienable rights, that among these are life, liberty and the pursuit of happiness. That to secure these rights, governments are instituted among men, deriving their just powers from the consent of the governed.

Jefferson served as the third president of the United States. The magnificent Thomas Jefferson Memorial is adapted from Jefferson's own design of the rotunda of the University of Virginia, which he based on the Pantheon in Rome. The cornerstone was laid in 1939 by Masonic President Franklin Roosevelt. It was dedicated in 1943. It was designed by John Russell Pope, the architect of the House of the Temple shown on page 171, headquarters of the Southern Jurisdiction of the Scottish Rite. (Photo above by Rachel Wasserman.)

THE NATIONAL MALL

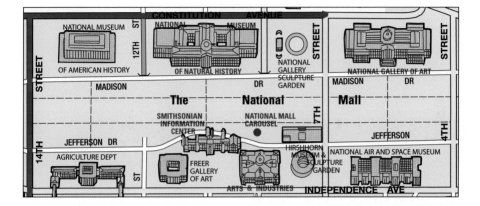

T HE NATIONAL MALL is the living embodiment of the Masonic spirit of the Enlightenment, for it houses several buildings of the Smithsonian Institution, the educational apparatus of the United States, in an elegant tree-lined expanse dedicated to the spirit of free inquiry.

As an additional benefit—and not dissimilar to the occasional and well-known cavorting of members of the Fraternity—there is a fun-filled opportunity for the kids provided by the vintage 1947 National Mall Carousel, and various refreshment stands that surround it. At this point of your tour, a drink of fresh water will be most welcome.

opposite. *Columbia Protecting Science and Industry* atop the Arts and Industries Building of the Smithsonian Institution. Columbia is the national female personification of the United States, identified with the Roman goddess Minerva and the earlier Greek Athena. Columbia is most often depicted as an armed figure of strength and national defense, a beautiful young woman wearing the helmet of a Roman centurion, carrying a sword and shield, wrapped in a white garment, and often with her right breast exposed. As a national personification, she is similar to Uncle Sam and the British Britannia.

above. Freedom is fun! The National Mall Carousel provides welcome play activity for kids and a chance for parents to sit down and rest their feet. Best advice for your Masonic walking tour of Washington, D.C.: Wear comfortable shoes!

opposite above. The Smithsonian Castle, now the Museum Information Center, was the first of the nineteen Smithsonian museums, nine research centers, and the National Zoo. The castle was built between 1847 and 1851 and today includes a public café.

James Smithson (1765–1829), a wealthy English scientist and Fellow of the Royal Society of London, willed that his considerable estate should be used "to found, at Washington, under the name of the Smithsonian Institution, an Establishment for the increase and diffusion of knowledge."

Constituted by an act of Congress in 1846, the institution has grown into the world's largest museum complex. It also serves as an international center for research. It preserves and cares for more than 140 million objects.

opposite below. The National Gallery of Art was created in 1937 by a joint resolution of Congress. It was a gift from Freemason, financier, and art collector Andrew W. Mellon, whose zodiacal fountain is shown on page 116. In 1999, the Gallery opened its six acre outdoor sculpture garden next door.

64 percent of the world's population.[3] (I place the word *democracies* in quotation marks because without a written constitution enshrining individual sovereignty, elections alone do not freedom make. Two wolves and a sheep voting on what to have for lunch may be an example of democracy, but it hardly serves as an enduring model of liberty.)

***

America continues the eternal human search for the right course of action in both domestic politics and international relations. I believe the answers we seek are "hidden in plain sight." The timeless truths upon which America was founded include the principles of Freemasonry and the Enlightenment, which are as relevant today as ever.

Of these, I believe the most important is the recognition of the **inherent dignity of the individual.** This is what has distinguished America from every other nation on earth, and it is the greatest ideological contribution we can offer to the rest of the world. The individual is the cornerstone of the social and political edifice.

The **spirit of open inquiry** in science has led this nation to the finest technological accomplishments and most widespread prosperity of any people in any time. Yet this fundamental principle is under attack. Science cannot be politicized to fit an agenda without dire consequences to the spirit of truth, let alone the practical reality of life on earth. Consensus is not a condition of empiricism. When scientists who question modern dogmas are labeled "deniers," we come perilously close to a modern Inquisition. Disagreement transforms into heresy, and the punitive removal of research opportunities is a form of house arrest Galileo would certainly recognize.

Freedom of thought and expression is the social corollary of unrestricted scientific inquiry. The ability of people to think for themselves and openly express ideas—good ideas and bad ideas—is a means by which a culture develops and maintains intellectual resilience and creativity. The marketplace of ideas rewards success and punishes failure. The most dangerous legacy of the "sixties generation" is political correctness. People who justified tearing down universities and burning flags in the name of free speech put a gag in the mouths of Americans when they came to power. The concertina-wired thought prison called "hate speech" is the most pernicious example of political correctness. Similarly, when people are discouraged from saying "Merry Christmas" in the name of religious freedom, it's time to remember the First Amendment was designed to protect something more than child pornography.

The **objective nature of reality,** celebrated by Enlightenment rationality, is another value that needs to be reacknowledged. People are what they are, rather than what we might like them to be. The Founders were realists: they assessed human nature for exactly what it is, eschewing fantasies of perfectibility. The pipe dreams espoused by Rousseau and his followers—who believed they could remake human nature—were responsible for the carnage of the French Revolution and the lives of countless millions since.[4] In the words of Thomas Jefferson, "In questions of power then, let no more be heard of confidence in man, but bind him down from mischief by the chains of the constitution."[5]

Until we find, or can create, a "cooperation gene" in the human DNA, the perception of man's actual nature as demonstrated in America's political design, will be more successful than "hopes and aspirations." A society that condones expelling six-year-olds from school for drawing pictures of guns, eliminating games of tag at recess because of the danger that someone might trip, and prescribing dangerous drugs to control rambunctious kids will not build the kind of citizens we need to remain a free people. For me, the quintessential example of the result of modern American social conditioning was the Virginia Tech massacre of 2007. Only one person—an elderly foreign-born professor—had the will to actively and aggressively resist evil and protect others from a lone maniac.

Self-reliance needs to be recovered as a modern virtue. We cannot allow ourselves to become a culture of spectators. The iconography of Washington, D.C., calls us to be heroes. Life is filled with danger. Suffering consequences teaches people to distinguish right from wrong. Overcoming adversity builds inner strength and self-confidence. If our goal is to make government the national caretaker—a nursery for the young and a nursing home for the old—we will become a nation of the dependent. Freedom is not free. It requires passion and determination. Perhaps the most accurate portrayal of the dangers we face is that presented in the novel *Brave New World* by Aldous Huxley. Will America succumb to the kinder, gentler tyranny of "managed care"?

Another issue that needs to be reexamined is the overextension of **America's mission in the world.** When George Washington warned against entangling ourselves in foreign alliances in his farewell address, his sentiments were not some quaint eighteenth-century truism to be discarded by future generations any more than the Ten Commandments are a survival from the tribal mentality. Truth is eternal. America needs a clear-eyed foreign policy working in the national self-interest. We can encourage those relationships that are compatible with our values and refuse to nurture those that are not. Propping up failed states is a recipe for greater suffering for those living in oppressive regimes. When people suffer enough, they will rebel. With an effective intelligence capacity providing accurate data, America can quietly manipulate the levers of power—with an economy of force—to help future allies succeed. Social and cultural change takes time.

We discussed the importance of the **meritocracy** in the chapter on Freemasonry. People are still free to rise on the basis of intellect, creativity, hard work, and the industrious spirit that has been the American legacy since the days when young Benjamin Franklin opened his print shop. But as we encourage trade with other nations and an expansion of our markets abroad, there are some industrial capabilities, consonant with self-defense that cannot be abandoned. "Free trade" agreements that require thousands of pages in description would appear to be the antithesis of "free." When America has the second highest rate of corporate taxation in the world, is it any wonder that corporations—and the jobs they provide—move to more business-friendly environments? Can a nation that has not built an oil refinery or nuclear plant in more than thirty years, and that refuses to extract energy within its own boundaries, realistically expect to become "energy-independent"?

Americans are the most charitable people of any country on earth. Witness the huge amounts of money contributed by our government, corporations, and individuals during the tsunami crisis in Southeast Asia in 2006. Such giving is commendable and consistent with our Judaeo-Christian roots, Masonic values, and the Founders' humanitarian sentiments. But, we need to be willing to distinguish **genuine charity** from encouraging unsuccessful behavior by paying for its consequences. Policies that reward failure will keep people in chains, whether domestically or internationally.

Should America fail—should "we the people" be unwilling to take responsibility for the dreams realized for a time by the luminaries we have visited in these pages—their words and deeds will live on. Like the ancient Egyptians, the Founders erected timeless structures, conceptual masterpieces that have lived beyond the lifetimes of their creators. If we, their beneficiaries, surrender to corruption and decline, becoming soft and self-indulgent, a leaner, hungrier, more motivated people will one day rediscover and embrace liberty—with all its demands. The Goddess of Democracy (see page 107) carries a torch whose flame is eternal.

My fervent prayer is that we Americans make ourselves worthy to continue to enjoy the gift of our freedom. The values our Founders espoused, and brought to life in this nation and its capital, are the highest and best of which humanity is capable. If we can summon the courage and will to face modern challenges, bringing to bear intelligence, through education, and apply the lessons taught by Washington, D.C., we can succeed.

Pages 102–3
The Contemplation of Justice and The Authority of Law
Supreme Court, 1st Street and Maryland Avenue, NE
Sculptor: James Earle Fraser

UNION STATION

Pages 64 and 104
The Progress of Railroading, 1908
Union Station, Massachusetts and Delaware Avenues, NE
Sculptor: Louis Saint-Gaudens

Page 107
Victims of Communism Memorial, 2007
Massachusetts and New Jersey Avenues, NW
Sculptor: Thomas Marsh

JUDICIARY SQUARE

Page 62
John Marshall, 1884
Judiciary Square, C Street and 4th Street
Sculptor: William Wetmore Story

Pages 108 and 111
Brigadier General Albert Pike, 1901
3rd and D Streets, NW
Sculptor: Gaetano Trentanove

Page 110 above
Dante and Michelangelo
Casa Italiana Cultural and Social Center, 3rd and F Streets

Page 110 below
Christopher Columbus
Holy Rosary Roman Catholic Church, 3rd and F Streets

Pages 112–13
Urban Life, 1941
Municipal Center Building, 300 Indiana Avenue, NW
Sculptor: John Gregory

FEDERAL TRIANGLE

Page 63
Captain Nathan Hale, ca. 1915
Department of Justice, Constitution Ave. between 9th and 10th Streets NW
Sculptor: Bela Lyon Pratt

Page 114
Past and Future, 1935
National Archives, Pennsylvania Avenue and 8th Street, NW
Sculptor: Robert Aitken

Page 116
Andrew W. Mellon Memorial Fountain, 1952
Constitution and Pennsylvania Avenues, NW
Sculptor: Sidney Waugh

Federal Trade Commission

Page 117
Man Controlling Trade, 1942
Federal Trade Commission, 6th Street and Pennsylania Avenue, NW
Sculptor: Michael Lantz

Page 117
American Transportation Doors, 1938
Federal Trade Commission, Pennsylvania Ave. between 6th and 7th Streets, NW
Sculptor: William M. McVey

Page 118
Americans at Work, Past and Present Limestone Reliefs, 1937
Federal Trade Commission, Constitution Ave. between 6th and 7th Streets, NW
Foreign Trade by Carl L. Schmitz
Agriculture by Concetta Scaravaglione

National Archives

Page 119
Heritage and Guardianship, 1935
National Archives, Constitution Avenue, between 7th and 9th Streets, NW
Sculptor: James Earle Fraser

Page 120 above
The Recorder of the Archives, 1935
National Archives, Constitution Avenue, between 7th and 9th Streets, NW
Sculptor: James Earle Fraser

Page 120 below
Destiny, 1935
National Archives, Pennsylvania Avenue and 8th Street, NW
Sculptor: Adolph Alexander Weinman

Department of Justice

Page 121 above and middle
Ars Boni and Ars Aequi, 1934
Department of Justice, Constitution Ave., between 9th and 10th Streets, NW
Sculptor: Carl Paul Jennewein

Page 121 below
Law and Order, 1934–1935
Department of Justice, Constitution Ave., between 9th and 10th Streets, NW
Sculptor: Carl Paul Jennewein

Interstate Commerce Commission (EPA)

Page 122 above
Interstate Transportation, 1935
Interstate Commerce Commission,
Constitution Avenue between 12th and 14th Streets, NW
Sculptor: Wheeler Williams

Page 122 below
Commerce and Communications, 1935
Interstate Commerce Commission,
Constitution Avenue between 12th and 14th Streets, NW
Sculptor: Wheeler Williams

Deptartment of Labor (EPA)

Page 123 above
Labor and Industry, 1935
Department of Labor, Constitution Ave. between 12th and 14th Streets, NW
Sculptor: Albert Stewart

Page 123 below
Abundance and Industry, 1935
Department of Labor, Constitution Ave. between 12th and 14th Streets, NW
Sculptor: Sherry Fry

Department of Commerce

Pages 124–25
Mining, Fisheries, Aeronautics, Foreign and Domestic Commerce, 1934
Department of Commerce
15th Street, between E Street and Constitution Avenue, NW
Sculptor: James Earle Fraser

Page 125 bottom
Griffins and Eagle, Parking Garage Ornaments
Department of Commerce, both 14th and 15th Street Entrances

Old Post Office

Page 127
Benjamin Franklin, 1889
Pennsylvania Avenue and 10th Street, NW
Sculptor: Jacques Jouvenal, after the design of Ernest Plassman

Page 128 above
The Advance of Civilization Through the Bond of World Postal Union, 1934
Department of the Post Office Building
Pennsylvania Avenue, between 12th and 13th Streets, NW
Sculptor: Adolph Alexander Weinman

Page 128 middle
The Spirit of Civilization and Progress, 1934
Department of the Post Office Building
12th Street between Pennsylvania and Constitution Avenues, NW
Sculptor: Adolph Alexander Weinman

D.C. Mayor's Executive Office

Page 128 below
Arts and Enterprises in the District of Columbia, 1908
D.C. Mayor's Executive Office
E Street between 13th and 14th Streets
Sculptor: Adolfo de Nesti

Freedom Plaza

Page 131
Brigadier General Count Casimir Pulaski, 1910
Pennsylvania Avenue and 13th Street, NW
Sculptor: Kasimiriez Chodzinski

THE WHITE HOUSE, ELLIPSE, AND LAFAYETTE PARK

Page 66
Second Division Memorial, 1936
The Ellipse, Constitution Avenue near 17th Street NW
Sculptor: James Earle Fraser

Page 132
First Division Monument, 1924
Ellipse, State Place and 17th Street, NW
Sculptor: Daniel Chester French

Page 136
Alexander Hamilton, 1923
Department of Treasury Building, South entrance,
Treasury Place between East Executive Avenue and 15th Street, NW
Sculptor: James Earle Fraser

Lafayette Park

Page 138
Major General Marquis Gilbert de Lafayette
Lafayette Park, Southeast corner
Sculptors: Jean Alexandre, Joseph Faulguiere, and Marius Jean Antonin Mercie

Page 139
Major General Andrew Jackson, 1853
Lafayette Park, Center axis
Sculptor: Clark Mills

Page 140
Major General Friedrich Wilhelm von Steuben, 1910
Lafayette Park, Northwest corner
Sculptor: Albert Jaggers

Page 141
Major General Comte Jean de Rochambeau, 1902
Lafayette Park, Southwest corner
Sculptor: J. J. Fernand Hamar

Page 142
Brigadier General Thaddeus Kosciuszko, 1910
Lafayette Park, Northeast corner
Sculptor: Antoni Popiel

Page 143
Navy Yard Urns, 1872
Lafayette Park, South side center
Sculptor: Ordnance Department, U.S. Navy Yard, Washington, D.C.

THE FEDERAL RESERVE

Page 144
The Prophet Daniel, 1962
Pan American Union Building, Constitution Avenue and 17th Street, NW
Sculptor: Antonio Francisco Lisboa

Page 148
America and the Federal Reserve Board, 1937
Federal Reserve Board Building, Constitution Avenue and 20th Street, NW
Sculptor: John Gregory

========== The National Academy of Sciences ==========

Page 150
Albert Einstein Memorial Statue, 1979
National Academy of Sciences,
Constitution Avenue and 22nd Street, NW
Sculptor: Robert Berks

Page 151
The Progress of Science, 1923
National Academy of Sciences Building, 2101 Constitution Avenue, NW
Sculptor: Lee Lawrie

WEST POTOMAC PARK AND THE TIDAL BASIN

Page 154
Lincoln Memorial, 1922
West Potomac Park, adjacent to Arlington Memorial Bridge
Sculptors: Daniel Chester French (statue); Ernest Bairstow (stonework)

Page 156
Commodore John Paul Jones, 1912
West Potomac Park, 17th Street and Independence Avenue, SW
Sculptor: Charles Henry Niehaus

Page 157
Washington Monument, 1848–1886
West Potomac Park between Constitution Avenue, NW and
Independence Avenue, SW
Architect: Robert Mills

========== The Thomas Jefferson Memorial ==========

Page 158
Thomas Jefferson Statue, 1943
Jefferson Memorial, Tidal Basin, East Potomac Park
Sculptor: Rudolph Evans

Page 159
Thomas Jefferson Memorial, 1943
Jefferson Memorial, Tidal Basin, East Potomac Park
Architect: John Russell Pope

NATIONAL MALL

Page 160
Columbia Protecting Science and Industry, 1881
Arts and Industries Building, Smithsonian Institution, 900 Jefferson Drive, SW
Sculptor: Casper Buberi

Page 162 above
The Smithsonian Museum, 1847–1851
The Smithsonian complex encompasses numerous buildings along the National Mall
from 4th Street to 14th Street between Constitution and Independence Avenues

Page 171
House of the Temple, 1911–1915
16th Street between R and S Streets
Architect: John Russell Pope

NOTES

FREEMASONRY AND THE CAUSE OF HUMAN LIBERTY

The chapter opening epigraph comes from George Washington's statement to the Massachusetts Grand Lodge, 1792, as quoted by Christopher Hodapp in *Solomon's Builders: Freemasons, Founding Fathers, and the Secrets of Washington, D.C.* (Berkeley: Ulysses Press, 2007), 50.

1. Steven Bullock, *Revolutionary Brotherhood: Freemasonry and the Transformation of the American Social Order, 1730–1840* (Chapel Hill: University of North Carolina Press, 1996), 13.

2. The development of Masonry from operative to speculative is known as the transitional theory. It has been accepted for nearly two hundred years. Modern research disputes that this was the case in England, although Scottish lodges are known to have grown on this pattern. A brief discussion and additional references may be found at http://freemasonry.bcy.ca/texts/transitiontheory.html.

3. Gen. 4:22 (King James Version).

4. Kim Sloan, ed., *Enlightenment: Discovering the World in the Eighteenth Century* (London: British Museum Press, 2003), 13.

5. Bullock, *Revolutionary Brotherhood*, 36.

6. W. Bro. Martin I. McGregor, "The Life and Times of Sir Christopher Wren," www.Freemasons-Freemasonry.com/christopher_wren_Freemasonry.html.

7. John Locke, *The Second Treatise on Civil Government* (Amherst, Mass.: Prometheus Books, 1986), 54.

8. Bullock, *Revolutionary Brotherhood*, 42.

9. Ibid., 53–54.

10. Christopher Hodapp, *Solomon's Builders: Freemasons, Founding Fathers, and the Secrets of Washington, D.C.* (Berkeley: Ulysses Press, 2007), 62.

11. Ibid., 83.

12. Bullock, *Revolutionary Brotherhood*, 108.

13. Ibid., 222, 223, 228, and 232.

14. Len Travers, "In the Greatest Solemn Dignity," in *A Republic for the Ages: The United States Capitol and the Political Culture of the Early Republic,* edited by Donald F. Kennon (Charlottesville and London: United States Capitol Historical Society by the University Press of Virginia, 1999), 171–73.

15. Judging people in the past by the ethical standards of modern society may not be the most successful method of understanding human progress.

16. Part of their argument is that Freemasons must be "freeborn." They say that Hall's birth into slavery was a disqualification for membership. All eleven of these grand lodges are in formerly Confederate states.

17. Mark Tabbert, *American Freemasons: Three Centuries of Building Communities* (New York: New York University Press, 2006), 65, 162–64.

THE MASONIC DESIGN OF WASHINGTON, D.C.

1. "Columbia" was the first popular name for the United States, and it nearly became the country's official name.

2. Jeffrey F. Meyer, *Myths in Stone: Religious Dimensions of Washington, D.C.* (Berkeley: University of California Press, 2001), 280.

3. Thomas Jefferson to Spencer Roane, 6 Sept. 1819, *Works 12:135–38,* University

Heath, Richard. *Sacred Number and the Origins of Civilization: The Unfolding of History through the Mystery of Number.* Rochester, Vt.: Inner Traditions, 2007.

Hieronimus, Robert. *The Two Great Seals of America: History and Interpretation.* Baltimore: Advance Publicity, 1976.

Hieronimus, Robert, and Laura Cortner. *Founding Fathers, Secret Societies: Freemasons, Illuminati, Rosicrucians, and the Decoding of the Great Seal.* Rochester, Vt.: Destiny Books, 2006.

———. *The United Symbolism of America: Deciphering Hidden Meanings in America's Most Familiar Art, Architecture and Logos.* Franklin Lakes, NJ.: New Page Books, 2008.

Hodapp, Christopher. *Solomon's Builders: Freemasons, Founding Fathers, and the Secrets of Washington, D.C.* Berkeley: Ulysses Press, 2007.

Huxley, Aldous. *Brave New World.* Garden City, NY: Sun Dial Press, 1932.

Jacob, Margaret C. *Living the Enlightenment: Freemasonry and Politics in Eighteenth-Century Europe.* New York: Oxford University Press, 1991.

Kennon, Donald F., ed. *A Republic for the Ages: The United States Capitol and the Political Culture of the Early Republic.* Charlottesville and London: United States Capitol Historical Society by the University Press of Virginia, 1999.

Ketcham, Ralph, ed. *The Anti-Federalist Papers and the Constitutional Convention Debates.* New York: Penguin Books, 1986.

Kohler, Sue, and Pamela Scott. *Designing the Nation's Capital: The 1901 Plan for Washington, D.C.* Washington, D.C.: U.S. Commission of Fine Arts, 2006.

Lamy, Lucy. *Egyptian Mysteries: New Light on Ancient Knowledge.* New York: Thames and Hudson, 1981.

Locke, John. *The Second Treatise of Civil Government.* Amherst, Mass.: Prometheus Books, 1986.

Mackey, Albert G. *The History of Freemasonry.* 7 volumes. New York and London: The Masonic History Company, 1906.

Macky, Albert G., and Charles T. McClenachan. *Encyclopedia of Freemasonry.* 2 volumes. New York: The Masonic History Company, 1920.

MacNulty, W. Kirk. *Freemasonry: A Journey through Ritual and Symbol.* London: Thames and Hudson, 1991.

———. *Freemasonry: Symbols, Secrets, Significance.* London: Thames and Hudson, 2006.

Mann, Nicholas R. *The Sacred Geometry of Washington, D.C.: The Integrity and Power of the Original Design.* Sutton Mallet, England: Green Magic, 2006.

Meyer, Jeffrey F. *Myths in Stone: Religious Dimensions of Washington, D.C.* Berkeley: University of California Press, 2001.

Morris, S. Brent. *Cornerstones of Freedom: A Masonic Tradition.* Washington, D.C.: The Supreme Council, 33°, S.J., 1993.

Naudon, Paul. *The Secret History of Freemasonry.* Rochester, Vt.: Inner Traditions, 1991.

Orwell, George. *Animal Farm.* New York: New American Library, 1964.

———. *Nineteen Eighty-Four.* New York: Signet Classic, 1949; reprint 1984.

Ovason, David. *The Secret Architecture of Our Nation's Capital: The Masons and the Building of Washington, D.C.* New York: HarperCollins Publishers, 1999.

Paine, Thomas. *Common Sense.* New York: Prometheus Books, 1995.

Pike, Albert. *Morals and Dogma of the Ancient and Accepted Scottish Rite of Freemasonry.* Washington, D.C.: House of the Temple, 1871; revised and expanded 1966.

Rand, Ayn. *Atlas Shrugged.* New York: Random House, 1957.

Robison, John. *Proofs of a Conspiracy.* Boston: Western Islands, 1967.

Rossiter, Clinton, ed. *The Federalist Papers.* New York: Penguin Books, 1961.

Rummel, R. J. *Death by Government.* New Brunswick, NJ: Transaction Publishers, 1994.

Shugarts, David A. *Secrets of the Widow's Son: The Mysteries Surrounding the Sequel to the Da Vinci Code.* New York: Sterling Publishing, 2005.

Sloan, Kim, ed. *Enlightenment: Discovering the World in the Eighteenth Century.* London: The British Museum Press, 2003.

Stavish, Mark. *Freemasonry: Rituals, Symbols and History of the Secret Society.* Woodbury, MN: Llewellyn, 2007.

Stevenson, David. *The Origins of Freemasonry.* New York: Cambridge University Press, 1988.

Tabbert, Mark A. *American Freemasons: Three Centuries of Building Communi-* *ties.* New York: New York University Press, 2006.

Wasserman, James. *The Mystery Traditions: Secret Symbols and Sacred Art.* Rochester, Vt.: Destiny Books, 2005.

———. *The Slaves Shall Serve: Meditations on Liberty.* New York: Sekmet Books, 2004.

———. *The Templars and the Assassins: The Militia of Heaven.* Rochester, Vt.: Inner Traditions, 2001.

USEFUL WEBSITES

http://freemasonry.bcy.ca/texts/index.html

http://bessel.org/masonic_info.htm

www.scottishrite.org/where/hq.html

www.gwmemorial.org

www.masonictours.com

http://web.mit.edu/dryfoo/Masonry/Misc/letter-G.html

http://en.wikipedia.org

DVD BROADCAST

Elias, Akram R. 33°. *Unveiling the Masonic Symbolism of Washington D.C.* Washington, D.C.: E-Square, 2005. Available at www.esquare-online.com.

Farkas, Mark. *The Capitol History.* West Lafayette, IN: C-Span, 2006. Available at www.c-span.org.

Hooper, Tom (director). *John Adams.* Miniseries. New York: HBO, 2008.

ACKNOWLEDGMENTS

A BRIEF WORD on my perspective may be helpful. I am not a Freemason. However, I have spent my entire adult life actively engaged in a derivative organization, Ordo Templi Orientis, founded by high-grade Freemasons in 1895 and in existence ever since. While a number of our early leaders identified the order as Masonic, we no longer make that claim. The distinguishing characteristics that prevent us from being Freemasons are that we accept women as full members and are specifically dedicated to the promulgation of a religious text received by one of our founders in 1904. We are, however, taught the highest regard for Freemasonry. On a personal level, I am proud to mention my father was a Freemason and member of the Scottish Rite of Freemasonry.

Throughout this project, I have been humbled by the warmth and cooperation extended to me by traditional Freemasons, without whose generosity this book would have not been possible. However, any errors in my interpretation of Masonic symbols, allegories, and rituals are solely my own.

So many people helped out with travel, research, permissions, photography, retouching, editorial, and artistic efforts that I can never thank all of you properly. I apologize if I have left anyone's name out of this list.

The credit for this book belongs to Ehud C. Sperling, founder of Inner Traditions, who originally suggested it and guided its progress during the conceptual stages. Thank you for helping me share my love for our country.

MASONS: Mark Tabbert, director of collections of the George Washington Masonic Memorial, provided valuable insights into Freemasonry for which I am grateful. Larissa Watkins, librarian of the House of the Temple of the

Scottish Rite, Southern Jurisdiction, was especially gracious. Arthur W. Pierson of Pierson Photography, a devoted Mason and a brilliant photographer, was generous with both his time and his photographs, and I deeply appreciate his help. Thanks to George Seghers, director of the George Washington Masonic Memorial, and Akram Elias, Grand Master of the Grand Lodge of Free and Accepted Masons of the District of Columbia. My friend Martin P. Starr facilitated critical introductions, and, as he has with all my books, provided especially valuable editorial assistance.

DESTINY BOOKS: I don't know if Jeanie Levitan works by sprinkling magic dust or by sonorous incantations in candlelit circles, but she brings a clarity to editorial work and book production that is nothing short of miraculous. We shared a wonderful day in Washington, D.C., with Don, Michael, Paige, and Rachel that will forever remain a treasured memory. Thanks to Jon Graham for our friendship and for communicating the essence of this book. Peri Ann Swan has once again created a superb cover. Thanks to Jon Desautels for his design collaboratoin, a creative first for me.

RESEARCH: Richard Kaczynski, Ph.D., was a key research ally, introduced me to Larissa Watkins, and provided the hospitality of his home for an extended visit. Thanks to Dan Burstein, Arne de Keijzer, Dr. Bob Hieronimus, and Peter Levenda for additional research help and contacts, and to Yvonne Paglia and Priscilla Costello.

TRAVEL: Kerry Kurowski, Jessica Melusine, and Ken Megill of William Blake Lodge of O.T.O. opened their homes and provided much needed logistical support, as did my friends Andrew Clarke and Tim Linn of Asia Pacific Offset. Thanks to Jim and Lisa Gannon for service above and beyond the call of duty!

EDITORIAL: My wife, Nancy, reviewed endless drafts and layout ideas and provided tremendous help in scheduling travel and keeping our home life on track during production. My friends Lindy Wisdom, Stella Grey, Anthony Carlson, Daniel Pineda, and Michael Antinori all provided editorial review and encouragement, as did Lon DuQuette. Nicole Laliberte has been a talented production assistant throughout.

PHOTOGRAPHY: Thanks to Carol M. Highsmith, who gave a generous gift to the American people by donating her extraordinary photography of the Library of Congress to the public domain. My daughter Rachel Wasserman's photo of the Jefferson Memorial is one of the best in the book, and I am grateful she helped immortalize one of my greatest heroes.

TECHNICAL: I thank Emma Gonzalez for teaching me to see by initiating me into the mysteries of photography. Steven Brooke, Allan Everett, and James Mason provided extremely useful guidance in the higher realms of Photoshop and Illustrator.

PERMISSIONS: I thank Dr. Barbara Wolanin, Jennifer Pullara, and Ann Kenny of the Architect of the Capitol's office, who were especially helpful in providing images and most hospitable to a weary traveler. Ben Hardaway of the Federal Reserve Board went out of his way to accommodate my needs during an enormously busy period for the board. Thanks to Marilyn Ibach, who introduced me to the Carol M. Highsmith archive, and to Mary Mundy, both of the Library of Congress Prints and Photographs Reading Room, and to Mariano Aquino of the U.S. Department of Commerce. Susan Raposa of the U.S. Commission of Fine Arts, Hillary Crehan of the White House Historical Association, Robin Webb of American Map Corporation, Andy Tuttle of CSI2, and my colleague Jennifer Belt of Art Resource were all especially competent and helpful.

IN WASHINGTON, D.C.: Bridget Zarate of the Senate Appropriations Committee and Nikki Greco of the Library of Congress brightened my visit with their warmth.

Finally, my daughter and I shared an unforgettable conversation with an Ethiopian-born cab driver who enthusiastically proclaimed his gratitude for the opportunities afforded him and his family by America. A naturalized citizen of some fifteen years, he had recently taken his three children, all born here, to the land of his birth. He wanted to give them an appreciation for their ancestral roots—but more importantly—for the country he had chosen to afford them the best opportunity in life. Thank you, sir, for sharing your love of America.

INDEX

About the Author

James Wasserman is a lifelong student of religion and spiritual development. In 1973, he began working at Samuel Weiser's, then the world's largest esoteric bookstore.

In 1976, he joined Ordo Templi Orientis (O.T.O.), having explored Aleister Crowley's system of Scientific Illuminism. In 1979, he founded TAHUTI Lodge, the third oldest O.T.O. Lodge in the world. He has played a key role in numerous seminal publications of the Crowley corpus.

His books on secret societies and Western spirituality include *An Illustrated History of the Knights Templar,* which offers the richest collection of Templar imagery in print. *The Mystery Traditions: Secret Symbols and Sacred Art* explains closely held esoteric teachings with rare clarity and understanding. His full-color restoration of the Papyrus of Ani (*The Egyptian Book of the Dead: The Book of Going Forth by Day*) with integrated English translation has been widely acclaimed.

The Templars and the Assassins: The Militia of Heaven is a detailed study of two medieval orders of warrior/monks during the Crusades. The book's insights into the underlying unity between Judaism, Christianity, and Islam are now particularly appropriate. He has also written a screenplay based on this research for an epic drama entitled *Divine Warriors: The Birth of Heresy.*

He edited, introduced, and expanded Una Birch's classic text, *Secret Societies: Illuminati, Freemasons, and the French Revolution,* examining the differences between the philosophical underpinnings of that revolution and its American counterpart. His *Aleister Crowley and the Practice of the Magical Diary* highlights the importance of recording one's spiritual practices. He is the overall editor of a series of books on practical occultism known as The Weiser Concise Guides.

His controversial collection of essays, *The Slaves Shall Serve: Meditations on Liberty,* examines political liberty as a spiritual value and eloquently advocates for the contemporary relevance of the Bill of Rights.

For more information, please visit
www.jameswassermanbooks.com

BOOKS OF RELATED INTEREST

The Templars and the Assassins
The Militia of Heaven
by James Wasserman

An Illustrated History of the Knights Templar
by James Wasserman

The Mystery Traditions
Secret Symbols and Sacred Art
by James Wasserman

Founding Fathers, Secret Societies
Freemasons, Illuminati, Rosicrucians,
and the Decoding of the Great Seal
by Robert Hieronimus, Ph.D., with Laura Cortner

Secret Societies of America's Elite
From the Knights Templar to Skull and Bones
by Steven Sora

Secret Societies
Their Influence and Power from Antiquity to the Present Day
by Michael Howard

The Secret Message of Jules Verne
Decoding His Masonic, Rosicrucian, and Occult Writings
by Michel Lamy

Secret Societies and the Hermetic Code
The Rosicrucian, Masonic,
and Esoteric Transmission in the Arts
by Ernesto Frers

Inner Traditions • Bear & Company
P.O. Box 388
Rochester, VT 05767
1-800-246-8648
www.InnerTraditions.com

Or contact your local bookseller

FREDERICK OF PRUSSIA

The Refutation of Machiavelli's *Prince* or

ANTI-MACHIAVEL

INTRODUCTION,
TRANSLATION,
AND NOTES BY

Paul   Sonnino

OHIO UNIVERSITY PRESS, ATHENS

Library of Congress Cataloging in Publication Data

Friedrich II, der Grosse, King of Prussia, 1712-1786.
   The refutation of Machiavelli's Prince.

   Translation of Anti-Machiavel.
   Bibliography: p. 25
   Includes index.
   1. Machiavelli, Niccolò, 1469-1527. Il principe.   I. Sonnino, Paul.
II. Title.   III. Title: Anti-Machiavel.
JC143.M3946F7413   320.1'01   80-15801
ISBN 0-8214-0559-4 cloth
ISBN 0-8214-0598-5 paper

Contents

INTRODUCTORY

an eventual republic. Not that the *Discourses* and the *Prince* are identical. There is a difference in mood. After arguing in the *Discourses* that only a tough prince can reform a corrupt people, Machiavelli adds, "and I do not know whether this has ever or can ever possibly happen."[6] This means that the author of *The Prince* is a desperate man virtually advocating the impossible and trying too hard, perhaps, to regain some favor with the Medici. But Machiavelli's desperation is not contradiction. It is a characteristic of the age in which the author lived and which was coming to an end by the time of his death in 1527.

Machiavelli and his fellow humanists dreamed of an earthly savior. They were rudely awakened by Martin Luther. Thus just as the Florentine's major works were being published posthumously during the first half of the sixteenth century,[7] the constricting and jaded Europe in which he had lived was giving way to the expanding and aggressive world of the "Reformations". He was read avidly in the new age, but the context in which he made his assertions rapidly grew incomprehensible to men who saw the highest good in the precise execution of certain inviolable Biblical formulas. He then became the incarnation of evil, the inspirer of all princely mischief, such as, for example, the massacre of St. Bartholomew in 1572.[8] Some, like Botero, attempted to moderate his ideas by refining them into the notion of "reason of state", an expression that the Florentine had never used and might well have deprecated.[9] The expression was the sixteenth century equivalent of our "national security" and implied that there were times when, for the good of the state, it was necessary to forego the normal standards of conduct. Only a few viewed Machiavelli favorably, and these pointed to his republicanism, maintaining that he had merely described princes as they were. An Italian wit, Traiano Boccalini had him asking Apollo, "Why should those who have invented the outrageous and desperate policies that I described be considered sacred, while I am made into a scoundrel and an atheist for publicizing them?"[10]

The mid-seventeenth century abandoned the religious reformers in favor of absolute monarchs. But for all the editions of the infamous Florentine that were issued in that period, the flesh and blood princes who appeared on the political scene were more interested in dominating an orderly society than in renovating it. Machiavelli did gain one distinction in this period, however. The most perfect, the most powerful, the most pretentious of the absolute monarchs deigned to comment on his works. Louis XIV, in the vigor of his youth and exceedingly proud of the first five years of his personal reign, began in 1666 to compose a set of *Mémoires* for the instruction of his son. The king was chiefly interested in describing his own political and military successes, but in the process, Louis turned his *Mémoires* into an implicit commentary on the *Prince* and the *Discourses*. The king goes a long way in sharing the Florentine's view of men: they are corrupt and selfish, and must be disciplined into shape, but Louis identifies this discipline with a traditional class structure functioning under a vigilant hereditary monarch. The king and Machiavelli both bewail the corruption of their age, but Louis does not believe that his age is all that sick. Kings are only occasionally reduced to extraordinary measures. "What they sometimes do against the common law," he feels compelled to explain, "is based on reason of state, which is the first of all laws by common consent." And while Louis, like the Florentine, appreciates the political utility of religion, he does not separate this utility from truth. The fact that Christianity so effectively teaches submission to kings is to him an additional proof of its veracity. Louis takes his most vainglorious departure from Machiavelli's *Prince* on the question of liberty versus fortune by insisting that kings, as opposed to the common run of humanity, should be able to change their temperament to fit the times. Louis always maintains his distance from the Florentine, whom he classes among "the most unscrupulous political thinkers, the least affected by principles of equity, of goodness, and of honor."[11]

By the end of the seventeenth century, however, Louis' complacent absolutism was joining Machiavelli's supposed cynicism in the trash heap of political fashions. The king's deepening financial straits, his bellicose foreign policy, and his persecution of the French Huguenots gradually transformed this model of monarchs into the ogre of Christendom. The list of princes who reaped the fruits of this unpopularity covers the map of Europe. It gave William of Orange occasion to preside refinement. It is not hard to guess which personality they came to prefer.[16]

The king's great ambition was to keep his domains populous and his subjects paying taxes so that the Prussian monarchy could stand alone militarily. He worked assiduously at this task himself, encouraging the less assiduous with his cane, or worse. His thrifty court, a place of hunting, drilling, and summary punishments, soon became famous for two bizarre institutions. The first, Frederick William's evening ritual, was the *tabagie*, a boisterous gathering of his old cronies and a few honored guests for an extended session of smoking, drinking, and barrack conviviality. The second of the king's extravagances was his beloved Potsdam regiment of giant grenadiers, 2000 men, at least six feet tall, recruited or abducted from every corner of Europe and disciplined to mechanical perfection. Frederick William, however, did not pass all of his time at court. He was always dashing off to one end of his kingdom or the other in order to insure that his officials were performing their duties and his subjects were at their labors. By these efforts the "sergeant king" achieved the desired results. He managed, in the course of his reign, to increase the size of his army from 40,000 nondescript soldiers to 81,000 spotless automatons. Yet the terror of the Prussians was a babe in the woods of European diplomacy. He dreaded embroilments with foreign powers, he hesitated to alienate the emperor, who could accord him the succession of Jülich and Berg, he could not bear to soil his beautiful army. Thus, except for an attack upon the Swedes at Stralsund in 1715 and some limited aid to the emperor in 1734, he always remained, as the English said of him, "a wolf only in his own sheepfold".[17]

It was in the trenches before Stralsund that Frederick William found a tutor for his son, a brave French Huguenot refugee named Jacques Egide Duhan. What the king did not realize was that this courageous soldier and firm Calvinist, who began to instruct the crown prince in 1716, was also a refined man of letters in contact with the emerging ideology of the "Enlightenment". In 1718 Frederick William drew up his instructions for the education of his son, a peculiar document for a man like Duhan to implement.[18] The king seemed primarily concerned with instilling the love—nay, the fear of God into the crown prince, as the only emotion capable of keeping absolute monarchs from abusing their power. Frederick William appeared almost as concerned with orthodoxy, or what he considered as such, insisting that his son be raised as a Calvinist, albeit one who believed that Christ had died for all mankind. These principles were to be inspired through an endless round of prayers, spiritual readings, and church attendance, as well as a careful avoidance of foul talk and worldly amusements. As to the crown prince's specific program of instruction, the king's inflexible first commandment was that his son be taught no Latin, but simply French and German. Arithmetic and mathematics were also on the curriculum, but history was to be limited to the last 150 years and was to center on the genealogy of the house of Hohenzollern. All in all, it was an education designed to produce a bluff unquestioning soldier and no intellectual fop. It was an education designed to reproduce a Frederick William I.

Duhan immediately unfolded an uncanny aptitude for following the king's instructions to the letter while totally violating their spirit. Since Latin was proscribed, the tutor began to accumulate for Frederick a library of ancient and modern classics, mostly in their French versions. One of the crown prince's earliest and dearest acquaintances was Fénelon's *Telemachus*, that pseudo-Homeric diatribe against Louis XIV. Duhan also acquired the library of Gabriel Naudé, a Huguenot savant residing in Berlin. This may have been the source of numerous old editions in Frederick's library, such as a 1597 French translation of Machiavelli's *Prince* and a 1700 edition of the works of Locke, which the crown prince could scarcely have mastered at a tender age. Frederick later acknowledged having read Sophocles, Horace, Cicero, Ovid, and Tasso in his teens, but much of his knowledge of authors like Machiavelli or Bayle always remained superficial. Still, while Frederick William was demanding that his son be turned into a military cadet, the tutor was fashioning a gentleman of refinement. Frederick's education merely confirmed his suspicion that there was a struggle in the world between the forces of authoritarianism, bigotry, and violence on the one hand, and those of reason, learning, and poetry on the other. And where his awesome father dictated a belief in free will; the crown prince opted for predestination. Frederick gradually developed a pattern of insolence covered by shyness, independence under a hunched posture, and impetuousness followed by terror which was to accompany him throughout his entire life.[19]

One fine day in March 1724, Frederick William suddenly turned to his courtiers and pointed to the crown prince. "I would like to know what goes on in that little head," he exclaimed, "I know that he does not think as I do and that there are people who incite him to criticize everything." The king's solution to this problem was characteristic: toughen the boy up. When the crown prince put on his gloves to keep from freezing during a hunt, the father exploded in a violent scene. When Frederick was injured in a fall from a horse, the king obliged him to ride again on the following day. The crown prince reacted just as characteristically. He manifested increasing aversion for things military and religious, increasing affection for letters and music. He required double lessons to get him through his confirmation in 1727, even though it would seem that he had no such difficulty during these years in absorbing Montesquieu's *Persian Letters* or Voltaire's *Henriade*. The first, a light hearted view of French society through the eyes of two itinerant Persians, pointed to the relativity of all human customs and the necessity, illustrated in the author's parable of the Troglodytes, of personal virtue to social survival. The second, an epic poem about Henry IV of France, depicts the heroic struggle of a legitimate king to secure his crown against the evil forces of religious persecution and political rebellion. Frederick William's exasperated ferocity toward his son reached its peak during a state visit to Saxony in June, 1730, and the crown prince began to think of flight. He plotted with two close friends, Lieutenants von Keith and von Katte. The occasion would be the king's forthcoming tour of the Rhineland, the destination England. But a younger brother of Keith who was a page to Frederick William panicked at the critical moment in August, 1730 and divulged the plot to the king at Mannheim. Keith was already in Holland, but Frederick and Katte were arrested and taken to the fortress of Küstrin. There Frederick William ordained a human sacrifice in order to regenerate his wayward son, forcing him to watch from a window the ghastly decapitation of Katte. Then, in the hope that he had finally broken Frederick's will, he gradually relented, offering the crown prince a regiment and graciously designating for him a wife, Princess Elizabeth Charlotte of Brunswick-Bevern.[20]

Frederick began to savor his return to grace in the summer of 1732, when he joined his regiment at Neu-Ruppin, a sleepy marsh town to the northwest of Berlin. The crown prince's duties consisted of drilling his troops, keeping account books on the royal lands, and, above all, mastering the role of obedient son. He also had ample leisure for reading, confident that time was on his side. In 1734, the king, who had reluctantly come to the aid of the emperor in the War of the Polish Succession, sent his son to the army of Prince Eugene camped along the Rhine. It was Frederick's first and only meeting with the legendary hero of the French and Turkish wars. Later that year, Frederick William fell grievously ill, hovering near death with a respiratory disease. The crown prince felt no sadness. "I think," he wrote to his older sister, "that he would be very easy to forget," and began negotiating underhandedly with the French ambassador regarding the future. But the king recovered, and Frederick went back to his books. He must have found some consolation in Montesquieu's *Considerations on the Causes of the Greatness of the Romans and Their Decline* and in Voltaire's *Philosophical Letters*, both of 1734. The crown prince even confessed his admiration for Voltaire to the French ambassador and asked him for help in obtaining some of the poet's unpublished works, but Frederick's greatest discovery in this period was the German philosopher Christian Wolff's metaphysical writings. Frederick William, that old enemy of predestination, had personally exiled this disciple of Leibnitz for maintaining that nothing happens without sufficient reason. The crown prince, the young enemy of free will, concluded that Wolff's doctrine should be read by everyone. And why not? For what doctrine excused as well as Wolff's the conduct which led up to the execution of Katte and Frederick's forced submission to his father?[21]

The crown prince continued his reconciliation with life in

August, 1736, when he and his wife took up residence in a newly reconstructed *château* in the town of Rheinsberg, some ten miles north of Neu-Ruppin. Frederick and Elizabeth collected around them a group of young friends, all acceptable to Frederick William, but also congenial to the crown prince. There was hunting, fishing, and strolling in the daytime for those who liked it, drama, music, and endless conversation in the evening. For privacy, Frederick would go up to his study in the old tower, read, and correspond. Just before moving into Rheinsberg, he had written for the first time to his idol Voltaire. The letter was strange, combining effusive praise for Voltaire's genius with an unseemly precipitation to acquaint him with the works of Christian Wolff. To Voltaire, who was then at Cirey with the Marquise du Châtelet and enjoying a mild exile of his own, the proffered friendship of the Prince of Prussia was a welcome acquisition. Thus began a correspondence in which the two men vied with each other in admiring virtue and abhorring vice, applauding monarchical government and decrying religious persecution, and in exchanging poems. But it was not all flattery. When pressed for his opinion of Wolff, Voltaire stated frankly that "all metaphysics contains two things: what all men of good sense know and what they will never know." When Voltaire sent Frederick the introduction to the *Age of Louis XIV*, with its evaluation of the good and bad ages of history, along with a substantial portion of the work, the crown prince admired the conception, but objected strenuously to Machiavelli's inclusion as a great man of Medicean Italy. Frederick and Voltaire debated at length the question of human liberty, the crown prince naturally opposed, with no agreement. There was more to this friendship than mutual convenience.[22]

Early in 1739 Frederick was struggling with Newton's *Optics*. "I am utterly persuaded," the crown prince wrote to Voltaire, "that we will never discover the secrets of nature. . . morality is the most necessary part of philosophy." What Frederick meant was that he had found another interest. "I am contemplating," he finally admitted, "a work on Machiavelli's *Prince*." Voltaire was most encouraging, but the crown prince discovered, like many scholars, that the research took longer than anticipated. We have his annotated copies of the *Prince* and of Montesquieu's *Considerations*, although it does not appear that Frederick ever touched the *Discourses*. In any case, he actually wrote his *Refutation* in the fall and winter of 1739–1740, criticizing Machiavelli chapter by chapter and sending revised portions of the work to Voltaire for editing. The crown prince intended the writing to be published anonymously, and Voltaire, though critical of Frederick's repetitious style, nevertheless volunteered to see the work, which he dubbed the *Anti-Machiavel*, through the press. He contacted Van Duren, a printer in The Hague, and conceived the idea of publishing the work in parallel columns with the *Prince*, which was also a tactful way of cutting out some of the crown prince's excess verbiage. Frederick, however, was beginning to have second thoughts about the *Refutation*. He asked Voltaire to tone down the passages which might be offensive to other princes, and when, on May 31, 1740, Frederick William died, the new King of Prussia did not wait long to change his mind completely. "By God," he entreated Voltaire, "buy up every edition of the *Anti-Machiavel*!" It was too late. Van Duren would not give up his prize, and Voltaire compounded the embarrassment by issuing a second, more moderate edition on the heels of the first.[23] As for Frederick, he no sooner saw the two editions than he was seized by an author's typical revulsion to being revised. "There is so much that is new in your edition," he complained to Voltaire, "that it is no longer my work." Frederick may have been exaggerating, but we must take him at his word. This is why it is his own pre-Voltaire text that we analyze and translate in this edition.

* * *

The Refutation of Machiavelli's *Prince* purports to be a thoroughgoing rejection of cruelty, duplicity, and superstition in favor of a new way of life in which humanity, forthrightness, and reason rule the day. It is more accurately the outpouring of an enthusiastic young man who seems unable to choose between optimism and pessimism, between liberty and determinism, between the vision of the "Enlightenment" which he professes without believing and the world of Machiavelli which he despises without understanding. Frederick almost expects to overwhelm his readers with a torrent of rhetoric, showing little regard for their patience and even less for their intelligence. He borrows here from the world as it should be and there from the world as it is, without making the slightest distinction between the two. In the process, the crown prince falls into considerably greater contradictions than those he claims to find in his *bête noire*, and utterly misses the glaring similarities between Machiavelli and himself.

Frederick has certainly contemplated the new vision of man, the reasonable, virtuous man à la Locke or Fénelon, who seeks only "to preserve his wealth and to increase it in legitimate ways."[24] All men love liberty, and "it is this spirit of pride and independence which has produced so many great men in the world."[25] Men may have passions, but "a reasonable being" will struggle against them for "his own good and the advantage of society."[26] This sanguine view of enlightened self-interest, however, is hardly consonant with the crown prince's assessment of the passions themselves. Man is their slave. He may have conceptions and combine ideas, but "few persons are rational,"[27] and "intemperate as we are, we want to conquer everything as if our life had no end."[28] Man's reason cannot sustain liberty for long. Much stronger, bewails the anti-clerical Frederick, "is the power of superstition upon idiots and of fanaticism on the human mind."[29] There would seem to be no remedy, for our passions depend on the "arrangement of certain organs in our body"[30] and other such physiological causes. Machiavelli would have had to ask his royal antagonist to think again.

It is the reasonable, virtuous man of the "Enlightenment" who is also at the heart of the crown prince's official theory of the state. Ignorant of the *Discourses* and critical of Machiavelli's pragmatic approach to this matter in the *Prince*, Frederick decides to be more philosophical in the *Anti-Machiavel*. He describes a kind of social contract in which men, out of enlightened self-interest, choose the most qualified and just among themselves to govern and protect them. Echoing Montesquieu's parable of the Troglodytes, the crown prince asserts that "there is no security for men without virtue."[31] Everyone must respect the laws, for without a rule of law each political unit would become "an empire of wolves."[32] Frederick has a special place in his heart for republics, like the Roman of old or the Dutch of his own time, although he concedes that in the long run the character of most men is best geared to a legitimate hereditary monarchy, sustained by a devoted nobility. Still, there is a cocky assurance in all this that government is a purely utilitarian arrangement that stands upon the services that it performs and needs no additional supernatural sanction. Yet the crown prince's simultaneous belief that the varieties in men's customs are caused by differences in climate, diets, and upbringing tears to shreds his political ideal, for he finds that the characteristic of men that makes them venerate the peculiarities of their environment is their stupidity. The stolid Chinese, the frivolous French, the passionate Italians all live under the regimes they deserve and blindly obey rulers who are fortunate enough to profit from the public ignorance. No rulers take better advantage of this human credulity than the priestly ones, for "religion is an old machine that will never wear out."[33] Machiavelli, who wants the lawgiver to draw virtue out of the worst passions of men, might have hoped that his critic was beginning to see the point.

Frederick is never so demanding as in his expectations of the sovereign. He wants him to be a paragon of virtue and justice, or in the phrase that he launched into the slogan of "Enlightened Despotism", the "first servant of his people".[34] The sovereign is to be guided in his fervor to uphold the laws by the same enlightened self-interest that inspires his people to obey him, a peculiar imperative since the crown prince is never so misanthropic as in his evaluation of sovereigns. He readily admits that "since the seduction of the throne is very powerful, it takes an uncommon virtue to resist it."[35] The only admirable princes that he can dredge up from antiquity are three Roman emperors, and neither the middle ages nor his own time seem to provide him with anything more worthy of praise than the beneficence of an obscure Duke of Lorraine. It is hard to escape the conclusion that Frederick ultimately believes that the only sovereign with the requisite virtues will be himself. But Machiavelli, too, did not think that Cesare Borgias were born every day.

The crown prince's ideal sovereign would not only be an example to his people, he would also participate in that happy diplomatic invention of modern times, "the balance of Europe, which establishes the alliance of some important princes in order to oppose the ambitious."[36] But the impression very definitely emerges in the course of the *Refutation* that this balance did not always function smoothly. Somehow, those incompetent sovereigns who occupied so many European thrones were also ambitious and dangerous. Frederick accuses the French monarchy of following Machiavellian principles and the emperor of acting imperiously in the Empire. It was a dangerous game, this balance of Europe, and so the crown prince, while roundly castigating Machiavelli for preaching faithlessness, admits "that there are some disturbing necessities when a prince cannot avoid breaking his treaties and alliances. He must, however, do it properly, by warning his allies in time and not unless the welfare of his people and extreme necessity oblige him."[37] But when did Machiavelli ever advise princes to violate treaties unnecessarily?

Frederick's indignant tirades against Machiavelli might well have turned to abject submission had it not been for the great weapons that the "Enlightenment" had placed at his disposal: its theory of history and its theory of progress; for the crown prince had joyously sensed what the introduction to Voltaire's *Age of Louis XIV* had so neatly confirmed; the world had changed. History, save for a few centuries of Greek and Roman grandeur, was indeed a dismal record of ignorance and of superstition in which men were the blind instruments of priestly obscurantism. The fifteenth century, both Voltaire and Frederick agreed, had seen a limited revival of the arts, but it was the modern era which had discovered the laws of motion along with all sorts of technological innovations. It was the modern era which had discovered the advantages to society of intellectual freedom and the costs of religious persecution. It was the modern era which cherished the thought that its discoveries held the key to the continued happiness and progress of mankind. To Voltaire's indices of advancement, however, the crown prince added a few criteria of his own. The uniform, the rifle, the standing army, all the instruments of eighteenth century warfare seem to have

been as important to him as the laws of universal gravitation
and of morality in conducting modern man toward virtue and
duty. These are the foundations of his new utilitarianism that
render the old divine right sanctions obsolete. These are the
reasons that he considers any popular revolt against the French,
Prussian, or most other contemporary monarchies out of the
question. Add to the military forces the balance of power
diplomacy that inspired even princes to be moderate, and we see
why Frederick believes that "all these things have produced
such a general change that they render most of Machiavelli's
maxims inapplicable."[38]

The crown prince's espousal of progress, however, was as
occasional in his volatile mind as his faith in the goodness of
man, and the spacious philosophy of the "Enlightenment" gave
him ample opportunity to shift his perspective merely by
dwelling on its mechanistic and deterministic implications.
Frederick was constantly returning to the idea that Wolff's
metaphysics had solidified in him. Everything in this world,
good or bad, progressive or regressive, had a cause. To this the
crown prince added the haunting possibility that nature's laws
were indifferent and that the appearance of progress was
nothing more than the rising curve of a cycle which led
inevitably to corruption. Republics, he graphically illustrates,
must eventually fall to the ambition of their most powerful
citizens, and Frederick is forced to admit, though with
considerably less gusto, that the same fate will ultimately lie in
store for monarchies. The crown prince thus eagerly grasps the
occasion of Machiavelli's Chapter XXV to reconsider whether
man has any control over the blows of fortune. After claiming
to scoff at this "metaphysical question",[39] he carefully weighs
both sides and, not surprisingly, concludes in favor of
determinism. "Chance, it is said, made my dice come out twelve
rather than seven," but what this really means is "how the dice
were inserted into the cup, the strength and repetition of the
shaking they receive."[40] It seems a clear victory for Frederick's
pessimism in spite of the fact that the crown prince ends up by
meekly agreeing with Machiavelli that men must do their best
to adapt themselves to circumstances.

The last chapter of Machiavelli's Prince, the "Exhortation to liberate Italy from the barbarians", posed a certain problem for Frederick. He could hardly attack patriotism or come out in favor of barbarians, but he could, like the Florentine, use the conclusion of his work in order to convey something of his highest aspirations to his readers. The crown prince thus entitled his last chapter, the only one on which he actually inscribed a title, "On different sorts of negotiations and on just reasons for waging war." Frederick is quite prepared to admit that he does not begrudge a little trickery in negotiations, "as long as it is not used for anything unworthy and dishonest,"[41] and his list of just causes for wars is impressive: defensive wars, wars for the maintenance of certain disputed rights or claims, preventive wars, for "prudence", says our anti-Machiavellian, "requires that small evils be preferred to greater ones and that one act while he is master."[42] Is it not clear by now, if there had been any doubt before, that this is the same man who would soon enforce his rights to Silesia, later launch a preventive attack against the Hapsburgs, and climax his humanitarian career with the first partition of Poland?

It would seem that, of all the philosophers and statesmen who attempted to criticize Machiavelli, the crown prince was one of the least removed from the Florentine in temperament, interests, and approach to life. A malicious wit, a man of letters who loved poetry, a pessimist who could entertain the loftiest visions, Frederick should of all people have managed to hear Machiavelli's voice crying in the wilderness. Yet the crown prince fell blindly into the same open trap which had already swallowed up Louis XIV and the other denigrators of the Florentine. The trap was this: they simply refused to acknowledge in him the very sentiment that they never questioned in themselves, a feeling of self-righteousness which automatically covered their most reprehensible actions under the mantle of virtue. They also, of course, failed to see any need in their more orderly world for the kinds of desperate expedients that Machiavelli advocated. But Frederick was faced with a more general difficulty that obscured his understanding. His own personal struggle between optimism and pessimism, liberty and determinism, the idea of progress and the indifference of nature was, as Carl Becker has shown, a common plight of the "Enlightenment" *philosophes*.[43] The Crown Prince of Prussia was not the only intellectual in this period who beat his breasts in the service of virtue and shed his tears to drown out doubt. The abbé de Saint-Pierre and Montesquieu, Hume and Diderot, Voltaire and Gibbon, each in his own way trod the same path. Frederick of Prussia may not be an enlightened man, but he is most certainly a man of the "Enlightenment".

NOTES

[1] See Robert S. Lopez and Harry Miskimin, "The Economic Depression of the Renaissance," *The Economic History Review*, XIV (1962), 408–426; Robert Davidsohn, *Geschichte von Florenz* (Berlin, 1896–1912), 2 vols.; Ferdinand Schevill, *History of Florence* (New York, 1936); and Johan Huizinga, *Herfsttij der Middeleeuwen* (Haarlem, 1919), or the English edition, *The Waning of the Middle Ages* (London, 1924).

[2] See Pasquale Villari, *Niccolò Machiavelli e i suoi tempi* (Milan, 1877–1882), 3 vols.; Oreste Tommasini, *La vita e gli scritti di Niccolò Machiavelli* (Turin–Rome, 1899–1911), 2 vols.; Roberto Ridolfi, *Vita di Niccolò Machiavelli* (Rome, 1954), 2 vols., or the English edition, *The Life of Niccolò Machiavelli* (Chicago, 1963).

[3] *Ibid.*

[4] *Discourses*, Bk. I, Ch. XVII.

[5] *Prince*, Ch. XVII.

[6] *Discourses*, Bk. I, Ch. XVII.

[7] The *Discourses* were first published in 1531, the *Prince* in 1532.

[8] See Innocent Gentillet, *Anti-Machiavel* (Geneva, 1576), republished by C. E. Rathé (Geneva, 1968).

[9] Giovanni Botero, *Regione di Stato* (Rome, 1589). See the English edition of P. J. and D. P. Waley (London, 1956).

[10] Traiano Boccalini, *Ragguagli di Parnasso* (Venice, 1612–1613) Centuria I, Capitolo LXXXIX.

[11] Louis XIV, *Mémoires for the Instruction of the Dauphin*, ed. Paul Sonnino (New York, 1970). See esp. 101–102, 168–170.

[12] John Locke, *Two Treatises of Government* (London, 1690). I cannot accept the wishful arguments of Peter Laslett in his edition of the *Treatises* (Cambridge, 1960) that Locke composed them prior to the "Glorious" Revolution of 1688.

[13] Pierre Bayle, *Dictionnaire historique et critique* (Rotterdam, 1697), 2 vols. See the excellent English abridgment by Richard H. Popkin (Indianapolis, 1965).

[14] François de La Mothe-Fénelon, *Télémaque* (Paris, 1699). See also the best English translation (London, 1793), 2 vols.

[15] See Johann G. Droysen, *Geschichte der preussischen Politik* (Berlin, 1855–

1886), 5 vols.; Otto Hintze, *Die Hohenzollern und Ihr Werk* (Berlin, 1915); and Sydney B. Fay, *The Rise of Brandenburg-Prussia to 1795* (New York, 1937).

16 See Friedrich Förster, *Friedrich Wilhelm I, König von Preussen* (Potsdam, 1834–1835), 5 vols.; Robert Ergang, *The Potsdam Führer* (New York, 1941), and Carl Hinrichs, *Friedrich Wilhelm I: König in Preussen* (Darmstadt, 1968).

17 *Ibid.*

18 See the instruction in Friedrich Kramer, *Zur Geschichte Friedrich Wilhelms I und Friedrichs II* (Hamburg, 1829), 3–25.

19 See Ernst Bratuscheck, *Die Erziehung Friedrichs des Grossen* (Berlin, 1885). See also Frederick to D'Argens, Oct. 22, 1762 in *Oeuvres de Frédéric le Grand*, ed. J. D. E. Preuss (Berlin, 1846–1857), XIX, 359.

20 See Ernest Lavisse, *La jeunesse du grand Frédéric* (Paris, 1891) and Carl Hinrichs, *Der Kronprinzenprozess* (Leipzig, 1936).

21 See Ernest Lavisse, *Le grand Frédéric avant l'avenement* (Paris, 1893). See also Christian Wolff, *Vernünftige Gedanken von Gott, der Welt, und der Seele des Menschen* (Halle, 1719), and his *Philosophia Rationalis sive Logica* (Frankfort and Leipzig, 1728).

22 The correspondence between Frederick and Voltaire can be conveniently followed in *Briefwechsel Friedrichs des Grossen mit Voltaire*, ed. Reinhold Koser and Hans Droysen (Leipzig, 1908–1911), 2 vols., republished (Osnabrück, 1965).

23 See an edition of Frederick's copy of Machiavelli's *Prince* (Amsterdam, 1696) in *Studies on Voltaire and the Eighteenth Century*, ed. Theodore Besterman (Geneva, 1958), vol. 5, 66–161. For the crown prince's copy of Montesquieu's *Considerations*, see the edition of that work published with Frederick's annotations (Paris, 1879). The two original editions of the *Anti-Machiavel* are *Examen du Prince de Machiavel* (The Hague, Van Duren, 1741 [1740]) and *Essai de critique sur le Prince de Machiavel* (The Hague, Paupie, 1740).

24 See p. 39.

25 See p. 71.

26 See p. 100-101.

27 See p. 49.

28 See p. 52.

29 See p. 82.

30 See p. 100.

31 See p. 41.

32 *Ibid.*

33 See p. 82.

34 See p. 34.

35 See p. 33.

36 See p. 76.

37 See p. 116.

38 See p. 76.

[39] See p. 150.

[40] See p. 150-151.

[41] See p. 159.

[42] See p. 161.

[43] See Carl Becker, *The Heavenly City of the Eighteenth Century Philosophers* (New Haven, 1932).

The Translation

The original manuscripts of Frederick of Prussia's *Refutation of Machiavelli's Prince* are only partially available. Some are in the German Democratic Republic Zentrales Staatsarchiv in Merseburg, Repositorium 92, Friedrich II, A Nr. 1. Others, once in the possession of Gottlieb Friedlander, are lost, and a final version of the Foreword is to be found in Paris, at the Bibliothèque Nationale, *Manuscrit Français* 15285, fol. 49. Excellent texts, however, have been published in the *Oeuvres de Frédérick le Grand*, ed. J. D. E. Preuss (Berlin, 1846–1857), VIII, 163–299, and in *Studies on Voltaire and the Eighteenth Century*, ed. Theodore Besterman (Geneva, 1958), V, 169–356. My translation presents the latest of Frederick's revisions by combining the Bibliothèque Nationale Foreword with the text published by Preuss. Both may also be followed in the Besterman edition.

Frederick's text is much longer than the ones published by Voltaire, and more cohesive. In the case of Chapter II, however, which is missing from the original manuscripts, I am obliged to translate Voltaire's version. I also provide indications of Voltaire's most substantive emendations, when these are particularly striking.

I have attempted in this translation to make Frederick sound in English as he would have sounded to his contemporaries, brash, wordy, and occasionally clumsy, although I have not been able to resist the temptation to reduce some of his most repetitious passages to their more simple meaning. The spelling of names and the punctuation have been modernized, and the notes are designed to complement the text rather than to compete with it.

I wish to thank Ragnhild Hatton, John Longhurst, and

Andrew Lossky for their support of this effort. Special thanks also go to David Young, Borimir Jordan, and Harold Drake for their advice in tracking down the classical references. For the shortcomings of this edition, the responsibility must be assumed by me.

Select Bibliography

THE "RENAISSANCE":

Baron, Hans, *The Crisis of the Early Italian Renaissance* (Princeton, 1955), 2 vols.

Brucker, Gene A., *Florentine Politics and Society: 1343–1378* (Princeton, 1962).

———, *The Civic World of Early Renaissance Florence*: 1378–1434 (Princeton, 1977).

Burckhardt, Jacob, *Die Kultur der Renaissance in Italien* (Basel, 1860). English edition, *The Civilization of the Renaissance in Italy* (London, 1878).

Davidsohn, Robert, *Geschichte von Florenz* (Berlin, 1896–1912), 2 vols.

Garin, Eugenio, *L'umanesimo italiano* (Bari, 1958). English edition, *Italian Humanism* (Oxford, 1959).

Huizinga, Johan, *Herfsttij der Middeleeuwen* (Haarlem, 1919). English edition, *The Waning of the Middle Ages* (London, 1924).

Kristeller, Paul O., *Studies in Renaissance Thought and Letters* (Rome, 1956).

Lopez, Robert S. and Miskimin, Harry A., "The Economic Depression of the Renaissance," *The Economic History Review*, XIV (1962), 408–426.

Miskimin, Harry A., *The Economy of Early Renaissance Europe: 1300–1460* (Englewood Cliffs, 1969).

———, *The Economy of Later Renaissance Europe: 1460–1600* (Cambridge, 1977).

Schevill, Ferdinand, *History of Florence* (New York, 1936).

MACHIAVELLI AND MACHIAVELLISM:

Bayle, Pierre, *Dictionnaire historique et critique* (Rotterdam, 1697), 2 vols. English abridgment, *Historical and Critical Dictionary*, by Richard H. Popkin (Indianapolis, 1965).

Boccalini, Traiano, *Ragguagli di Parnasso* (Venice, 1612–1613).

Botero, Giovanni, *Regione di Stato* (Rome, 1589). English edition, *Reason of State*, by P. J. and D. P. Waley (London, 1956).

Chabod, Frederico, *Machiavelli and the Renaissance* (London, 1958).

Church, William F., *Richelieu and Reason of State* (Princeton, 1973).

Fénelon, François de La Mothe, *Télémaque* (Paris, 1699). English edition, *The Adventures of Telemachus* (London, 1793), 2 vols.

Gentillet, Innocent, *Anti-Machiavel* (Geneva, 1576). Republished by C. E. Rathé (Geneva, 1968).

Gilbert, Felix, *Machiavelli and Guicciardini* (Princeton, 1965).

Hale, John R., *Machiavelli and Renaissance Italy* (New York, 1960).

Hazard, Paul, *La crise de la conscience européenne* (Paris, 1935). English edition, *The European Mind: 1680–1715* (London, 1953).

Locke, John, *Two Treatises of Government* (London, 1690). Edited by Peter Laslett (Cambridge, 1960).

Louis XIV, *Oeuvres*, ed. Ph. A. Grouvelle (Paris, 1806), 6 vols. English edition, *Mémoires for the Instruction of the Dauphin* by Paul Sonnino (New York, 1970).

Machiavelli, Niccolò, *The Chief Works and Others*, ed. Allan Gilbert (Durham, 1965), 3 vols.

———, *Discorsi sopra la prima deca di Tito Livio* (Florence, 1531).

———, *Opere*, ed. Giuliano Procacci and Sergio Bertelli (Milan, 1960–1965), 8 vols.

———, *Il Principe* (Rome, 1532).

Mattingly, Garret, "Machiavelli's *Prince*: Political Science or Political Satire?" *The American Scholar*, XXVII (1958), 482–491.

Meinecke, Friedrich, *Die Idee der Staatsraison in der neueren Geschichte* (Munich and Berlin, 1924). English edition, *Machiavellism: The Doctrine of Raison d'Etat and its Place in Modern History* (New Haven, 1957).

Pocock, J. G. A., *The Machiavellian Moment* (Princeton, 1975).

Ridolfi, Roberto, *Vita di Niccolò Machiavelli* (Rome, 1954), 2 vols. English edition, *The Life of Niccolò Machiavelli* (Chicago, 1963).

Tommasini, Tommaso, *La vita e gli scritti di Niccolò Machiavelli* (Turin-Rome, 1899–1911), 2 vols.

Villari, Pascuale, *Niccolò Machiavelli e i suoi tempi* (Milan, 1877–1882), 3 vols.

THE "ENLIGHTENMENT":

Becker, Carl, *The Heavenly City of the Eighteenth Century Philosophers* (New Haven, 1932).

Cassirer, Ernst, *Die Philosophie der Aufklärung* (Tübingen, 1932). English edition, *The Philosophy of the Enlightenment* (Princeton, 1951).

Gay, Peter, *Voltaire's Politics* (Princeton, 1959).

Hampson, Norman, *The Enlightenment* (Penguin, 1968).

Havens, George, *The Age of Ideas* (New York, 1955).

Lanson, Gustave, *Voltaire* (Paris, 1909).

Manuel, Frank E., *The Age of Reason* (Ithaca, 1951).

Montesquieu, Charles de, *Considérations sur les causes de la grandeur des Romains et de leur décadence* (Amsterdam, 1734). English edition, *Considerations on the Causes of the Greatness of the Romans and Their Decline*, by David Lowenthal (New York, 1965).

——, *Lettres persanes* (Amsterdam, 1721), 2 vols. English edition, *Persian Letters*, by J. Robert Loy (New York, 1961).

——, *Oeuvres complètes* (Paris, 1875–1879), 7 vols.

Rockwood, Raymond O., ed., *Carl Becker's Heavenly City Revisited* (Ithaca, 1958).

Shackleton, Robert, *Montesquieu: a critical biography* (Oxford, 1955).

Voltaire, *Correspondence*, ed. Theodore Besterman (Geneva, 1953–1975), 108 vols.

——, *La Henriade* (London, 1728).

——, *Histoire de Charles XII* (London, 1731). English edition, *History of Charles XII*, by Winfred Todhunter (London, 1908).

——, *Lettres écrites de Londres sur les Anglois et autres sujets* (Basel and London, 1734). English edition, *Philosophical Letters*, by Ernest Dilworth (New York, 1961).

——, *Oeuvres complètes* (Paris, 1877–1885). 52 vols.

——, *Le siècle de Louis XIV* (Berlin, 1751). English edition, *The Age of Louis XIV*, by Martyn P. Pollack (London, 1926).

Wolff, Christian, *Philosophia Rationalis sive Logica* (Frankfort and Leipzig, 1728).

——, *Vernunftige Gedanken von Gott, der Welt, und der Seele des Menschen* (Halle, 1719).

FREDERICK WILLIAM I—CROWN PRINCE FREDERICK:

Bratuscheck, Ernst, *Die Erziehung Friedrichs des Grossen* (Berlin, 1885).

Droysen, Hans, "Beiträge zur Textkritik einiger Werke Friedrichs des Grossen aus Voltaires handschriftlichem Nachlasse," *Zeitschrift für französische Sprache und Literatur* (1906) 118–131.

Droysen, Johann G., *Geschichte der preussischen Politik* (Berlin, 1855–1886), 5 vols.

Ergang, Robert, *The Potsdam Führer* (New York, 1941).

Fay, Sidney B., *The Rise of Brandenburg-Prussia to 1795* (New York, 1937).

Förster, Friedrich, *Friedrich Wilhelm I, König von Preussen* (Potsdam, 1834–1835), 5 vols.

Frederick II, *Anti-Machiavel*, in *Studies on Voltaire and the Eighteenth Century*, ed. Theodore Besterman (Geneva, 1958), V.

———, *Anti-Machiavel*, ed. Gottlieb Friedlander (Hamburg, 1834).

———, *Briefwechsel Friedrichs des Grossen mit Voltaire*, ed. Reinhold Koser and Hans Droysen (Leipzig, 1908–1911), 2 vols., republished (Osnabrück, 1965).

———, *Essai de critique sur le Prince de Machiavel* (The Hague, Paupie, 1740).

———, *Examen du Prince de Machiavel* (The Hague, Van Duren, 1741 [1740]. English edition, *An Examination of Machiavel's Prince* (London, 1741).

———, *Frederick the Great on the Art of War*, ed. Jay Luvaas (New York, 1966).

———, *Oeuvres de Frédéric le Grand*, ed. J. D. E. Preuss (Berlin, 1846–1857), 30 vols.

———, *Oeuvres posthumes* (Berlin and Cologne, 1788–1789), 22 vols. Partial English edition, *Posthumous Works*, by Thomas Holcroft (London, 1789), 13 vols.

Gaxotte, Pierre, *Frédéric II* (Paris, 1938). English edition, *Frederick the Great* (London, 1941).

Hinrichs, Carl, *Friedrich Wilhelm I: König in Preussen* (Darmstadt, 1968).

———, *Der Kronprinzenprozess* (Leipzig, 1936).

Hintze, Otto, *Die Hohenzollern und Ihr Werk* (Berlin, 1915).

Hubatsch, Walther, *Frederick the Great* (London, 1973).

———, *Das Problem der Staatsraison bei Friedrich dem Grossen* (Göttingen, 1956).

Koser, Reinhold, *König Friedrich der Grosse* (Stuttgart and Berlin, 1901–1903), 2 vols., (1921), 4 vols., republished (Darmstadt, 1963).

Kramer Friedrich, *Zur Geschichte Friedrich Wilhelms I und Friedrichs II* (Hamburg, 1829).

Lavisse, Ernest, *Le grand Frédéric avant l'avenement* (Paris, 1893).

———, *La jeunesse du grand Frédéric* (Paris, 1891).

Ranke, Leopold von, *Neun Bücher preussischer Geschichte* (Berlin, 1847), 3 vols. English edition, *Memoirs of the House of Brandenburg* (London, 1849), 3 vols.

The Refutation of Machiavelli's *Prince* or
ANTI-MACHIAVEL

Foreword

Machiavelli's *Prince* is to morality what the work of Spinoza is to faith: Spinoza sapped the foundations of faith and aimed at no less than to overthrow the edifice of religion; Machiavelli corrupted politics and undertook to destroy the precepts of sound morality. The errors of one were only errors of speculation; those of the other regarded practice. However, while the theologians have sounded the tocsin and raised the alarm against Spinoza, while his work has been formally refuted, and while the Divinity has been defended against the attacks of this impious man, Machiavelli has been harried only by some moralists and has maintained himself, in spite of them and in spite of his pernicious morality, as an authority on politics to our day.[1]

I dare come to the defense of humanity against this monster who would destroy it, I dare to oppose reason and justice to iniquity and crime, and I have ventured my reflections on Machiavelli's *Prince* following each chapter, so that the antidote may be found right next to the poison.

I have always considered Machiavelli's *Prince* as one of the most dangerous works ever to be disseminated in the world. It is a book which falls naturally into the hands of princes and of those with a taste for politics. Since it is very easy for an ambitious young man, whose heart and judgment are not sufficiently developed to distinguish clearly between good and evil, to be corrupted by maxims which flatter the impetuosity of his passions, any book which can contribute to this must be regarded as absolutely pernicious and contrary to the good of mankind.

But if it is bad to seduce the innocence of a private individual who has only limited influence over the affairs of the world, it is all the worse to corrupt princes who must govern people, administer justice, set an example for their subjects, be the living images of the Divinity by their goodness, magnanimity, and mercy; and who must be kings less by greatness and power than by personal qualities and virtues.

The floods that ravage the countryside, the lightning that reduces towns to ashes, the deadly and contagious plague that desolates provinces are not as ghastly for the world as the dangerous morality and the unbridled passions of kings. The chastisements of Heaven last only for a time, they ravage only certain countrysides, and these losses, though painful, are repaired; but the crimes of kings make whole peoples suffer, the misfortune of the state weighs upon their heavy arms, and the oppressed people do not even have the feeble consolation, without committing a crime, of wishing for the end of their miseries.

Just as kings can do good when they want to do it, they can do evil whenever they please. And how deplorable is the condition of the people when they have everything to fear from the abuse of sovereign power, when their goods are prey to the avarice of the prince, their liberty to his caprice, their tranquillity to his ambition, their security to his perfidy, and their life to his cruelties! This is the tragic picture of a state ruled by Machiavelli's monster.

Let me say more. Even if the venom of the author did not reach as far as the throne, even if it is spread only to those political organs which sustain it, I maintain that a single disciple of Machiavelli and of Cesare Borgia in the world would suffice to make the execrable principles of his awful political theory abhorrent.

I must not finish this foreword without saying a word to those persons who believe that Machiavelli wrote about what princes do rather than what they must do. This thought has been popular because it is wry and has some appearance of truth. This brilliant falsehood had merely to be said before it was repeated.

May I come to the defense of princes against those who would slander them and save from this awful accusation those whose only function must be to work for the happiness of mankind.

Those who have pronounced this final decree against princes have been seduced no doubt by the examples of some bad princes, contemporaries of Machiavelli cited by the author, by the life of some tyrants who have earned the opprobrium of humanity, and by a perverse spirit of contradiction. I answer to these misanthropic censors that in every country there are honest and dishonest people just as in every family there are handsome persons along with one-eyed, hunchbacks, blind, and cripples; that there are and always will be monsters among princes, unworthy of the character with which they are invested. I ask them to consider that since the seduction of the throne is very powerful, it takes an uncommon virtue to resist it; and thus it is hardly astonishing that in an order as numerous as that of princes, there are some bad ones among the good, and that among the same Roman emperors where one finds the Neros, Caligulas, and Tiberiuses, the world recalls with joy the virtuous names of the Tituses, Trajans, and Antoninuses.[2]

It is thus rank injustice to attribute to an entire body what is applicable only to some of its members.

History should only preserve the names of good princes and let die forever those of the others with their indolence, their injustice, and their crimes. There would be many less history books, it is true, but humanity would profit and the honor of living in history and of seeing one's name pass into eternity would only be the reward of virtue. Machiavelli's book would no longer infest the schools of politics, his pitiful self-contradictions would be scorned, and the world would see that the true policy of kings, founded solely on justice, prudence, and goodness is preferable in every way to the disjointed, horrible, and cruel system that Machiavelli has had the impudence to present to the public.

NOTES

[1] Compare with Bayle's *Dictionary*: articles, "Machiavelli" and "Spinoza". Bayle gives a rather balanced treatment to Machiavelli, but betrays a violent passion against Spinoza.

[2] Nero (54–68), Caligula (37–41), Tiberius (14–37), Titus (70–81), Trajan (98–117), Antoninus Pius (138–161), Roman emperors.

On the kinds of principalities and how they are acquired   **Chapter 1**

In order to reason justly in the world, it is necessary to begin with the nature of the subject under consideration, to go back to the origin of things, and to learn as much as one can of their first principles. It is then easy to deduce their results and consequences. Instead of noting the different kinds of states which have sovereigns, Machiavelli would, it seems to me, have done better to examine the origin of princes, the source of their power, and to discuss what might have engaged free men to give themselves masters.

Perhaps it would not have been proper in a book intended to sanctify crime and tyranny to mention what should destroy it forever. Machiavelli would have hated to say that people, having found it necessary for their tranquillity and preservation to have judges to regulate their differences, protectors to defend them and their goods against their enemies, and sovereigns to unite all their different interests into a single common one, had chosen those amongst themselves whom they thought most wise, equitable, disinterested, humane, and valiant in order to govern over them and to assume the painful burden of their affairs.

It is thus justice, one might have said, which must be the principal object of a sovereign. It is thus the good of the people he governs that he must prefer to every other interest. It is thus their happiness and felicity that he must augment—or procure if they do not have it. What becomes then of such ideas as of interest, greatness, ambition, and despotism? The sovereign, far from being the absolute master of the people under his dominion, is nothing else but their first servant[1] and must be the instrument of their felicity as they are of his glory. Machiavelli obviously sensed that such details would have covered him with shame and that such an investigation would only have increased the number of pitiful contradictions in his political theory.

The maxims of Machiavelli are as contrary to good morality as the system of Descartes is to that of Newton.[2] Interest does everything in Machiavelli just as the vortices do everything in Descartes. The morality of the political thinker is as depraved as the ideas of the philosopher are frivolous. Nothing can equal the effrontery with which this abominable political thinker teaches the most awful crimes. To his way of thinking, the most unjust and atrocious actions become legitimate when they have interest or ambition as their goal. Subjects are slaves whose life and death depends on the arbitrary will of the prince, almost like a flock of lambs whose milk and wool is for the use of their master, who even slaughters them whenever he sees fit.

Since it is my intention to refute these erroneous and pernicious principles in detail, I shall reserve to speak of them in their place and as the subject matter of each chapter furnishes the occasion.

I must however say in general that what I have related on the origin of sovereigns renders the action of usurpers more atrocious than it would be in simply considering their violence, since they go entirely counter to the intention of the people who have given themselves sovereigns for protection and have submitted themselves only under this condition; whereas by obeying an usurper they sacrifice themselves and their goods in order to satiate the avarice and the caprices of an often cruel and frequently detested tyrant. There are thus only three legitimate manners of becoming masters of a country: by succession, by election when the people have this power, or by conquering some provinces from the enemy in a just war.

I beg the reader not to forget these remarks on the first chapter of Machiavelli, since they are like a pivot on which all of my subsequent reflections will turn.

NOTES

[1] Voltaire changed first *servant* to first *magistrate* in the second of his editions.

² This learned comparison of Descartes with Newton is clearly inspired by Voltaire's *Philosophical Letters*, XIV–XV. Both Voltaire and Frederick feel that Descartes' excessive reliance on metaphysics and deduction sometimes led him into absurdities, such as his belief that there had to be invisible "vortices" guiding planetary motion.

Chapter 11

On hereditary principalities*   **Chapter II**

Men have a certain respect for everything that is old, amounting to a superstition, and when the right of inheritance is joined to the power of time, no yoke is greater nor more easily borne. Thus I am far from challenging Machiavelli on what everyone will grant him, that hereditary kingdoms are the easiest to govern.

I shall only add that hereditary princes are fortified in their possession by an intimate bond between themselves and the most powerful families in the state, most of whom owe their goods and greatness to the sovereign house, and whose fortune is so inseparable from that of the prince that his fall would inevitably be followed by theirs.

In our day, the large and powerful armies that princes maintain in both peace and war contribute even more to the security of states. They restrain the ambition of neighboring princes, like naked swords which keep those of others in the scabbard.

But it is not enough for the prince to be, as Machiavelli says, *di ordinaria industria*.[1] I would also want him to think about making his people happy. Contented people will not think of revolting. Happy people fear losing their prince and benefactor more than their sovereign fears losing his power. The Dutch would never have revolted against the Spanish if their tyranny had not reached such extreme proportions as to become unbearable.[2]

The kingdoms of Naples and Sicily have repeatedly passed from the Spanish to the emperor and back again.[3] Their conquest has always been easy because both dominations were very rigorous and the people always hoped to find liberators in their new masters.

What a difference between the Neapolitans and the Lorrainers! When these were obliged to change domination all Lorraine was in tears over the loss of that line of dukes which had so long possessed that flourishing country, some of whom are worthy to serve as examples to kings. The memory of Duke Leopold was so dear to the Lorrainers that when his widow was obliged to leave Lunéville, the people fell on their knees in front of the coach and kept stopping the horses.[4] There was nothing but wailing and tears.

NOTES

* Since this chapter is missing from Frederick's original manuscripts, I am inserting the text from Voltaire's first edition in its place.

[1] Of ordinary industriousness.

[2] The Dutch Revolt against Spain: 1567–1609. Compare with Gregorio Leti's *Vita del catolico re Filippo II* (Cologne, 1679), 2 vols., in its revised French translation, *Histoire du Roi Philippe II* (Amsterdam, 1734), 6 vols. See especially the editor's or translator's addition in II, 63–66.

[3] Ferdinand of Aragon established himself in Naples and Sicily between 1500 and 1504, and the Spanish remained in possession until 1707 when, in the course of the War of the Spanish Succession: 1701–1713/4, the Emperor Joseph conquered the kingdom. The Spanish, however, subsequently intervened in the War of the Polish Succession: 1733–1735 and reconquered the area for Philip V's younger son Don Carlos.

[4] Leopold (1679–1729), Duke of Lorraine since 1697, and his wife Elizabeth-Charlotte d'Orléans (1676–1744) were extremely beneficent and popular rulers. Their son Francis III (1708–1765), Duke of Lorraine since 1729, had, as a result of the War of the Polish Succession, been obliged to give up Lorraine to the deposed King of Poland, Stanislas Leszczynski, in return for the upcoming succession to the Grand Duchy of Tuscany.

On mixed
principalities

Chapter III

The fifteenth century was like the childhood of the arts and sciences. Lorenzo de Medici revived them in Italy through his protection, but they were still feeble in the time of Machiavelli, as if recovered from a long illness. Philosophy and the geometric spirit had made little or no progress, and reasoning was not as consistent as it is in our day. Even the learned were seduced by brilliant appearances. Then, the ghastly glory of conquerors and their striking actions of imposing grandeur were preferred to mildness, equity, clemency, and all the virtues. Now, humanity is preferred to all the qualities of a conqueror. We are no longer demented enough to encourage, through praise, the furious and cruel passions that overturn the world and make innumerable men perish. Everything is submitted to justice, and the valor and military capacity of conquerors is abhorred whenever it is fatal to the human race.

Machiavelli could thus say in his time that it was natural for man to wish after conquests and that a conqueror could not fail to acquire glory. We answer him today that it is natural for a man to wish to preserve his wealth and to increase it in legitimate ways, but that envy is natural only to bad characters and that the desire for self-aggrandizement through the despoiling of another will not easily come to the mind of an honest man nor to those who want to be esteemed in the world.

The political theory of Machiavelli can only be applicable to one man to the detriment of the entire human race, for what would happen in the world if many ambitious men wanted to become conquerors, if they wanted to seize each other's goods, if, envious of whatever was not theirs, they thought only of

invading everything, of destroying everything, and of dispossessing every one? There would at the end be only one
master in the world, who would have collected the succession of
all the others and would preserve it only as long as the ambition
of a newcomer permitted it.

I ask what can bring a man to self-aggrandizement, why he
should form the plan of raising his power upon the misery and
destruction of other men, and how he can believe that he will
become illustrious by creating misery. The new conquests of a
sovereign do not render his old possessions any more opulent or
rich, his people do not profit from them at all, and he is deluding
himself if he imagines that they will make him any happier. His
ambition will not be limited to this simple conquest. He will be
insatiable and, consequently, always dissatisfied with himself.
How many great princes have never seen the conquests that
their generals have made! These conquests are thus imaginary
and unrealistic as far as the prince is concerned. This is making
many people miserable in order to satisfy the fantasy of a single
man who is hardly worthy of notice in the world.

But let us suppose that this conqueror submits the whole
world to his domination. After subjugating the world, could he
govern it? However great a prince may be, he is but a limited
being, an atom, a miserable individual, hardly noticeable as he
crawls upon this globe. He will scarcely remember the names of
his provinces, and his greatness will only serve to expose his
true smallness.

Besides, it is not the size of a prince's country that contributes
to his glory, it is not some additional leagues of territory that
render him illustrious: otherwise, those who possessed the
most acres of land would be the most esteemed.

The valor of a conqueror, his capacity, his experience, and the
art of leadership are qualities which may be admired separately
in him, but he will never be anything but an ambitious and very
vicious man if he uses them unjustly. He can acquire glory only
if he uses his talents to support equity and if he becomes a
conqueror by necessity rather than by temperament. Heroes
are like surgeons, who are esteemed when their barbarous
operations save men from a present danger but are detested
when they execrably abuse their craft and perform unnecessary
operations simply to show off their skill.

If men thought solely of their own interest, there would be no more society; for instead of abandoning private advantages for the common good, the common good would be sacrificed to personal advantages. Why not contribute to that charming harmony that makes for the mildness of life and the happiness of society and be great only by obliging others and showering them with favors? One should always remember not to do to others what one would not want them to do to us: by this means one would not seize the riches of others and would be satisfied with his own condition.

The error of Machiavelli on the glory of conquerors might be characteristic of his time, but his viciousness assuredly is not. There is nothing more awful than certain means he proposes for preserving one's conquests: on careful scrutiny, there is not a single one that is reasonable or just. "One must," says this monster, "extinguish the race of the princes who reigned before your conquest." Can anyone read such precepts without shuddering with horror and indignation? This is trampling underfoot all that is holy and sacred in the world; this is overthrowing of all laws the one that men must respect the most; this is opening to interest the path of all violences and crimes; this is approving murder, treason, assassination, and everything that is most destestable in the world. How can magistrates have permitted Machiavelli to publish his abominable political theory? And how can the world have tolerated this infamous scoundrel who overthrows all right of possession and security, everything that men hold most sacred, the laws most august, and humanity most inviolable? Since an ambitious person has violently seized the states of a prince, shall he have the right to have him assassinated, poisoned? But this same conqueror thereby introduces a practice into the world which can turn only to his own confusion. Another, more able and more ambitious than he will punish him in kind, invade his states, and make him perish as unjustly as his predecessor. What a wave of crimes, what cruelties, what barbarities would afflict humanity! Such a monarchy would be an empire of wolves, of which a tiger like Machiavelli merits to be the legislator. If there were nothing but crime in the world, it would destroy the human race. There is no security for men without virtue.[1]

"A prince must establish his residence in his new conquests."

This is the second maxim of Machiavelli for fortifying the conqueror in his new states. It is not cruel and even appears good in some regards, but one must consider that most of the states of the great princes are so situated that they cannot very well abandon the center without the entire state feeling it. As the first principle of its activity, they cannot leave the center without its extremities languishing.

The third maxim of the political thinker is "that colonies must be established in the new conquests so as to insure their fidelity." The author relies on the practice of the Romans, and he believes that he triumphs when he finds some examples in history of injustices similar to the ones he teaches. This practice of the Romans is as unjust as it is old. By what right could they dispossess the legal owners of their homes and goods? Machiavelli reasons that it can be done with impunity because those you dispossess are poor and incapable of avenging themselves. What reasoning! You are powerful, those who obey you are feeble, thus you can oppress them without fear. It is thus only fear, according to Machiavelli, which can restrain men from crime. But then, by what right can a man assume such absolute power over his fellows as to dispose of their life, their goods, and to render them miserable whenever he sees fit? The right of conquest assuredly does not extend that far. Are societies formed only to serve as victims to the furor of a selfish or ambitious criminal? And is this world made only to satiate the folly and rage of an unnatural tyrant? I don't think that a reasonable man would ever maintain such a thing, unless an immoderate ambition blinds and hardens him to the lights of good sense and humanity.

It is very false that a prince can do evil with impunity, for even if his subjects did not initially punish him, even if the thunderbolts of heaven did not crush him at a given point, his reputation with the public would be no less shattered, his name would be cited among the horrors of humanity, and the abomination of his subjects would be his punishment. What maxims of politics: take no half measures, totally exterminate a people—or at least reduce it, after mistreating them, to the harsh condition of not being redoubtable to you—extinguish the least spark of liberty, extend despotism to the goods and violence to the life of sovereigns! No, there is nothing more awful! These maxims are unworthy of a reasonable being and a man of integrity.

Let us examine now if these colonies, for whose establishment Machiavelli has his prince commit so many injustices, are as useful as the author says. Either you send powerful colonies into the recently conquered country or you send weak ones. If these colonies are strong, you depopulate your state considerably and you dispossess a great number of your newly conquered subjects, weakening yourself since the power of a prince consists of the number of men who obey him. If you send weak colonies into this conquered country, they will not guarantee your security, for this small number of men cannot compare to that of the inhabitants. Thus you would have dissatisfied those whom you dispossess without profiting at all.

It is thus much better to send some disciplined and well-ordered troops into the newly subjugated countries, which will not press the people nor be a burden on the cities that they garrison. I must say, however, so as not to betray the truth, that in the time of Machiavelli troops were entirely different from what they are now. Sovereigns did not maintain large armies: their troops were for the most part a collection of bandits who ordinarily lived from violence and rapine. Nothing was known then of barracks and a thousand other arrangements which put a brake in time of peace on the licence and indiscipline of the soldier.

In these disturbing cases, the mildest means always appear the best to me.

"A prince must attract to himself and protect the small princes in his vicinity, sowing dissention among them so as to raise and humble whomever he wishes." This is the fourth maxim of Machiavelli, and it is the maxim of a man who thinks the world is created only for him. The trickery and scoundreliness of Machiavelli permeate his work as the smelly odor of a privy contaminates the surrounding air. An honest man would act as mediator of these small princes. He would terminate their differences amicably and gain their confidence by his integrity, impartiality, and disinterestedness. His power would make him the father of his neighbors instead of their oppressor, and his greatness would protect them instead of ruining them.

It is true, besides, that princes who have wanted to raise others have ruined themselves. Our age has furnished two examples of this: one is Charles XII, who raised Stanislas to the throne of Poland, and the other is more recent.[2] I conclude then that an usurper will never merit glory, that assassination will always be abhorred by the human race, and that princes who commit injustices and violences toward their new subjects will alienate hearts instead of gaining them. It is not possible to justify crime, and all its would-be apologists reason as badly as Machiavelli. One merits to lose his reason and babble like an idiot when he turns the art of reasoning so abominably against the good of humanity. This is wounding ourselves with a sword that is only given to us for our defense.

I repeat what I have said in the first chapter. Princes are born to be the judges of the people. It is from justice that they derive their greatness. Thus they must never renounce the foundation of their power and the origin of their institution.

NOTES

[1] This is the moral of Montesquieu's striking parable of the Troglodytes in the *Persian Letters*: XI–XIV. These mythical people became nearly extinct when they abandoned good faith, but achieved happiness and dignity once they began to practice it.

[2] Charles XII (1682–1718), who became King of Sweden in 1697, successively defeated Frederick IV of Denmark, Peter I of Russia, and Augustus II of Poland in the Great Northern War: 1699–1721, but his efforts to establish Stanislas Leszczynski on the Polish throne permitted Peter I to recoup his losses and win a smashing victory at Poltava. Charles XII's brilliant extravagance is the theme of Voltaire's *Histoire de Charles XII* (London, 1731). Frederick feels that Charles VI (1685–1740), emperor since 1711, made a similar mistake in the recent War of the Polish Succession by supporting the candidacy of Augustus II's son, Augustus III, while France, Spain, and Sardinia took up the cause of the same Stanislas Leszczynski. The emperor won his point, but in the process lost part of his possessions in Italy (see Ch. II, note 3), while his future son-in-law Francis III of Lorraine had to exchange the Duchy of Lorraine for the ultimate succession in Tuscany (see Ch. II, note 4). Voltaire suppressed the criticisms of both Charles XII and Charles VI in the second of his editions.

Why the kingdom **Chapter IV** of Darius which was conquered by Alexander did not revolt against Alexander's successors after his death

In order to judge the spirit of nations, one has but to compare them with each other. Machiavelli in this chapter draws a parallel between the Turks and the French, very different in customs, morals, and opinions. He examines the reasons which render the conquest of this first empire difficult to achieve but easy to preserve, while noting what makes France easy to subjugate and troublesome to possess.

The author envisages things only from one point of view: he stops only at the constitution of governments. He appears to think that the power of the Persian and Turkish Empires was founded only on the general slavishness of these nations and on the unique position of a single man who is at their head. He has the notion that a well established and unbridled despotism is the surest means for a prince to reign without trouble and to resist his enemies vigorously.

In the time of Machiavelli, the great and the nobles were still viewed in France as little sovereigns who shared somehow in the power of the prince, which gave rise to divisions, fortified the parties, and fomented frequent revolts. I don't know, however, if the grand seigneur is not more exposed to being dethroned than a king of France. The difference between them is that a Turkish emperor is ordinarily strangled by the Janissaries while the kings of France have customarily been assassinated by monks.[1] But Machiavelli speaks in this chapter of general revolutions rather than of particular cases. He has hit in truth upon some springs of a very complicated machine, but he has spoken only as a political thinker. Let us see what he could have added as a philosopher.

The difference in climates, diets, and upbringing of men establish a total difference in their way of living and thinking; whence it comes that an American savage acts in an entirely opposite manner from a Chinese scholar, that the temperament of an Englishman—profound as Seneca but a hypochondriac—is entirely different from the stupid and ridiculous courage and haughtiness of a Spaniard, and that a Frenchman has as little resemblance to a Dutchman as the vivacity of a monkey has to the phlegma of a turtle.

The spirit of oriental peoples has always been noted for its constancy in that they never depart from their old practices and customs. Their religion is different from that of the Europeans in that it obliges them somehow not to favor the undertakings of infidels to the prejudice of their masters and to avoid carefully anything which might threaten their religion and overturn their governments. Thus the sensuality of their religion and the ignorance which helps to attach them so inviolably to their customs insures the throne of their masters against the ambition of conquerors, and their way of thinking rather than their government contributes to the perpetuity of their powerful monarchy.

The spirit of the French nation is entirely different from that of the Moslems and is partially if not entirely the cause of the frequent revolutions in this empire. Flightiness and inconstancy have always marked the character of this charming nation. The French are restless, libertines, and easily bored with everything that does not appear new to them. Their love for change is manifest even in the greatest things. It appears that those cardinals, hated and esteemed by the French, who have successfully governed this empire have profited from the maxims of Machiavelli and from their knowledge of the spirit of the nation to humble the great and to divert the frequent storms by which the flightiness of the subjects constantly menaced the throne.

The policy of Cardinal Richelieu had no other goal than to humble the great so as to raise the power of the king to the level of despotism. He succeeded so well that at this moment there remain no more vestiges in France of the power which the kings sometimes accused the lords and nobles of abusing.[2]

Cardinal Mazarin followed in the traces of Richelieu. He experienced much opposition, but he succeeded and despoiled, moreover, the *parlement* of its old prerogatives, so that in our days this respectable body has only the shadow of its old authority. It is a phantom which sometimes imagines that it still has a body, although it is ordinarily made to repent of this error.[3]

The same policy which brought these two great men to establish an absolute despotism in France taught them how to humor the flightiness and inconstancy of the nation so as to render it less dangerous. A thousand frivolous occupations, trifles, and pleasures took in the spirit of the French, so that these same men who had revolted under Caesar, who called foreigners to their aid in the time of the Valois, who leagued against Henry IV, who cabaled under the minority,[4] these same French, I say, do nothing today but follow the torrent of fashion and change their tastes from one day to the next in mistresses, whereabouts, amusements, opinions, and crazes. This is not all, for powerful armies and a vast number of fortresses insure forever the possession of this kingdom to its sovereigns, and they have nothing to fear now either from internal wars or from conquest by their neighbors.

It is to be believed that the French ministry, after having found so much to its liking in some of Machiavelli's maxims, will not stop there and that it will not fail to put all the lessons of this political thinker into practice. There is no reason to doubt of its success, in view of the wisdom and ability of the minister who is now at the helm of affairs. But let us finish, as the Curate of Colignac used to say, before we say anything foolish.[5]

NOTES

[1] The grand seigneur was indeed much more liable to being deposed than a

king of France. Between 1500 and 1739, the elite Janissary infantry corps helped to overthrow seven Ottoman sultans, executing two of them, Othman II (1618–1622) and Ibrahim I (1640–1648). During the same period, in spite of the bloody civil and religious wars of the late sixteenth century, no French king was actually overthrown, although the Dominican Jacques Clément (Frère Jacques) managed to assassinate Henry III (1574–1589) and the schoolmaster François Ravaillac, who was accused of being influenced by the Jesuits, dispatched Henry IV (1589–1610). The anti-clerical Frederick, however, will not let exaggeration deprive him of his witticism.

    2 Armand du Plessis (1589–1642) Cardinal de Richelieu, prime minister of France from 1624. Severe and authoritarian, he sapped the power of the nobles and of the Huguenots at home and arrested the progress of the Hapsburgs in the Thirty Years' War abroad.

    3 Giulio Mazarini (1602–1661) or Mazarin, who succeeded Richelieu as prime minister. Supple and insinuating, Mazarin governed France during the youth of Louis XIV and carried Richelieu's policies to a successful conclusion.

    4 The revolt of Vercingetorix in 52. See Caesar's *Gallic Wars*, VII. The French civil and religious wars. See Voltaire's *Henriade*. The minority of Louis XIII, between 1610 and 1614, was also a period of great unrest, leading to the calling of an Estates-General.

    5 André-Hercule (1653–1743) Cardinal de Fleury, prime minister of France since 1726. An old man of kindly bearing, he was no less effective than Richelieu or Mazarin. Fleury maintained order at home and supported the candidacy of Louis XV's father-in-law, Stanislas Leszczynski, in the War of the Polish Succession, obtaining for him as compensation the Duchy of Lorraine, which was to revert to the French crown upon the new duke's death. Voltaire entirely suppressed Frederick's hostile remarks against Fleury in his editions. I have not been able to identify the Curate of Colignac.

Chapter V

How cities or principalities that lived by their own laws before being conquered should be administered

Man is a rational animal, has two feet and no feathers: this is what the schools have decided about our being. This definition might be just in relation to some individuals, but it is very false in regard to the vast majority since few persons are rational, and even if they were on one subject, there are an infinity of others on which the contrary is true. Man is an animal, one might say, who has conceptions and who combines ideas: this is characteristic generally of the entire race and can relate the wise man to the idiot, the man who thinks well to the man who thinks badly, the friend of humanity to its persecutor, the respectable Archbishop of Cambrai[1] to the infamous political thinker of Florence.

If Machiavelli has ever renounced reason, if he has ever thought in a manner unworthy of his being, it is in this chapter. He proposes in it three means for a prince to preserve a free republican state which he has conquered.

The first gives no security to the prince, the second can only be used by a wild man, and the third, the least bad, is not without obstacles.

Why conquer a republic, why put the whole human race in irons, why reduce free men to slavery? To manifest your injustice and viciousness before the whole earth and to divert to your interest a power which should make for the happiness of

49

the citizens—abominable maxims which would not fail to destroy the world if they made any disciples! It is all too obvious that Machiavelli sins against good morals. Let us see now how he sins against sense and prudence.

"One must render a free state that has been recently conquered tributary by establishing in authority a small number of people who will preserve it for you." This is the first maxim of the political thinker by which a prince would never find any security; for it is not plausible that a republic restrained simply by a few persons attached to the new sovereign would remain loyal to him. It will naturally prefer its liberty to slavery and escape from the power of its conqueror. The revolution would not fail to break out on the first favorable occasion.

"There is no sure means to preserve a free state that has been conquered other than to destroy it." This is the surest means of not fearing a revolt. A deranged Englishman killed himself some years ago in London; a note was found on his table in which he justified his strange action by explaining that he had taken his life in order to avoid ever getting sick.[2] I don't know which was worse, the pain or the remedy. I would not speak of humanity to a monster like Machiavelli: this would be profaning the respectable name of virtue which makes for the happiness of mankind. Even without the assistance of religion and morality, Machiavelli can be refuted on his own ground, on interest, the soul of his book, the god of politics and crime, the only god he adores.

You say, Machiavelli, that a prince must destroy a free country recently conquered in order to possess it more surely; but answer me; for what purpose has he undertaken this conquest? You will tell me that it is in order to augment his power and to render himself more formidable. This is what I wanted to hear so as to prove to you that in following your maxims he does exactly the contrary, for he ruins himself in making the conquest and then he ruins the only country that could reimburse him for his losses. You will admit that possession of a country that is devastated, sacked, and denuded of inhabitants, people, cities—in short—of everything that constitutes a state could not render a prince formidable and powerful. I don't believe that a monarch who possessed the vast deserts of Libya and Barca would be very formidable, nor that a million panthers, lions, and crocodiles are worth a million subjects, rich cities, navigable ports filled with ships, industrious citizens, troops, and all the products of a populous country.[3] Everyone agrees that the strength of a state does not consist in its size, but in the number of its inhabitants. Compare Holland with Russia: see some marshy and sterile islands rising from the depth of the ocean, a small republic only [48] leagues long and [40] wide; but this small body is all nerves, an immense number of people inhabit it, and this industrious people are very powerful and rich. It shook off the yoke of Spain when it was the most formidable monarchy in Europe. The commerce of this republic extends to the ends of the world. It ranks immediately after kings. It can maintain an army of one hundred thousand men in wartime, aside from a large and well equipped fleet.[4]

Then cast your eyes on Russia: an immense country comes into view, similar to the world when it emerged from chaos. This country borders on one side, Great Tartary and the Indies, on the other, the Black Sea and Hungary. On the European side its frontiers extend to Poland, Lithuania, and Kurland. Sweden borders it on the northern side. Russia may be 300 German miles wide by 300 miles long. The country is fertile in wheat and furnishes all the commodities necessary to life, particularly around Moscow and Little Tartary. However, with all these advantages it contains at the most [15 million] inhabitants. This once barbarous nation which is now beginning to figure in Europe is hardly more powerful than Holland at sea and in land troops, and much inferior to it in riches and resources.[5]

Since the strength of a state does not consist in the possession of a vast wilderness or of an immense desert, but in the wealth and number of its inhabitants, it is in the interest of a prince to populate a country and to render it flourishing, rather than to devastate or destroy it. If Machiavelli's viciousness is horrifying, his reasoning is pitiful, and he would have done better to learn how to reason well than to teach his monstrous politics.

"A prince must establish his residence in a newly conquered republic." This is the third maxim of the author. It is more moderate than the others, but I have shown in the third chapter the difficulties that can attend it.

It seems to me that a prince who conquers a republic after having had just reasons for waging war against it might merely punish it and then restore its liberty, though few people would agree. Those who don't might retain possession by establishing strong garrisons in the principal strongholds of their new conquest, otherwise letting the people enjoy their full liberty.

Intemperate as we are, we want to conquer everything as if we had time to possess everything, as if our life had no end. Our time passes too quickly and often when one thinks he is working for himself, he is merely working for unworthy or ungrateful successors.

NOTES

[1] François de La Mothe-Fénelon (1651–1715), Archbishop of Cambrai from 1695 and author of *Télémaque*.

[2] The English were notorious in the eighteenth century for their inclination to suicide, but this story sounds more like a joke that Frederick has taken seriously.

[3] Barca was a part of ancient Lybia, even though Frederick seems to draw a distinction between the two.

[4] Compare with Leti's *Histoire du Roi Philippe II* (Amsterdam, 1734), the editor's or translator's addition in II, 52–62, and with Voltaire's *Histoire de Charles XII*, Bk. I. Voltaire also inserted the number of leagues in his editions.

[5] A German mile is the equivalent of about five English miles. Frederick is, of course, considering only European Russia, west of the Urals, even though the Russian Empire already stretched to the Pacific in the eighteenth century. Voltaire, without changing the description, added to Russia's length in his editions as well as inserted the number of inhabitants.

On new principalities which are acquired by one's own arms and virtue

Chapter VI

If men were without passions, it would be pardonable for Machiavelli to want to give them some. He would be a new Prometheus stealing the celestial fire in order to animate insensitive machines incapable of benefiting the human race. This is not how things are, actually, for no man is without passions. When these are moderated, they can contribute to the happiness of society; but when they are unleashed, they become harmful and often very pernicious.

Of all the sentiments that tyrannize over our soul, none is more ghastly to experience, nor more contrary to humanity, nor more fatal to the tranquillity of the world than a disordered ambition or an excessive desire for false glory.

A private person who has the misfortune of being born with such ambitions is even more wretched than he is insane. He is insensitive to the present and lives only in the future. His imagination is continually filling him with vague projects, and since his ghastly passion has no limits, nothing in the world can satisfy him, and the absynth of his ambition is always mixing some bitterness into the mildness of his pleasures.

An ambitious prince is at least as unfortunate as a private individual, for his insanity being proportional to his greatness is all the more vague, indocile, and insatiable. If honors and greatness serve to feed the passion of private individuals, provinces and kingdoms nourish the ambition of monarchs; and since it is easier to obtain posts and employments than to conquer kingdoms, private individuals can be satisfied more easily than princes.

How many restless and turbulent spirits are there whose impetuosity and desire for self-aggrandizement would overturn the world and whose love for a false and vain glory is all too deeply rooted? These firebrands should be carefully extinguished rather than stirred up. The maxims of Machiavelli are all the more dangerous to them in that they flatter their passions and give them ideas that they might not perhaps have come up with by themselves.

Machiavelli proposes to them the examples of Moses, Cyrus, Romulus, Theseus, and Hiero. One can easily enlarge this list with certain founders of sects like Mohammed and William Penn; and may the Jesuits of Paraguay permit me to offer them a small but glorious place here by including them among the heroes.[1]

The bad faith of the author in using these examples should be evoked. It is good to discover all the subtleties and ruses of this infamous seducer.

A man of integrity must not present things simply from one point of view, but from all sides so as not to disguise the truth even if it is contrary to his principles. Machiavelli, on the contrary, shows ambition only in its best light. It is a painted face which he makes appear only by candlelight and which he hides carefully from the rays of the sun. He speaks only of ambitious men who have been favored by fortune, but he maintains a profound silence on those who have been the victims of their passions; almost like the convents of virgins, which recruit young girls by making them relish beforehand all the mildness of heaven without speaking to them of the bitterness and restrictions awaiting them in this world. This is imposing on people, this is misleading the public, and it cannot be denied that Machiavelli in this chapter plays the charlatan of crime.

Why, in speaking of the leader, prince, and legislator of the Jews, of the liberator of the Greeks, of the conqueror of the Medes, and of the founder of Rome, whose successes corresponded to their designs, doesn't Machiavelli add the examples of some unfortunate heads of parties, so as to show that if some men attain their ambition, the vast majority are ruined by it. The fortune of Moses could thus be opposed to the misfortune of the first Goths who ravaged the Roman Empire, the success of Romulus with the failure of Masaniello, the Neapolitan butcher who rose to royalty by his daring but was the victim of his crime, the crowned ambition of Hiero with the punished ambition of Wallenstein, the bloody throne of Cromwell, the murderer of his king, would be placed next to the fallen throne of the proud Guise, assassinated at Blois.[2] Thus the antidote following so closely upon the poison would forestall its dangerous effects. This would be a lance of Achilles which both makes and heals the wound.

It seems to me, besides, that Machiavelli classes Moses rather haphazardly with Romulus, Cyrus, and Theseus. Either Moses was inspired or he was not. If he was not, he can only be regarded as an archscoundrel, a trickster, and an impostor, who used God as poets use the *deus ex machina* to bring a play to a conclusion when they are in a bind. Moses was, besides, so inept that he led the Jewish people for forty years over a distance that they could have very conveniently covered in six weeks. He had profited very little from the lights of the Egyptians, and he was in that sense much inferior to Romulus, Theseus, and the other heroes. If Moses was inspired by God, he can only be regarded as the blind organ of divine omnipotence; and the leader of the Jews was greatly inferior to the founder of the Roman Empire, to the Persian monarch, and to the Greek heroes who performed greater actions by their own valor and strength than he ever performed with the immediate assistance of God.

I admit in general and without hesitation that it takes a lot of spirit, courage, skill, and confidence to equal the men we have just discussed, but I don't know if the epithet "virtuous" fits them. Valor and skill are found both in highwaymen and heroes: the difference is that the conqueror is an illustrious thief who impresses by the grandeur of his actions and gains respect by his power, while the ordinary thief is an obscure nobody who is scorned for his abjectness. One receives laurels as the prize of his violences: the other is punished by the ultimate punishment. We never judge things by their just value. An infinity of clouds blinds us. We admire in some what we blame in others, and as long as a scoundrel is illustrious he can count on the support of most men.

Although it may be true that whenever one tries to introduce novelties into the world, a thousand obstacles will arise to prevent it and that a prophet makes more proselytes with an army than with arguments *in barbara* or *in ferio*[3]—the proof being that the Christian religion was weak and oppressed when it maintained itself only by arguments and spread in Europe only after shedding much blood—it is no less true that some opinions and novelties have been accepted easily. How many religions and sects have been introduced with infinite ease! There is nothing like fanaticism for accrediting novelties, and it seems to me that Machiavelli has overstated the case in this matter.

It remains for me to make some reflections on the example of Hiero of Syracuse, which Machiavelli proposes to those who rise with the aid of their friends and their troops.

Hiero got rid of the friends and soldiers who had aided him in the execution of his designs. He made new friendships and raised other troops. I maintain, in spite of Machiavelli and of the ingrate, that Hiero's policy was very bad and that it is much more prudent to rely on experienced troops and proven friends than on unknown quantities. The reader can take my reasoning from there. Whoever abhors ingratitude and knows friendship will not remain indifferent on this matter.

I must, however, warn the reader to pay attention to the different senses that Machiavelli assigns to words. Let no one be fooled when he says, "Without opportunity, virtue dies." This scoundrel means that without favorable circumstances, the sly and the bold would not be able to use their talents. Only the code words of crime can explain the obscurities of this contemptible author.

It seems to me in general, to conclude this chapter, that the only occasion in which a private individual can without criminality think of his fortune is when he is born in an elective monarchy or when an oppressed people chooses him as its liberator. The height of glory would be to restore liberty to a people. But let us not paint men like Corneille's heroes. Let us content ourselves with Racine's, and even that is asking a good deal.[4]

NOTES

[1] Moses (c. 1215 B.C.), founder of Judaism. Cyrus (d. 530 B.C.), founder of the Persian Empire. Romulus (c. 753 B.C.), traditional founder of Rome. Theseus (c. 1460 B.C.), traditional King of Athens who unified Attica. Hiero (d. 457 B.C.), unscrupulous and successful tyrant of Syracuse. Mohammed (570–632 A.D.), founder of Islam. William Penn (1644–1718), English Quaker and founder of Pennsylvania. See Voltaire's *Philosophical Letters*, IV. The Jesuits of Paraguay had established themselves there in the early seventeenth century and were governing a virtually independent state in the time of Frederick. See the scurrilous *Mémoire touchant l'établissement des pères Jesuites dans les Indes d'Espagne* (1712).

[2] Tommaso Aniello (1622–1647), a fisherman from Amalfi who became the leader of the unsuccessful Neapolitan revolt of 1647 against Spain. Albrecht von Wallenstein (1583–1634), enterprising and ambitious Imperial general during the Thirty Years' War, who was ultimately assassinated by order of the Emperor Ferdinand II. Oliver Cromwell (1599–1658), the English squire who fought for the parliament in the civil wars against Charles I and became Lord Protector of England in 1653. Henry of Lorraine, (1550–1588) Duke de Guise, leader of the Catholic League in the French civil wars, who was assassinated in the very chamber of King Henry III. The lance of Achilles, which wounded King Telephus in a battle, was the only instrument that could heal him. See Ovid's *Metamorphoses*, XIII:171–172.

[3] Designations used by medieval scholastics to identify different moods in syllogisms.

[4] Pierre Corneille and Jean Racine, the celebrated French playwrights of the seventeenth century, presented entirely different types of heroes and heroines in their tragedies. Corneille's, like Rodrigue in *Le Cid*, were inspired by the loftiest motives in their struggle against an external dilemma. Racine's, like *Phèdre*, struggled helplessly against their own conflicting passions.

On new principalities which are acquired by the arms of others and by fortune

Chapter VII

It is extremely difficult for an author to hide the depths of his character. He covers so many subjects that he always betrays some imprudent features which tacitly depict his morals.

Compare Fénelon's prince with Machiavelli's:[1] you will see in the one the character of an honest man, goodness, justice, equity, all the virtues—in short—pressed to the highest degree. They seem like those pure intelligences by which wisdom is said to watch over the government of the world. You will see in the other scoundreliness, trickery, treason, and all the crimes. He is a monster—in short—that hell itself would be hard put to produce. But if in reading M. de Fénelon's *Telemachus* it seems as if our nature approaches that of the angels, it appears to approach the demons of hell when one reads the *Prince*. Cesare Borgia, or the Duke of Valentinois, is the model on which the author forms his prince and which he has the impudence to propose as an example to those who rise in the world through the aid of their friends and their arms. It is thus very necessary to know what Cesare Borgia was, so as to get an idea of the hero and of the author who toasts him.[2]

There is no crime that Cesare Borgia did not commit, no viciousness of which he did not give the example, no kind of assaults of which he was not guilty. He had his brother assassinated, his rival for glory in the world and for the love of his sister. He had the pope's Swiss guards massacred as vengeance against some Swiss who had offended his mother. He despoiled an infinity of cardinals and rich men in order to satiate his cupidity. He invaded the Romagna against the Duke of Urbino and had the cruel De Orco, his sub-tyrant, executed. He committed a frightful treachery at Sinigaglia upon some princes whose existence he believed contrary to his interests. He had a Venetian lady whom he had violated drowned. But what cruelties were not committed by his orders? Who can count the number of his crimes? This is the man whom Machiavelli prefers to all the great spirits of his time, to the heroes of antiquity, and whose life and actions he finds worthy of serving as an example of those raised by fortune!

Since I dare take the part of humanity against one who would destroy it, I must combat Machiavelli in greater detail, so that those who think like him will find no more subterfuges or defenses for their viciousness.

Cesare Borgia based his plan for greatness on the dissention between the princes of Italy. He resolved to embroil them with each other so as to profit from the spoils. This is an awful combination of crimes. Nothing was unjust to Borgia when his ambition was at stake. One fall led to another: in order to usurp the possessions of my neighbors, they must be weakened; and in order to weaken them, they must be embroiled. This is the logic of scoundrels.

Borgia wanted to be sure of support. It was thus necessary for Alexander VI to accord a marriage dispensation to Louis XII in return for aid. This is how clergymen often make fools of the world and think only of their interests when they appear most attached to those of heaven. If the marriage of Louis XII could have been dissolved, the pope should have done it without political considerations. If the marriage could not have been dissolved, nothing should have decided the head of the Church and the vicar of Jesus Christ to do it.

Borgia needed creatures. Thus he corrupted the faction of the Urbinos by his presents and liberalities. The corrupter is somehow as criminal as the corrupted, since he plays the role of tempter and without his temptation the other could not succumb. But let us not look for more of Borgia's crimes and let us pass over his corruptions if only because they have at least some resemblance to favors, with the difference that the corrupter is generous only to himself and the benefactor is to others. Borgia wanted to get rid of some princes of the house of Urbino,[3] of Vitellozzo, Oliverotto da Fermo, etc., and Machiavelli says that he had the prudence to have them come to Sinigaglia where he treacherously executed them.

Abusing the good faith of men, dissimulating one's viciousness, using infamous ruses, betraying and perjuring oneself, assassinating—this is what the doctor of scoundreliness calls prudence! I do not speak to him of religion, nor of morality, but simply of interest. It will suffice to confound him. I ask if it is prudent for men to show how not to keep faith and how to perjure oneself. If you overthrow good faith and oaths, what guarantees of men's fidelity will you have? If you overthrow oaths, how can you oblige your subjects and people to respect your dominion? If you annihilate good faith, how can you have confidence in anyone or rely on any promises? Give examples of treachery—there will always be traitors to imitate you. Give examples of perfidy—how many of the perfidious will pay you back in kind? Teach assassination—watch out that one of your disciples does not begin by practicing on you and that you will retain only the precedence in crime and the honor of having shown the path to monsters as unnatural as yourself! This is how vices become prejudicial and dangerous to their own adherents. A prince will never have the monopoly on crime: thus he will never find impunity in his scoundreliness. Crime is like a falling mountainside which breaks everything in its path and finally fragments of its own weight. What abominable error, what loss of reason can make Machiavelli relish maxims as contrary to humanity as they are detestable and depraved?

Borgia established the cruel De Orco as governor of the Romagna in order to suppress the disorders, thefts, and assassinations that were committed there. What a pitiful contradiction! Borgia should have blushed to punish in others the vices that he tolerated in himself. Could the most violent of usurpers, the most false of perjurers, the most cruel of assassins and of poisoners condemn to death swindlers and scoundrels who mimicked the character of their new master to the best of their feeble capacity?

That king of Poland whose death has just caused so many troubles in Europe acted much more consistently and nobly toward his Saxon subjects.[4] The laws of Saxony condemned all philanderers to have their head severed. I wouldn't know about the origin of this barbarous law, which appears more proper to Italian jealousy than to German patience. An unfortunate transgressor of this law, driven by love to flaunt both custom and punishment—which is no small thing—was condemned. Augustus had to sign the decree of death, but he was sensitive to love and to humanity. He pardoned the criminal and abrogated a law by which he tacitly condemned himself whenever he enforced it. From that time on, gallantry went unchecked in Saxony.

The king conducted himself as a sensitive and humane man, Cesare Borgia like a scoundrel and a tyrant. The one, as father of his people, was indulgent toward weaknesses which he knew to be inseparable from humanity: the other, always rigorous and ferocious, persecuted those of his subjects whose vices he feared to be similar to his own. The one could stand the sight of his weakness, and the other did not dare to see his crimes. Borgia had the cruel De Orco, who had so perfectly fulfilled his intentions, torn to pieces so as to please the people. The weight of tyranny is never more heavy than when the tyrant wants to put on a façade of innocence and oppression takes place under the shadow of the laws. The tyrant does not even leave the people with the feeble consolation of knowing about his injustices. To disavow his cruelties, he makes others bear the guilt and the punishment. I see him as an assassin who believes that he can deceive the public and gain absolution by throwing the instrument of his fury into the flames. This is what the unworthy ministers of criminal princes can expect: even if they are rewarded in time of need, sooner or later they serve as the victims of their masters; which is at the same time a fine lesson for those who commit themselves lightly to tricksters like Cesare Borgia and deliver themselves without reservation and with no regard for virtue to the service of their sovereign. Thus crime is always accompanied by punishment.

Borgia, extending his foresight beyond the death of the pope his father, began by exterminating all those whom he had despoiled, so that the new pope could not use them against him.

Look at the cascade of crime: in order to meet expenses, it is necessary to have goods; in order to obtain them, it is necessary to despoil the possessors; and in order to enjoy all of this in security, it is necessary to exterminate them. Count Horn, executed in the public square, could not have said more.[5] Bad actions are like a horde of deer: when one crosses the nets, the others all follow. Beware, then, of making the first step!

Borgia, in order to poison some cardinals, invites them to supper at his father's. The pope and he inadvertently drink some of the brew. Alexander VI dies of it, Borgia recovers— worthy reward for poisoners and assassins!

This is the prudence, wisdom, ability, and virtue that Machiavelli never tires of praising. The famous Bishop of Meaux, the celebrated Bishop of Nîmes, the eloquent pan- egyrist of Trajan could not have said more for their heroes than Machiavelli does for Cesare Borgia.[6] If his eulogy had been but an ode or an exercise in rhetoric, one could admire his subtlety while despising his choice, but it is just the contrary. It is a treatise on politics which is to pass to the most remote posterity. It is a very serious work in which Machiavelli is so impudent as to accord praises to the most abominable monster that hell has ever spewed upon the earth. This is coldly exposing oneself to the hatred of the human race and to the horror of honest men.

Cesare Borgia would have been perfect, according to Machiavelli, if he had not subscribed to the elevation of the Cardinal of Saint Peter in Vincoli[7] to the pontificate "because," he says, "with great men, present favors never efface past injuries." I don't define a great man as the author does. All right- thinking people would forever reject the title of "great" if it could only be merited through a spirit of vindictiveness, ingratitude, or perfidy.

The pains and cares of Cesare Borgia for his aggrandizement and ambition were badly recompensed, for he lost the Romagna and all his goods after the death of the pope. He took refuge with the King of Navarre in Spain, where he perished through one of those treacheries which he had used so often in the course of his life.

Thus vanished so many ambitious plans and secret projects. Thus so many combats, murders, cruelties, perjuries, and perfidies became useless. So many personal dangers, disturbing situations, and embarrassing fixes from which Borgia successfully extricated himself did nothing for his fortune and rendered his fall greater and more remarkable. Such is ambition: this phantom promises goods that it is in no position to give and does not itself possess. The ambitious man is like a second Tantalus who, in the very river in which he is swimming, cannot even quench his thirst.[8]

Is the ambitious man searching for glory? This is false, for he is running after false glory, and the true kind is but a puff of smoke. The great men of our days are to the infinite number of those who have performed great and heroic actions as small rivers flowing into an immense ocean.

Are the ambitious searching for happiness then? They will find it even less than glory. Their path is strewn with thorns, and they meet only cares, vexations, and innumerable labors. True happiness is as little connected to fortune as the body of Hector was to the skin of Achilles. There is no happiness for man except in himself, and only wisdom makes him discover this treasure.

NOTES

[1] In the *Telemachus*. See above, pp. 7, 10.

[2] Compare with Francesco Guicciardini's *History of Italy*, Bk. IV and especially with Tomaso Tomasi's *La Vita del Duca Valentino*, first published in 1655. Frederick probably used the French translation, titled *Mémoires pour servir à l'histoire de la vie de Cesar Borgia* (Amsterdam, 1739).

[3] Frederick meant to say *Orsini*. See *ibid.*, pt. 2, 253–256.

[4] Augustus of Saxony (1670–1733), Elector of Saxony from 1694 and King of Poland from 1697 (see Ch. III, n. 2), was one of the greatest royal lovers of all time, fathering over 300 illegitimate children. It was this achievement rather than any military prowess that earned him the title of "the Strong".

[5] Antoine-Joseph (1698–1720) Count Horn, was a Flemish nobleman of illustrious ancestry who had killed a stockbroker in Paris in order to steal his wallet. The Duke d'Orléans, Regent of France, decided to make an example of him. See Joseph de La Grange-Chancel, *Odes Philippiques*, IV, verse 12n. in the Labbessade edition (Paris, 1876), 405–406.

[6] Bénigne Bossuet (1627–1704), Bishop of Meaux and Esprit Fléchier (1632–1710). Bishop of Nîmes, were famous for their sermons and funeral

orations at the court of Louis XIV, whereas Pliny the Younger (61/2–c. 133), delivered a panegyric of the Emperor Trajan in the year 100.

[7] Giuliano della Rovere (1443–1513), who had been Cardinal-priest of Saint Peter in Vincoli prior to his election as Pope Julius II in 1503. See Guicciardini's *History of Italy*, Bk. VI.

[8] Tantalus, mythical King of Phrygia, was condemned in Hades to standing up to his neck in water which receded into the ground when he sought to drink it, while the thick branches of fruit that dangled over his head were lifted by the wind whenever he attempted to reach for them. See Homer's *Odyssey*, XI:582–592 and Ovid's *Metamorphoses*, IV:457–458.

On those who become princes by crime

Chapter VIII

M. de La Grange's *Philippics* are regarded in Europe as one of the strongest defamatory libels which has ever been composed, and rightfully so.[1] However, what I have to say against Machiavelli is stronger than what M. de La Grange said against the Regent of France; for his work is pure calumny, and what I have against Machiavelli is true. I use his very words in order to refute him. Could I say anything more atrocious about him than that he has laid down the rules of politics for those who rise to supremacy through crime? That is the title of this chapter.

If Machiavelli taught crime in a seminary of scoundrels, if he sanctified perfidy in a university of traitors, it would not be astonishing for him to treat matters of this nature; but he speaks to all men, for an author who comes out in print communicates with the entire world, and he addresses himself primarily to those who should be the most virtuous since they are destined to govern others. What then is more infamous or insolent than to teach them treachery, perfidy, murder, and all the crimes? It would be more desirable for the good of the world if examples such as those of Agathocles and Oliverotto da Fermo, which Machiavelli cites with such pleasure, were never to be found or at least relegated to perpetual oblivion.

Nothing is more seductive than a bad example. The lives of an Agathocles[2] or an Oliverotto da Fermo are capable of developing the dangerous germ that an incipient scoundrel carries unsuspectedly within himself. How many young men who have been spoiled by the reading of novels saw and thought only like Gandalin or Medor?[3] There is something epidemic in ways of thinking, if I may say so, which spreads from one mind to another. That extraordinary man, that adventurer king worthy of the old chivalry, that vagabond hero all of whose virtues when pushed too far degenerated into vices—Charles XII, that is—carried the life of Alexander the Great with him from his earliest childhood, and many people who knew this Alexander of the North personally, assure us that it was Quintus Curtius who ravaged Poland, that Stanislas became king in the manner of Porus, and that the battle of Arbela occasioned the defeat of Poltava.[4]

May I be permitted to descend from such a great example to some lesser ones? It seems to me that when it is a question of the human mind, the differences in conditions and estates disappear. Kings are only men philosophically, and all men are equal, but for some general impressions or modifications produced by certain external causes on the human mind.

All England knows what happened some years ago in London. A rather bad comedy entitled *Cartouche* was presented. The subject of this play was the agility and slight of hand of this famous thief. On leaving the performance, many persons noticed the loss of their rings, snuff boxes, and watches. Cartouche had made disciples so promptly that they practiced his lessons in the pit itself, obliging the police to prohibit the performance of such a dangerous comedy.[5] This is sufficient proof, it seems to me, that one can't be too careful or prudent in setting examples and of how pernicious it is to offer bad ones.

Machiavelli's first reflection on Agathocles and on Fermo turns on how they managed to maintain themselves in power in spite of their cruelties. The author attributes this to their having committed these cruelties opportunely. Now, being a prudent barbarian and exercising tyranny consistently means, according to this abominable political thinker, executing in one fell swoop all the violences and crimes that one considers useful for his interests.

Have those you suspect, have those you distrust, have your declared enemies assassinated—but don't drag out your vengeance! Machiavelli approves such actions as the Sicilian Vespers and the massacre of St. Bartholomew, where the cruelties that were committed are enough to make humanity blush.[6] This unnatural monster completely ignores the horror of his crimes, provided that they are committed in a manner that impresses the people and has an immediate impact upon them; his reason being that memories vanish more easily for the public than do the successive and continual cruelties by which princes perpetuate the memory of their ferocity and barbarity—as if it were not just as bad and abominable to execute a thousand persons in a day as to assassinate them by intervals! The prompt and determined barbarism of the first imposes more fright and fear: the slower and premeditated viciousness of the second imposes more aversion and horror. The Emperor Augustus should have been cited by Machiavelli; this emperor who ascends the throne still dripping with the blood of his fellow citizens and besmirched by the perfidy of his proscriptions, but who, through the counsels of Maecenas and Agrippa, followed so many cruelties by mildness and who, it is said, should never have been born or never have died.[7] Perhaps it was just because Machiavelli regretted that Augustus finished better than he had begun that he failed to include him among his great men.

But what abominable policy does this author not advocate? The interest of a single individual should overturn the world, and his ambition should choose between good and evil?—the awful prudence of monsters who know and love only themselves and who infringe upon all justice and humanity in order to follow the furious torrent of their caprices and excesses!

It is not enough to refute the awful morality of Machiavelli. He must also be convicted of error and bad faith.

It is first of all false, as Machiavelli relates, that Agathocles enjoyed the fruit of his crimes in peace. He was almost always at war with the Carthaginians: he was even obliged to abandon his army—which massacred his children after his departure—in Africa; and he himself died of a poisoned brew given to him by his grandson. Oliverotto da Fermo perished through the perfidy of Borgia, worthy reward for his crimes; and since this was a year after his elevation, his sudden fall would appear to have anticipated the punishment that the public hatred was preparing for him.

The example of Oliverotto da Fermo should not have been cited by the author since it proves nothing. Machiavelli would like crime to pay, and he flatters himself that he has here a good reason or, at least, a passable argument in his favor.

But let us suppose that crime can be committed in safety and that a tyrant can exercise his scoundreliness with impunity. Even if he did not fear a tragic death, he would be equally miserable to see himself surrounded by the opprobrium of the human race. He could not extinguish the internal testimony of his conscience. He could not impose silence on that powerful voice which is heard on the thrones of kings as well as in the tribunals of tyrants. He could not avoid being struck by a ghastly melancholy at seeing the bloody spirits which his cruelty had sent to their graves appearing to violate the laws of nature in order to vindicate their unfortunate and tragic end.

Read the life of a Dionysius, a Tiberius, a Nero, a Louis XI, an Ivan Basilevich and see how these insane and ferocious monsters ended up in the most ghastly and miserable manner in the world![8] The cruel man is of a misanthropic and arbitrary temperament. If he does not combat his miserable disposition from an early age, he will not fail to become as ferocious as he is insane. Thus even if there were no justice on earth and no Divinity in heaven, men would need to be all the more virtuous; since virtue unites them and is absolutely necessary for their preservation, while crime can only render them unfortunate and destroy them.

Machiavelli lacks feeling, good faith, and reason. I have demonstrated his bad morality and the inaccuracy of his examples. I shall now convict him of gross and manifest contradictions. Let the most intrepid commentator, let the most subtle interpreter reconcile Machiavelli with himself here. He says in this chapter "that Agathocles sustained his greatness with heroic courage. However, one cannot give the name of virtue to the assassinations and treacheries which he committed." And in the seventh chapter he says of Cesare Borgia "that he waited for the occasion to get rid of the Orsinis and that he used it prudently." Ibid. "If one examines, in general, all of Borgia's actions, it is difficult to blame them." Ibid. "He could not act otherwise than he did."

May I ask the author how Agathocles differs from Cesare Borgia? I see in them only the same crimes and viciousness. If one compares them, the only problem would be to decide which of the two was the greater scoundrel.

Truth, however, sometimes obliges Machiavelli to make admissions by which he seems to offer an apology to virtue. The force of evidence obliges him to say "that a prince must always conduct himself in a steadfast manner so that in bad times he is not obliged to make concessions to his subjects, for such extorted mildness would be without merit and his people would not appreciate it." Thus, Machiavelli, cruelty and the art of making oneself feared are not the only springs of politics, as you appear to insinuate, and you yourself grant that the art of gaining hearts is the most secure foundation for the security of a prince and the fidelity of his subjects. I don't ask for anything more: this admission from the mouth of my enemy is sufficient. It is a lack of respect for oneself and for the public to produce and publish a work without form, connection, or order, and full of contradictions. Machiavelli's *Prince*, by generalizing upon the author's pernicious morality, can merit only scorn for him. It is properly only a dream in which all sorts of ideas bump and jostle each other, the fit of an insane man who sometimes has intervals of good sense.

Such is the reward of scoundreliness that even if those who embrace crime to the prejudice of virtue escape the rigor of the laws, they lose, like Machiavelli, both their judgment and reason.

NOTES

[1] Joseph de La Grange-Chancel (1677–1758), famous French playwright. His *Odes Philippiques* were directed against Philippe d'Orléans, Regent of France. They first appeared in 1720 and were disseminated, with explanatory notes, in various manuscript and printed editions. Frederick would seem to have used an edition whose notes generally correspond with the Léon de Labbessade edition published in Paris in 1876.

[2] Agathocles (362–289 B.C.), became tyrant of Syracuse in 317. He gained fame for his cruel executions and his wars against the Carthaginians.

[3] Gandalin was a personage in the chivalric *Amadis of Gaul* romances, put together by Vasco Lobeira and later revised by Garciadoñez de Montalvo. Medor was a hero in Ariosto's chivalric poem *Orlando Furioso*.

[4] See Voltaire's *Histoire de Charles XII*, Bks. I–II. Voltaire, however, identifies

Stanislas Leszczynski with the scholarly Abdalonymus, whom Alexander raised from obscurity to be King of Sidon, (see Quintus Curtius, *History of Alexander*, Bk. IV, Ch. I:15–26) rather than with the brave Porus, whom Alexander restored to the throne after defeating on the Hydapses (see *ibid.*, Bk. VIII, Chs. XIII–XIV).

5 A play by Marc-Antoine Legrand (1673–1728), about the dashing and notorious Parisian bandit chief, Louis-Dominique Cartouche. It was first performed in Paris in 1721, the year of Cartouche's capture and execution.

6 The Sicilian Vespers was the rising of 1282 when the people of the island revolted and slaughtered their French occupiers. The massacre of St. Bartholomew was the Queen mother Catherine de Medici's effort in 1572 to rid herself of the French Huguenot leaders who were conveniently gathered in Paris on the occasion of a royal wedding.

7 See La Grange-Chancel's *Odes Philippiques*, I, verse 16n. in the Labbessade edition, 271–272.

8 Dionysius (c. 432–367 B.C.), Tyrant of Syracuse from 405. Tiberius (42 B.C.–37 A.D.), Roman emperor from 14 A.D. Nero (37–68 A.D.), Roman emperor from 54. Louis XI (1423–1483), King of France from 1461. Ivan the Terrible (1530–1584), Russian emperor from 1533.

On the civil
principality

Chapter IX

There is no sentiment more inseparable from our being than that of liberty: all men are permeated by it from the most civilized to the most barbaric; for since we are born without chains, we presume to live without constraint; and since we want to be independent, we don't like to accede to the caprices of others. It is this spirit of pride and independence which has produced so many great men in the world and has given rise to those sorts of governments that are called republican, which by the aid of wise laws defend the liberty of the citizens against oppression and establish a kind of equality between the members closely approximating the state of nature.

Machiavelli gives in this chapter some very excellent political maxims to those who rise to supreme power with the assistance of the leaders or the people of a republic, which furnishes me with two reflections: one on politics and the other on morality.

Although the maxims of the author are very suitable for those who rise through the favor of their fellow citizens, it seems to me, nevertheless, that examples of these sorts of elevations are very rare in history. The republican spirit is so jealous of its liberty that it takes umbrage at whatever might curtail it and revolts at the very idea of a master. There are people in Europe who have shaken off the yoke of tyrants in favor of a happy independence, but there are none who have voluntarily exchanged their liberty for slavery.

Many republics have relapsed with the passage of time into despotism. This would appear to be an inevitable misfortune which awaits them all and an effect of those vicissitudes and changes that all things of this world experience. For how could a

republic forever resist all the causes which undermine its
liberty? How could it always contain the great ambitions that it
nourishes within its breast—ambitions that are constantly
reborn and never die? How could it in the long run watch over
the seductions and underhanded practices of its neighbors and
the corruption of its members, as long as interest is all-powerful
among men? How can it always hope to emerge happily from
the wars it will have to sustain? How could it forestall those
circumstances menacing to its liberty, those critical and decisive
moments, and those gambles that favor the rash and the
audacious? If its troops are commanded by cowardly and timid
leaders, it will fall prey to its enemies; and if they are led by
valiant and daring men, these will be no less enterprising in time
of peace than in time of war. The defect in its constitution will
thus make it perish sooner or later.

But if civil wars are ghastly for a monarchical state, they are
all the more so in a free one. They are a malady fatal to it.
Thanks to them Sulla preserved the dictatorship in Rome,
Caesar became master through the arms that had been placed in
his hands, and Cromwell succeeded in mounting to the throne.[1]
Republics are almost all raised from the abyss of tyranny to
the height of liberty, and they have almost always relapsed from
this liberty into slavery. The same Athenians who in the time of
Demosthenes defied Philip of Macedon groveled before
Alexander,[2] the same Romans who abhorred royalty after the
expulsion of the kings suffered patiently after the passage of
some centuries all the cruelties of their emperors, and the same
English who put Charles I to death for encroaching upon their
rights bent their stiff courage under the haughty power of their
protector. Thus it is not republics which have given themselves
masters by choice, but enterprising men who, aided by some
favorable circumstances, have subjugated them by force against
their will.

Just as men are born, live a while, and die of sickness or old
age, so republics are founded, flourish for some centuries, and
finally perish from the audacity of a citizen or from the arms of
their enemies. Everything comes to an end, the greatest empires
and monarchies even have their time, and there is nothing in the
world which is not subject to the laws of change and

destruction. Sooner or later, despotism deals the death blow to liberty and seals the fate of a republic. Some last longer than others: depending on the strength of their temperament they defer, insofar as they can, the fatal moment of their ruin and utilize all the remedies suggested by wisdom in order to prolong their destiny; but they must finally submit to the eternal and immutable laws of nature and perish in the long run.

There is no point, besides, in asking men who know and want happiness, to give up their liberty.

No one will ever persuade a republican, a Cato or a Littleton,[3] that monarchy is the best form of government if a king has the will and power to perform his duty effectively. I agree, they will say to you, but where can this phoenix of princes be found? He would be a platonic man, another Venus of the Medicis which a sculptor assembled out of forty different beauties and existed only in marble.[4] We know what humanity is like and that few virtues can resist the unlimited power and seductions of the throne. Your metaphysical monarchy, if it existed, would be an earthly paradise; but despotism, as it really is, more or less changes this world into a real hell.

My second reflection regards Machiavelli's morality. I cannot refrain from criticizing his assertion that interest is the key to all actions, both good and bad. It is true that according to popular opinion interest plays a big part in a despotic system, while justice and integrity play none; but this awful political theory does not rest on the maxims of a sound and pure morality and should be exterminated forever. Machiavelli would have everything in the world done from interest, just like the Jesuits would save men solely through fear of the devil to the exclusion of the love of God. Virtue should be the only motive for our actions, for virtue and reason are and always will be inseparable if one wants to act consistently. Let us then be reasonable, since it is only a little reason that distinguishes us from the beasts and a little goodness that brings us closer to that infinitely good being from which we draw our existence.

NOTES

[1] Cornelius Sulla (138–78 B.C.), was Dictator of Rome from 82 until he

resigned in 79. Julius Caesar (c. 100–44 B.C.), was dictator from 49 until his assassination. On Cromwell, see Ch. VI, note 2.

2 Demosthenes (384/3–322 B.C.), the Athenian orator and statesman, delivered his famous *Philippics* between 351 and 341.

3 Frederick is evidently referring here to Cato the Younger (95–46 B.C.), the inveterate enemy of Julius Caesar, and has apparently transformed the name of John Lilburne (c. 1614–1657), the Leveller champion in the English civil wars, into Littleton.

4 Zeuxis (fl. 400 B.C.), chose a number of models out of whom he painted a single beauty, according to Cicero's *De inventione*, II, Dionysius of Halicarnassus, *De oratoribus veteribus*, I, and Pliny the Elder's *Natural History*, XXXV:9. Frederick probably got this story from Ariosto's *Orlando Furioso*, XI:71 and Montesquieu's *Persian Letters*, LXIX, although Frederick inexplicably turns the painter into a sculptor, numbers the models at 40, and, possibly because it was sometimes attributed to Phidias, identifies the sculpture with the famous Venus of the Medici.

How the strength of all principalities should be measured

Chapter X

Since the time that Machiavelli wrote his *Prince* the world has changed so much that it is hardly recognizable any more. The arts and sciences which were then beginning to revive from their ashes were still suffering from the barbarism in which the establishment of Christianity, the frequent invasions of Italy by the Goths, and a succession of cruel and bloody wars had plunged them. Now, nations have almost all exchanged their ancient customs for new ones, weak princes have become powerful, the arts have been perfected, and the face of Europe is entirely different from what it was in the age of Machiavelli.

If a philosopher from those remote times returned to the world, he would feel very stupid and ignorant. He wouldn't even understand the terminology of the new philosophy. He would find new heavens and a new earth. Instead of that inactivity and rest that he attributed to our globe, he would see the world and all the planets subject to the laws of impetus and attraction, turning in ellipses around the sun, which itself revolves upon its axis: instead of great bizarre words whose pompous sound obscured the nonsense of his thought and hid his proud ignorance, he would be taught to recognize truth and evidence simply and clearly; and for the miserable fantasies of his physics, he would be shown admirable, conclusive, and astonishing experiments.

If some able captain of Louis XII reappeared in our days, he would be entirely disoriented.[1] He would see wars waged by

75

huge armies which can hardly even be supplied in the field because of their size and are maintained by princes in both peace and war; whereas in his time, in order to strike great blows and to execute great undertakings, a handful of men sufficed who were dismissed at the end of the war. Instead of suits of armor, lances, and muskets, he would find uniforms, rifles, and bayonets, new methods of warfare, an infinity of murderous inventions for the attack and defense of strongholds, and the art of supplying troops just as necessary now as the art of beating the enemy once was.

But what would Machiavelli himself say if he could see the new form of the European body politic: so many great princes figuring now in the world who didn't amount to anything then, the power of kings solidly established, the manner in which sovereigns negotiate—those privileged spies maintained reciprocally in all the courts, and the balance of Europe which establishes the alliance of some important princes in order to oppose the ambitious—wisely maintaining equality with no other goal than the tranquillity of the world?

All these things have produced such a general and universal change that they render most of Machiavelli's maxims inapplicable and useless to modern politics. This is primarily what this chapter shows. Here are some examples.

Machiavelli supposes "that a prince whose country is large and who has a lot of money and troops can maintain himself by his own strength without the assistance of any ally against the attacks of his enemies."

This I dare very modestly to dispute; and I even venture to say that no matter how redoubtable a prince is, he could not resist his powerful enemies by himself and that he absolutely needs the aid of some ally against their attacks. If the greatest, the most formidable, the most powerful prince in Europe, if Louis XIV was on the point of succumbing during the War of the Spanish Succession; if from lack of alliances he could hardly offer any more resistance to the redoubtable league of kings and princes which almost overwhelmed him, any sovereign who is inferior to him cannot for all the more reason take the chance of remaining isolated.[2]

It is said over and over again without much reflection that treaties are useless because their provisions are hardly ever fulfilled and that we are less scrupulous about this in our age than in any other. I answer that there can undoubtedly be found both old and recent examples of princes who have not scrupulously kept their commitments, but that it is still very advantageous to make treaties. If nothing else, your allies will be so many less enemies; and even if they are of no help to you, you will still reduce them to observing a strict neutrality.

Machiavelli then speaks of the *principini*, those miniature sovereigns who having only small states cannot put an army into the field, and he urges them to fortify their capital so as to take refuge in it with their troops in case of war.

The princes of whom Machiavelli speaks are only hermaphrodites of sovereigns and private individuals. They play the great lords only with their servants. The best counsel one could give them would, it seems to me, be to diminish somewhat their infinite opinion of their greatness, their extreme veneration for their ancient and illustrious race, and their inviolable zeal for their coat of arms. Common sense suggests that they would do better to figure in the world only as well-to-do private individuals, to quit once and for all the stilts on which their pride has mounted them, to maintain at the most a guard sufficient to chase hungry thieves away from their *châteaux*, and to raze the ramparts, walls, and everything that can give their residence the air of a stronghold.

Here are my reasons. Most of the petty princes, and notably those of Germany, ruin themselves by excessive expenses out of inebriation with this vain grandeur. They crush themselves in order to sustain the honor of their house, and their vanity leads them down the path to indigence. Even the cadet of a cadet of an apanaged line imagines that he is similar to Louis XIV. He builds his Versailles, he kisses his Maintenon, and he maintains his armies.[3]

There is now a certain prince in Germany, apanaged to a great house, who through a refinement of grandeur maintains in his service the exact bodies of troops that compose the household of a king, but on such a small scale that it would take a microscope to identify each particular body.[4] His army might perhaps be strong enough to stage a battle in the theater of Verona, but don't ask him for anything more.

I have said, in the second place, that the petty princes were wrong to fortify their residence, and the reason is quite simple. They are not liable to be besieged by their equals because their more powerful neighbors intervene in their squabbles and offer them a mediation that they are in no position to refuse. Thus instead of bloodshed, two strokes of a pen conclude their petty quarrels.

What then is the good of their fortresses? Even if they could sustain a siege as long as Troy's against their petty enemies, they would not last as long as Jericho against the armies of a powerful king. If, besides, great wars are waged in their vicinity, they are in no position to remain neutral without being totally ruined; and if they join one of the warring parties, their capital becomes its military stronghold.

Victor Amadeus, infinitely superior in power to the order of princes that we have just described, experienced a great deal of trouble with his fortresses in the Italian wars.[5] Even Turin experienced an ebb and flow of French and Imperial domination.

The advantage of open cities is that no one bothers with them in time of war. They are regarded as useless and thus left to the peaceful possession of their owner.

The idea that Machiavelli gives us of the Imperial cities of Germany is entirely different from what they are now. An order from the emperor or, that failing, a firecracker would suffice to render him their master. They are all badly fortified, most of them with old walls flanked here and there by great towers and surrounded by moats that the crumbling earth has almost entirely filled in. They have few troops, and those that they maintain are poorly disciplined. Their officers are either the rejects of Germany or old men who are no longer fit to serve. Some of these cities have rather good artillery, but it is not sufficient to oppose the emperor, who is accustomed to make them feel their inferiority quite often.

In short, waging war, giving battle, attacking or defending fortresses is solely the affair of great princes; and those who would imitate them without having the power are as foolish as

Domitian, who counterfeited the sound of thunder in the hope of persuading the Roman people that he was Jupiter.[6]

NOTES

[1] Louis XII (1462–1515), King of France from 1498.

[2] See Voltaire's *Age of Louis XIV*, Ch. XXII.

[3] Françoise d'Aubigné (1635–1719), Marquise de Maintenon, mistress and later the secret wife of Louis XIV.

[4] Duke Ernest-August of Saxe-Weimar (d. 1748), whose troops Frederick had seen during his visit to Saxony in 1730.

[5] Victor Amadeus II (1666–1732), Duke of Savoy from 1675. He extricated his country from French domination, exhibited great vacillation in his alliances, and ultimately obtained the title of king in 1713.

[6] Actually, Salmoneus, the mythical King of Elis. See Virgil's *Aeneid*, VI:585–586.

On ecclesiastical principalities   **Chapter XI**

I have always found it very strange that those who call themselves successors of the apostles, I mean of some beggars—preachers of humility and repentance—should possess great wealth, wallow in luxury, and fill posts more proper to satisfy the vanity of the age and the ostentation of the great than to occupy men who must meditate on the nothingness of human life and on the quest for salvation. However, the clergy of the Roman church is extremely rich. Bishops hold the rank of sovereign princes, and the temporal and spiritual power of the first bishop of Christendom renders him somehow the arbiter of kings and the fourth person of the Divinity.

Clergymen and theologians separate the attributes of the body from those of the soul more scrupulously than anyone else, but their arguments might better be applied to the subject of their ambition. You, they could be told, whose ministry is restricted to the spiritual realm, how can you have so grossly confused it with the temporal? You who so subtly employ the *distinguo* when it comes to the mind, which you do not understand at all, and to matter, which you understand very little, how does it come that you reject these distinctions when it comes to your interest?[1] Is it because these gentlemen worry very little about the unintelligible jargon that they spout out and very much about the great revenues that they take in. It is because their fashion of reasoning must conform to orthodoxy and their fashion of acting to their passions; and that the tangible objects of nature are as dominant over their intellect as the real happiness of this life is over the ideal happiness of the next world.

The astonishing power of clergymen as well as everything which regards their temporal government is the subject of this chapter.

Machiavelli finds that ecclesiastical princes are very happy because they have to fear neither the rebellion of their subjects nor the ambition of their neighbors. The respectable and impressive name of the Divinity shelters them from whatever could oppose their interest and greatness. The princes who attack them would fear the fate of the Titans and the people who disobey them that of the sacrilegious.[2] The pious policy of this kind of sovereign aims at persuading the world of what Despréaux expresses so well in the verse:

"He who loves not Cotin loves neither God nor king."[3]

What is strange is that these princes find enough credulous dupes who adhere blindly to whatever they want them to believe.

It is certain, however, that no country swarms with more beggars than one run by priests. There one can see a touching picture of all the human miseries, not of those poor attracted by the alms of sovereigns or of those insects who attach themselves to the rich, but of starving beggars deprived of necessities by the charity of their bishops so as to prevent them from becoming corrupted by affluence.

It is undoubtedly upon the laws of Sparta where money was prohibited that the principles of these ecclesiastical governments are founded, with the difference that the prelates reserve for themselves the use of the wealth of which they most devoutly despoil their subjects. Blessed, they say, are the poor, for they shall inherit the kingdom of heaven! And since they want everybody to be saved, they make sure that everyone is poor. Oh, ecclesiastical piety, is there anything that escapes your wise foresight?

Nothing should be more edifying than the story of the heads of the Church or vicars of Jesus Christ. One expects to find examples of irreproachable and saintly morals there. However, it is just the contrary. There are only obscenities, abominations, and sources of scandal; and one cannot read the lives of the popes without detesting their cruelty and perfidy.[4]

One sees there their immense ambition to augment their

temporal power, their sordid avarice in transferring great wealth unjustly and dishonestly to their families in order to enrich their nephews, mistresses, or bastards.

Those who reflect insufficiently find it peculiar that people suffer the oppression of this kind of sovereign with docility and patience, that they do not open their eyes to the vices and excesses of the clergymen who degrade them, and that they endure from a head that is shorn what they would not suffer from a head crowned with laurels. This phenomenon appears less strange to those who know the power of superstition upon idiots and of fanaticism on the human mind. They know that religion is an old machine that will never wear out and that has always been used to insure the fidelity of people and put a brake on the restlessness of human reason. They know that error can blind the most penetrating men and that there is nothing more triumphant than the policy of those who put heaven and hell, God and the devil into play in order to attain their designs. Even the true religion itself, the purest source of all our good, is most deplorably abused and often becomes the origin and principle of all our misfortunes.

The author most judiciously notes what contributed to the elevation of the Holy See. He attributes it principally to the able conduct of Alexander VI, a pontiff who pushed cruelty to the extreme and who knew no justice but perfidy. One could not thus confuse the product of the ambition of this pontiff with the work of the Divinity. Heaven could not have played any direct part in the elevation of this temporal greatness, which is only the work of a very vicious and depraved man. One could thus do no better than to distinguish carefully among clergymen between the mark of God when they announce the divine orders and the corrupt man when they are thinking only of satisfying their passions.

The eulogy of Leo X concludes this chapter,[5] but this eulogy doesn't carry much weight since Machiavelli was the contemporary of this pope. Any praise by a subject to his master or by an author to a prince appears, whatever one may say, as very close to flattery. Our life can only be judged by posterity, which judges without passions or interest. Machiavelli should have been the last to make an attempt at flattery, for he was not a competent judge of true merit, not even knowing what virtue was; and I don't know if it is better to have been praised than blamed by him. I leave this question for the reader to judge.

NOTES

[1] Like so many men of the "Enlightenment", Frederick was highly contemptuous of the scholastics and their subtle philosophical and theological distinctions.

[2] Zeus, in Greek mythology, defeated the Titans and imprisoned them below Hades in Tartarus. See Hesiod's *Theogony*: 617–735 and Ovid's *Metamorphoses*, I:113.

[3] Nicolas Boileau, *Satires*, IX.

[4] Compare with Guicciardini, *op. cit.* and Tomasi, *op. cit.* Voltaire, who usually cut down on Frederick's text, expanded greatly on his criticism of the papacy.

[5] Giovanni de Medici (1475–1521), who became Pope Leo X in 1513. See Guicciardini, *op. cit.*, Bk. XI.

On the kinds of troops and on mercenaries   **Chapter XII**

Everything in the world is varied. The fecundity of nature manifests itself in productions which, though of the same species, are nevertheless different from each other. This operation of nature is so universal, so general, that it is not only seen in plants, animals, countrysides, and in the features, complexions, faces, and constitutions of men, but it extends, if I may say so, to the temperament of empires and monarchies. By the temperament of an empire I mean, in general, its size, population, strategic situation, commerce, customs, laws, strengths, weaknesses, wealth, and resources.

This difference in governments is considerable and even infinite if one wants to go into details. Just as physicians possess no secret panacea to cure all maladies nor any remedy suitable to all complications, the most expert and able political thinkers cannot prescribe any general rules of politics which are applicable to all forms of government and to each particular country.

This reflection leads me naturally to examine Machiavelli's sentiments on foreign and mercenary troops. The author entirely rejects their use by claiming to prove that these troops have done more harm than good to the states that have used them.

It is sure and experience has generally shown that the best troops of any state are the national ones. This opinion is supported by such examples as the valorous resistance of Leonidas at Thermopylae, the inferiority of the Lacedaemonians to the other Greeks when they let their slaves fight for them, and the astonishing progress of the Roman Empire when its legions were made up only of Roman citizens. It was the nationals and not foreigners who subjected the entire world to the domination of this haughty and proud republic.[1] The maxim of Machiavelli is thus suitable to all people who can furnish a sufficient number of soldiers for their defense. I am persuaded, like the author, that an empire is badly served by mercenaries and that the fidelity and courage of indigenous soldiers greatly surpasses them. It is particularly dangerous to let one's subjects languish and grow effeminate in inactivity and sloth while the labors of wars and battles harden one's neighbors.

It has been noted repeatedly that states which were emerging from civil wars have been infinitely superior to their enemies, since in a civil war everyone is a soldier, merit outshines favor, and since men are creatures of habit.

There are cases, however, which seem to be an exception to this rule. If some kingdoms or empires do not produce enough men for their military needs, necessity obliges them to supplement this deficiency by recourse to mercenaries.

Some expedients may then be found to eliminate most of Machiavelli's objections to this kind of militia: such as carefully mixing them with the nationals so as to prevent them from forming a band apart, and by accustoming them to the same order, discipline, and fidelity; with particular attention that the number of foreigners does not exceed the number of nationals.

There is a king in the North whose army is no less powerful and formidable for being composed of this sort of mixture.[2] Most European troops are composed of nationals and mercenaries. Those who cultivate the soil and live in the cities no longer go to war. They pay a tax to maintain the troops who defend them. The soldiers come from the dregs of the people; and do-nothings who prefer idleness to work, debauchees who hope for licence and impunity with the troops, wayward and emptyheaded youth who enlist out of libertinage and serve out of flightiness have as little inclination and attachment for their master as do foreigners. How different are these troops from the Romans who conquered the world! The desertions so

frequent in all the armies of our day were unknown among the
Romans. Men who fought for their families, their gods, their
fellow citizens, and for all that they held most dear would never
have betrayed so many interests by a cowardly desertion.

What makes for the security of the great princes of Europe is
that their troops are nearly all the same, and none has, in that
respect, any advantages over the others. Only the Swedish
troops are burghers, peasants, and soldiers at the same time; but
when they go to war, no one stays at home to till the soil. Thus
their power is in no way formidable, since they can do nothing
over the long haul without ruining themselves more than their
enemies.

So much for mercenaries. As to the manner in which a great
prince must wage war, I am entirely of Machiavelli's opinion.
Indeed, why shouldn't a great prince lead his own troops and
preside over his army as he does over his own residence? His
interest, duty, and glory all engage him to it. Just as he is the
leader in distributing justice, he is also the protector and
defender of his people; and he must view the defense of his
subjects as one of the most important objects of his ministry,
and one which he can for this reason entrust only to himself. His
interest seems to require absolutely that he serve in person with
his army; since when all orders emanate from his person,
counsel and execution follow each other in rapid succession.
The august presence of a prince puts an end to the dissensions
of the generals, so ghastly for armies and so prejudicial to the
interests of the master: it establishes more order into the stores,
munitions, and provisions or war, without which a Caesar at
the head of a hundred thousand troops could never do anything
great or heroic; and since it is the prince who orders the battles,
it would seem that he should direct them and communicate by
his presence a spirit of valor and confidence to his troops. He
should show them how victory is inseparable from his plans,
how fortune is captive to his prudence, and give them an
illustrious example of how to scorn peril, danger, and even
death when duty, honor, and immortal reputation demand it.

How glorious for the ability, wisdom, and valor of a prince if
he protects his states from the incursion of his enemies,
triumphs by his courage and dexterity over the violent

undertakings of his adversaries, and upholds his rights with firmness, prudence, and military virtue when they are challenged by injustice and usurpation!

All these reasons must, it seems to me, oblige princes to take charge of their own troops and to share with their subjects all the perils and dangers to which they expose them.

But, it will be said, everyone is not born a soldier, and many princes have neither the intelligence nor experience necessary for commanding an army. This is true, I admit. However, this objection does not bother me very much, for there are always experienced generals in an army and the prince has but to follow their counsels. The war will still be waged more successfully than when the general is in the care of a minister who is too far away from the army to judge things and who often renders the most able general incapable of exhibiting his capacity.

I shall finish this chapter by pointing out a most singular sentence of Machiavelli. "The Venetians," he says, "mistrusting the Duke of Carmagnola, who commanded their troops, were obliged to make him leave this world."[3]

I don't understand, I admit, what it is to make someone leave this world, unless it is to betray him, poison him, assassinate him—in short—have him killed. This is how this doctor of scoundreliness seeks to render the blackest and most guilty actions innocent by softening his terminology!

The Greeks were accustomed to use circumlocutions when they spoke of death, since they could not bear the thought of it without horror. Machiavelli circumlocutes crimes since his heart revolts against his mind and cannot entirely swallow the execrable morality that he teaches.

What a sad situation when one blushes to show himself to others as he really is and flees from the opportunity to examine himself!

NOTES

[1] Leonidas (d. 480 B.C.), King of Sparta who fought to the death in the legendary defense of Thermopylae against the Persians. See Herodotus, *Histories*, VII:204–233. Frederick seems to contrast his reign to the tyranny of Nabis (d. 192 B.C.), a Spartan social reformer who freed the helots in an

unsuccessful effort to maintain the independence of the city against the
Achaean League. See Polybius, *Histories*, XIII–XX. On the rise and fall of Rome,
compare with Polybius, *Histories*, Livy's *History of Rome*, and Montesquieu's
Considerations on the Causes of the Greatness of the Romans and Their Decline, Chs. IX,
XVIII.

[2] Frederick is referring to his own father.

[3] These are the terms of the Desbordes edition used by Frederick, but
Machiavelli explicitly states that the Venetians were forced "to kill him". The
La Houssaye translation, which Voltaire inserted in columns parallel to the
Anti-Machiavel, employs the expression "take his life", thus permitting Voltaire
to save Frederick's point—more or less. In either case, however, Frederick is
attacking Machiavelli on the basis of liberties taken by his translators.

On auxiliary, **Chapter XIII**
mixed, and local troops

Of all the philosophers of antiquity, the most wise, judicious, and modest were undoubtedly those of the New Academy.[1] Circumspect in their decisions, they were never hasty in affirming or denying nor swayed by presumption or anger.

Machiavelli should have profited from the moderation of these philosophers rather than abandon himself to the impetuosity of his imagination, which so often diverted him from the path of reason and good sense.

Machiavelli pushes hyperbole to the extreme when he maintains that a prudent prince should prefer to die with his own troops rather than win with foreign assistance. It is not possible to push exaggeration any further; and I maintain that this is the greatest absurdity of all time, unless saying that Machiavelli's *Prince* is a good book is greater.

Such a preposterous assertion is not only blameworthy, it is also inconsistent with politics and experience. What sovereign would not prefer the preservation of his states to their ruin, regardless of the means or persons employed?

I don't think that a dying man would pay any attention if someone told him that because he should not owe his life to others, he should perish rather than clasp the line that was extended to him. Experience shows us that man's first concern is self-preservation and that the second is happiness, which completely destroys the author's fallacy.

On deeper consideration, Machiavelli is only striving by this maxim to inspire princes with a secret jealousy for their generals and allies. It is, however, this very jealousy and the unwillingness of princes to wait for aid from fear of having to share their glory which has always been prejudicial to their interests. An infinite number of battles have been lost for this reason, and petty jealousies have often caused more harm to princes than the superiority of their enemies.

Envy is one of the most harmful vices to society, and it is all the more serious in princes. A state governed by a prince who is envious of his subjects will furnish only timid citizens incapable of great actions. Envious princes stifle in their infancy those geniuses created for illustrious undertakings. The Eastern Empire owed its ruin to the jealousy of the emperors for the successes of their generals as well as to the religious pedantry of its last rulers.[2] Instead of rewarding able generals, they were punished for their successes, while inexperienced captains accelerated the ruin of the state. Thus the Empire could not fail to perish.

The first sentiment of a prince must be the love of country, and his only concern should be to work for the good of the state, to which he must sacrifice his pride and all of his passions, and to profit from all the advice, assistance, and great men he can find—in short—from all that can contribute to fulfilling his good intentions for the happiness of his subjects.

The powers that can do without mixed or auxiliary troops do well to exclude them from their armies, but since few princes of Europe are in this position, I believe that there is no risk in auxiliaries as long as the number of nationals is greater.

Machiavelli wrote only for petty princes. His work is composed only of theories: there is hardly a place where he is not contradicted by experience. I could advance an infinity of examples of successful armies composed of auxiliaries and of princes who have been well served by them.

The wars of Brabant, the Rhine, and Italy in which the emperor, united with the Empire, England, and Holland, defeated the French, expelled them from Germany and Italy, and mastered them in Flanders were fought with auxiliaries. The undertaking by which three northern kings despoiled Charles XII of a part of his German states was similarly executed by the troops of three masters allied together, and in the war of 1734, which France began on the pretext of maintaining the rights of that on again off again king of Poland, the French allied with the Savoyards conquered the Milanese and most of Lombardy.[3]

Where do these examples leave Machiavelli, and what comes of the ingenious allegory of David refusing to fight Goliath with the armor of Saul because of its weight? It is a lot of whipped cream! I admit that auxiliaries sometimes inconvenience princes, but I ask if conquering cities and provinces is not worth a little inconvenience.

On the topic of these auxiliaries, Machiavelli spews his venom upon the Swiss in the service of France. I must say one thing on the subject of these brave troops: there is no doubt that the French have won more than one battle with their assistance, that they have rendered signal services to this empire, and that if France dismissed the Swiss and Germans who serve in her infantry, her armies would be much less formidable than they are now.

So much for errors of judgment. Let us come now to the moral ones. The bad examples proposed by Machiavelli cannot be overlooked. He cites in this chapter Hiero of Syracuse who, considering that his troops were as dangerous to keep as to dismiss, had them cut in pieces.[4] Such historical facts are revolting, but they are infuriating in a book devoted to the instruction of princes.

Cruelty and barbarism are often fatal and thus, for the most part, held in horror by private individuals; but princes, placed by Providence far above the common lot, have nothing to fear and are less averse to them. Those who govern men must thus be imbued with all the more revulsion against abusing their unlimited power.

The same Machiavelli who says in this chapter "that nothing is as fragile as influence and reputation when they are not founded on virtue," now finds that his own fragile reputation has vanished and that if he was esteemed for his intelligence during his life, he is detested for his viciousness after his death. How true it is that the public can be fooled for a time, but that it will not be fooled forever and that it judges men regardless of their rank as severely after their death as the ancient kings of Egypt were supposedly judged after theirs.[5]

There is thus only one sure and infallible means of preserving a good reputation in the world. It is to be in fact what one purports to be in public.

NOTES

[1] Carneades of Cyrene (214–129 B.C.), founded this school of philosophical skepticism which maintained that man could not discover truth and had to content himself with probabilities. He shocked the Romans in 155 by giving two convincing speeches on two successive days, one in favor of justice and the other against it. See Charles Rollin, *Histoire Ancienne* (Paris, 1733–1738), XII, 563–570.

[2] See Montesquieu's *Considerations on the Causes of the Greatness of the Romans and Their Decline*, Chs. XXII–XXIII.

[3] The War of the Spanish Succession (1701–1713). The alliance of Hanover, Denmark, and Prussia in 1715, an episode in the Great Northern War (1699–1721). The War of the Polish Succession (1733–1735).

[4] On Hiero, see Ch. VI, note 1.

[5] See Rollin, *op. cit.*, I, 88–89.

What a prince
ought to do
about troops

Chapter XIV

There is a kind of pedantry common to all the crafts which derives from the exaggeration and intemperance of those who practice them, making those affected by it seem extravagant and ridiculous.

We smile with indulgence upon those drudges of the republic of letters who bury themselves in the learned dust of antiquity for the good of science, bestow the light from this darkness upon the human race, and commune with the dead whom they know intimately for the benefit of the living whom they scarcely know.

This pedantry which is excusable somehow in scholars of the first order, prevented by their profession from circulating in the civilized world, is entirely unbearable in military men for just the opposite reason.

A soldier is pedantic when he is too meticulous, when he blusters, or when he plays the Don Quixote. These faults render him as ridiculous in his profession as a musty appearance and Latin affectations render a scholar.

Machiavelli's enthusiasm exposes his prince to similar ridicule. He exaggerates so much that he wants his prince to be nothing but a soldier. He makes him into a complete Don Quixote, his head full of battlefields, entrenchments, sieges, and fortifications. I am surprised that it has not occurred to the author to feed him advance post soup, bomb *pâté*, and horn work tarts, and that he doesn't have him attacking windmills, sheep, and ostriches like the lovable eccentric of Miguel de Cervantes.

These are the inconveniences of departing from that golden

mean which is to morality what the center of gravity is to mechanics.

A prince fulfills only half of his calling if he dedicates himself only to the craft of war. It is patently false that he must be only a soldier if one recalls what I have said on the origin of princes in the first chapter of this work. They are instituted as judges and are generals only as a side line. Machiavelli is like the Homeric gods who were always pictured as strong, robust, and powerful, but never as just and equitable.[1] The author ignores even the essentials of justice: he knows only interest and violence.

The author presents only little ideas. His limited intellect embraces only subjects suitable to the policy of petty princes. Nothing is more pitiful than his reasons for recommending hunting to princes. He is of the opinion that princes will thereby get to know the topography of their country.

If a king of France or an emperor sought to get to know his states in this manner, he would have to go hunting for an entire year.

Let me go into a kind of digression on the subject of hunting, since this sport is something of a passion with nobles, great lords, and kings.

Most kings and princes spend at least three quarters of their lives racing through forests, chasing and killing animals. If this work falls into their hands—although I am not so vain as to presume that they would interrupt their humanitarian pursuits long enough to read it—I ask them to excuse my honest sentiments in case they are contrary to theirs. I am not a flatterer. My pen is not for sale. My intention in this work is to satisfy myself and to express my true convictions freely. If the reader is sufficiently depraved not to like truth or contradictions, he can throw away this book. No one, assuredly, is forcing him to read it.

I return to my subject. The hunt is one of those sensual pleasures which excite the body but do nothing for the mind. It is a lethal skill which is used against savage animals. It is a continual dissipation, a tumultuous pleasure which fills the emptiness of the soul, rendering it incapable of any other reflection. It is the ardent desire to pursue some wild beast and the cruel satisfaction of killing it. In short, it is an amusement which builds up the body but leaves the mind fallow.

Hunters will no doubt reproach me with taking things too seriously, with playing the dour and severe critic, and with being like a priest who can say whatever he wants from the pulpit without fear of opposition.

I shall not exploit these advantages and will advance in good faith all the specious reasons advanced by hunters. They will tell me initially that the hunt is the noblest and oldest pleasure of men, that the patriarchs and many great men were hunters, and that hunters are merely exercising the power over animals that God gave to Adam. I agree that the hunt may be as old as the world. This proves that men have been hunting for a long time, but what is old is not necessarily better. I admit that some great men have loved hunting, but they had their faults and weaknesses too. Let us imitate their great qualities and not their petty ones!

It is true that the patriarchs hunted. They also married their sisters and practiced polygamy. But these good patriarchs and our dear ancestors often reflected the barbarous age in which they lived. They were very crude, ignorant, and idle people trying to drown their boredom in the hunt, wasting in the woods chasing after beasts the time that they did not have the wit or intelligence to pass in the company of reasonable people.

Whether or not Adam received the empire over the beasts, I wouldn't know; but I do know that we are more cruel and rapacious than the beasts themselves and that we act like tyrants over this supposed empire. If anything should give us an advantage over animals, it is assuredly our reason; and great hunters ordinarily have nothing else but horses, dogs, and all sorts of animals on their minds. Ordinarily crude, they surrender wholeheartedly to their passion; and it is to be feared that they will become as inhuman toward men as they are toward beasts or, at least, that their cruel indifference to suffering will make them less compassionate to their fellow men. Is this such a noble pleasure? Is this such a rational occupation?

One might object, perhaps, that hunting is healthy, that

hunters live longer, that it is an innocent pleasure proper for great lords since it displays their magnificence, dissipates their vexations, preserves the image of war in time of peace, and teaches princes topography, passages, and—in short—all about a country.

If you tell me that hunting is a passion, I would pity you for not having a better one. I would even excuse you somehow and counsel you to moderate a passion that you cannot destroy. If you tell me that hunting is a pleasure, I would answer that you should enjoy it without overdoing it, for God forbid that I should condemn any pleasure. I am, on the contrary, all for them. But when you tell me that hunting is very good and useful for a hundred reasons suggested by your false pride and misleading passions, I answer that your frivolous reasons cannot disguise the ugly reality and that for lack of proof you try to dazzle. What good is the long life of an idle and indolent man to society? Let us remember these lines:

"The life of a hero is not measured by its length."[2]

It is not a question of a man indolently and uselessly reaching the age of Methuselah. The more he has thought, the greater and more useful his actions, the longer he will have lived.

Besides, of all the amusements hunting is the least suitable for princes. They can manifest their magnificence in a manner much more useful to their subjects, and if the abundance of game should be ruining the country folk, the care of destroying these animals could very well be committed to hunters. Princes should only properly occupy themselves with acquiring more knowledge and greater ability to reason. Their profession is to think well and justly: that is what they should be practicing. Since men are creatures of habit and their occupations dominate their thinking, they should prefer the company of mild and sensible people to that of ferocious and savage animals; for how much better it is to have developed one's mind than to be the slave of one's sensations! Moderation, that virtue so necessary to princes, is not found in hunters; and this should be enough to render hunting odious.

I must add, to answer all possible objections and to return to Machiavelli, that it is not necessary to be a hunter in order to be a great captain, that Gustavus Adolphus, the Duke of

Marlborough, and Prince Eugene—to whom no one would dispute the quality of illustrious men and able officers—were not hunters,[3] and that it is much easier to reflect judiciously and solidly upon topography and the art of war while strolling than when distracted by partridges, dogs, stags, a bevy of animals, and the ardor of hunting. A great prince who participated in the second Hungarian campaign with the Imperialists was almost taken prisoner by the Turks while hunting.[4] Hunting should actually be forbidden in armies, for it causes many disorders during the marches with the officers neglecting their troops and going every which way. Detachments have even been surprised and cut to pieces by the enemy for similar reasons.

I thus conclude that it is pardonable for princes to go hunting if this is done rarely and as a distraction from their serious and sometimes vexing occupations. Hunting is proper for professional hunters, but rational men are in this world to think and act; and life is too short for them to waste its precious moments.

I have said above that the first duty of the prince was the administration of justice. I add here that a close second is the protection and defense of his states.

Sovereigns are obliged to maintain order and discipline among their troops. They must devote themselves seriously to the craft of war so that they can command armies, sustain labors, choose camps, secure victuals, make dispositions, react rapidly, get out of tight spots, profit from good as well as bad fortune, and never lack for counsel or prudence.

This is in truth asking a lot of humanity. It may, however, be expected more of a prince who devotes his attention to cultivating his mind than of those who think only of material things and follow the crude impulses of their senses. The mind is like the body. If you practice dancing, it becomes graceful, supple, and skillful. If you neglect it, it will stiffen, lose its grace, and become incapable of exercise.

NOTES

[1] Frederick undoubtedly meant to say, "Machiavelli's *prince* is like the Homeric gods . . ."

2 Jean-Baptiste Rousseau, *Odes*, Bk. II, Ode X.

3 Gustavus II Adolphus (1594–1632), became King of Sweden in 1611 and achieved a brilliant military reputation in the Polish and Thirty Years' wars. John Churchill (1650–1722), Duke of Marlborough, famed English commander in the War of the Spanish Succession. Eugene of Savoy (1663–1736), renowned Imperial general who won his laurels both in the French and Turkish wars.

4 Duke Francis III of Lorraine (see Ch. II, note 4), now husband of the Archduchess Maria Theresa and Grand Duke of Tuscany, commanded the Imperial armies against the Turks in 1738. He proved to be an indifferent soldier and was almost captured while hunting near Kolari, Serbia.

On those things **Chapter XV** about which men and particularly princes are praised or blamed

Painters and historians have this one thing in common: that the first paint the traits and complexions of men; and the others their characters, actions, and the history of the human spirit, in order to transmit it to the most remote posterity. There are painters whose brush, inspired by the graces, corrects the negligence of nature, supplements the defects of age, and softens the deformity of the original. The eloquent tongues of the Bossuets and the Fléchiers have repeatedly transformed merely great men into heroes.[1] There are, on the contrary, painters who catch only the ugly. Their coloring sullies the most beautifully tinted lilies and roses, they give a certain strangeness to the most regular features and traits, so that their copies of *Aphrodite* and *Eros*, the masterpieces of Praxiteles, would be unrecognizable.[2] Party spirit makes historians fall into the same error. Father Daniel, in his *History of France*, entirely distorts the events of the Reformation,[3] and some Protestant authors who are as immoderate and unwise as this reverend father have been cowardly enough to prefer the falsehoods suggested by their passions to the impartial testimony of truth, without considering that the first duty of a historian is to report the facts faithfully without twisting or changing them. Still another category of painters has mixed history and fiction in order to portray monsters more hideous than hell could ever spawn. Their brushes seem to catch only the features of devils. Their fertile and ghastly imagination imprints on canvas the somberness of the damned and the ferocity of the monsters of hell. What the Callots and the Pietro Testas are to this type of painting, Machiavelli is to writing.[4] He portrays the world as a hell and all men as demons. One might say that this misanthropic and hypochondriac political thinker had wanted to libel all mankind out of pure hatred for the species or that he had taken it upon himself to crush virtue in order perhaps to make all the inhabitants of this continent into his likeness.

Machiavelli makes himself ridiculous by speaking of virtue without understanding it, and he falls into the very excess which he condemns in others; for if some authors have made the world too good, he portrays it as vicious to the extreme. Starting from a principle laid down in his drunkenness, he can only deduce false consequences from it. It is as impossible to reason justly without the right principle as it is to draw a circle without a common center.

The author's political morality is reduced to having no vices but those which contribute to self-interest, sacrificing all others to ambition and to conformity with the scoundreliness of the world in order to avoid an otherwise inevitable ruin.

Interest is the key word of this political system. It is the vortex of Descartes, the gravitation of Newton.[5] According to Machiavelli, interest is the soul of the world. Everything bends before it, even the passions. It is, however, a grievous sin against knowledge to suppose that men can choose their passions. The mechanism of the human body is such that our gaiety, our sadness, our mildness, our anger, our love, our indifference, our sobriety, our intemperance—in short—all our passions depend on the arrangement of certain organs in our body, on the tightness or looseness of some small fibers and membranes, on the thickness or fluidity of our blood, on the facility or difficulty of its circulation, on the strength of our heart, on the nature of our bile, on the size of our stomach, etc. Now I ask if all these parts of our body are sufficiently docile to conform to the laws of our interest and if it is not more reasonable to assume that they will do nothing about it. Machiavelli would find, besides, many heretics who would prefer the god of Epicurus to the god of Caesar.

The only legitimate reason which can engage a reasonable

being to struggle against his passions is his own good and the advantage of society. The passions debase our nature and ruin our body when we abandon ourselves to them and give them free reign. They must be moderated without being destroyed and directed toward the good of society; and even if we do not win any pitched battles against them, we must consider the slightest advantage as the beginning of an empire over ourselves.

I must also call the attention of the reader to a most flagrant contradiction of Machiavelli in this chapter. He says at the beginning "that there is such a difference between what one does and what one should do that any man who bases his conduct on the duties of men and not on what they actually are will not fail to perish." The author had perhaps forgotten what he expresses in the sixth chapter where he says: "Since it is impossible to imitate one's model perfectly, a wise man must always imitate the greatest, so that he can at least lend their color to his actions." Machiavelli should be pitied for his poor memory if he shouldn't be all the more so for his incoherence.

Machiavelli pushes his errors and the maxims of his abominable false wisdom even further. He asserts that it is not possible to be entirely good in this corrupt and scoundrelly world without perishing. They say that if triangles could make a god, he would have three sides. This vicious and corrupted world is no less a creation of Machiavelli.

An honest man can be circumspect and prudent without this preventing him from penetrating the designs of his enemies and avoiding their traps.

But what is it not to be entirely good among scoundrels? It is nothing else than to be a scoundrel oneself. A man who begins by not being entirely good ordinarily ends by being very bad, and he will share the fate of the Danube which gets no better as it flows downstream. It begins by being Swiss and ends up by being Tartar.

I admit that one learns new and singular things in Machiavelli. I was sufficiently stupid and uncouth to ignore, until I read the *Prince*, that there were cases in which it was permitted for an honest man to become a scoundrel. I had ignored in my simplicity that the Catilines, the Cartouches,[6] and the Mir Vais[7] were to be models for the world; and I was convinced, along with most persons, that virtue was superior to vice.

Is it necessary to dispute, is it necessary to argue in order to demonstrate the advantages of virtue over vice, of beneficence over mischievousness, and of generosity over treason? I think that any reasonable man knows well enough which is the more profitable of the two and abhors a man who has no doubt or hesitation about deciding for crime.

NOTES

[1] See Ch. VII, note 5.

[2] Praxiteles (fl. 364 B.C.), the famous Athenian sculptor. The Aphrodite of Knidos and Eros of Messene are his most famous statues.

[3] Gabriel Daniel, S.J., *Histoire de France* (Paris, 1713), 3 vols. See Etienne Laval's *A compendius history of the reformation in France . . . wherein the many falsifications of the Jesuit Daniel . . . are set forth* (London, 1737–1743), 6 vols., which was just beginning to come out.

[4] Jacques Callot (1592–1635), Lorrainian engraver whose gruesome collection of plates, *Les misères de la guerre*, first appeared in 1633 and represents a stark indictment of the military profession. Pietro Testa (1611–1650), Italian engraver and painter best known for his baroque depictions of massacres and sacrifices. There seems to be little ground for placing Callot's brutal realism and Testa's voluptuous idealizations in the same category.

[5] See Ch. I, note 1.

[6] Sergius Catilina (c. 108–62 B.C.), the famous conspirator against the Roman Republic. See Cicero's *Catilinarian Orations* and Sallust's *Conspiracy of Catiline*. On Cartouche, see Ch. VIII, note 5.

[7] Mir Vais (1675–1715) was an intriguing Afghan chieftan from Kandahar who in 1709 managed to stage a bloody coup against its Persian governor and established an independent principality in the area. Mir Vais' son, Mir Mohammed, later conquered Persia and founded a short-lived Afghan dynasty there. See Jean-Antoine Du Cereau's *Histoire de la dernière revolution de Perse* (Paris, 1728), 2 vols.

On liberality and parsimony   **Chapter XVI**

Two famous sculptors, Phidias and Alcamenes, each made a statue of Minerva, so that the Athenians could choose the most beautiful to place at the top of a column. Both were presented to the public. Alcamenes' won—the other was considered too roughly shaped. Phidias, undisturbed by the judgment of the vulgar, asked that both statues be placed upon the column before deciding on their beauty. The two statues were indeed raised, and then the rules of proportion, perspective, and elegance of design were found to have been much better observed by Phidias than by his adversary.[1]

Phidias owed his success to the study of optics and proportions. What is on an elevation is subject to different rules than what is on a plane. But this law of proportion is just as applicable to politics as to sculpture. In politics, a difference in place makes for a difference in maxims: applying them generally renders them vicious. What would be admirable for a great kingdom would not be suitable to a small state. What would serve for the rise of one would only contribute to the fall of the other. If such different interests were confused, it would result in strange errors and false applications of principles which might in themselves be very salutary. The luxury which comes from abundance and makes riches circulate through all the veins of a state makes a great kingdom flourish. It maintains industry and multiplies the needs of the rich and opulent, thus tying them to the poor and indigent. Luxury is to a great empire what the diastolic and systolic movements of the heart are to the human body. It is the spring which sends the blood through the great arteries to our extremities and makes it circulate through the small veins back to the heart for redistribution.

If it occurred to some incompetent politician to banish luxury from a great state, the state would begin to languish and get weaker. Money, useless, would remain in the coffers of the wealthy. Commerce would languish, manufactures would decline for lack of markets, industry would perish, rich families would always remain so, and indigents would have no recourse against their poverty.

On the contrary, luxury would destroy a small state. Private individuals would go broke, and the flow of more money out of the country than was coming in would make its delicate body die of consumption. Thus political thinkers should never confuse small states with big ones, which is precisely what Machiavelli does in this chapter.

The first fault that I find with him is that he defines the word liberality too vaguely. There is a clear difference between a lavish man and a liberal one. The first spends all his wealth with profusion, disorder, and impropriety. This is a censurable excess, a kind of folly, and a fault of judgment. Consequently, a wise prince will not be lavish. On the contrary, the liberal man is generous and reasonable. His income is the barometer of his expenses; and although he may be stingy with his favors, his compassion leads him to deprive himself of his surplus in order to assist the unfortunate. His goodness is limited only by his forces. This, I maintain, is one of the foremost qualities of a great prince and of all those who are born to relieve the poverty of others.

The second fault that I find with Machiavelli is his ignorance of character in attributing to liberality the faults of avarice. "A prince," he says, "cannot maintain his reputation for liberality without overburdening his subjects, confiscating their goods, and resorting to disreputable ways of filling his coffers." These are precisely the traits of a miser. It was Vespasian and not Trajan who taxed the Roman people.[2] Avarice is a voracious hunger that is never satiated, a cancer that corrupts everything around it. A miser desires riches, he envies those who possess them, and he takes all he can. Greedy men fall to the lure of profit, and avaricious judges are corruptible. The vice is such that it can eclipse the greatest virtues.

The liberal man is just the opposite of the miser. Goodness and compassion underlie his generosity. If he does good, it is in order to aid the unfortunate and to contribute to the happiness of persons of merit whose fortune does not correspond to their worth. A prince of this type, far from oppressing the people and spending for his pleasures what his subjects have amassed by their industry, thinks only of augmenting their opulence. Unjust or bad actions are done only without his knowledge, and his good heart inspires him to procure for the people under his dominion all the happiness that they can achieve.

This is the ordinary meaning of liberality and avarice. Petty princes with restricted domains and large families do well to push economy to the limits of avarice. Sovereigns who, for all their states, are not among the greatest princes, are obliged to administer their revenues carefully and measure their liberalities according to their means; but the more powerful princes are, the more liberal they should be.

Perhaps objection might be made with the example of Francis I of France, whose excessive expenses were in part the cause of his misfortunes.[3] It is true that his pleasures exhausted the resources needed for his glory. But there are two answers to this objection: the first is that the France of his time was not comparable in power, revenue, and forces to what she is now; and the second is that he was not liberal but lavish.

Far from condemning good order and economy in a sovereign, I am the first to praise it. A prince, as the guardian of his subjects, has the administration of the public moneys. He is responsible for this to his subjects, and he must wisely assemble sufficient funds so that he can furnish the necessary expenses in time of war without imposing new burdens. Prudence and circumspection are necessary in administering the goods of the state, but it is always for the good of the state that a prince is liberal and generous. This is how he encourages industry, solidifies glory, and inspires virtue.

It only remains for me to evoke an error of morality in which Machiavelli has fallen. "Liberality," he says, "makes one poor and consequently contemptible." What pitiful reasoning! What false ideas of what is worthy of praise or blame! What,

Machiavelli, the treasures of a rich man should serve as the measure of public esteem? A metal in itself contemptible and arbitrarily priced should render its possessor worthy of praise? It is thus not man, but the grains of gold that are venerated. How can a rational mind get such an idea? Riches are acquired by industry, inheritance, or what is worse, by violence. All these goods are external to man—he may keep or lose them. How can one thus confuse objects as different in themselves as virtue and filthy lucre? The Duke of Newcastle, Samuel Bernard, and Pels are known for their riches, but there is a difference between being known and being esteemed.[4] The proud Croesus and his treasures, the avaricious Crassus and his riches have struck people as singular phenomena without touching the heart or being esteemed. The just Aristides and the wise Philopoemen, Marshal de Turenne and M. de Catinat, equal to the legendary morals of the early centuries, were the admiration of their time and an example to upright people in all ages in spite of their frugality and disinterestedness.[5]

It is thus not power, force, or wealth which win the hearts of men, but personal qualities, goodness, and virtue. Poverty or indigence can no more tarnish virtue than external advantages can ennoble vice.

The vulgar and the indigent have a certain respect for wealth which comes to them precisely because they do not know it. Rich persons, on the contrary, and those who think justly, have a sovereign contempt for everything that comes through fortune or chance, and their possessions make them better aware of the empty vanity of worldly goods.

It is not a question of dazzling the public and absconding, so to speak, with their esteem. It is a question of meriting it.

NOTES

[1] See Charles Rollin, *Histoire Ancienne* (Paris, 1733–1738), XI, pt. 1, 83.

[2] See Suetonius, *Lives of the Twelve Caesars*, "Vespasian", XVI.

[3] Francis I (1494–1547), King of France from 1515.

[4] Thomas Pelham (1693–1768), Duke of Newcastle, affluent English peer and a collaborator of Robert Walpole in maintaining the Whig supremacy in parliament. Samuel Bernard (c. 1651–1739), French banker and former

Protestant who helped to support Louis XIV's sagging fortunes in the War of the Spanish Succession. Andries Pels (1655–1731), Dutch banker who sustained the English cause in the same war.

5 Croesus (d. 546 B.C.), King of Lydia from 560 famous for his riches. Crassus (c. 115–53 B.C.), Roman financier and collaborator of Julius Caesar. Aristides (c. 530–468 B.C.), Athenian statesman who organized the Confederacy of Delos, for which he became known as "the just". Philopoemen (253–184 B.C.), Megalopolitan soldier and statesman who led the Achaean League. Henri de La Tour-d'Auvergne (1611–1675), the renowned Marshal de Turenne, one of Louis XIV's greatest generals. Nicolas Catinat (1637–1712), Marshal of France from 1693, another of Louis XIV's distinguished commanders.

On cruelty and pity; and if it is better to be loved than to be feared, or the contrary   **Chapter XVII**

The most precious trust that is placed in the hands of princes is the life of their subjects. Their post gives them the power of condemning the guilty to death or of pardoning them. As supreme arbiters of justice, a word from their mouth sets in motion the sinister instruments of death and destruction or gives wing to the speedy agents of their graces bearing good news. But such absolute power demands circumspection, prudence, and wisdom if it is not to be abused.

Tyrants set no value on human life. Their position prevents them from sympathizing with misfortunes that they do not experience. They are short-sighted people who cannot see beyond the tip of their nose and do not notice the rest of humanity. Perhaps if they could sense the horror of the punishments that they have ordered, of the cruelties committed out of their sight, and of everything that accompanies an execution, their hearts would not be so hard as to continue renouncing humanity and their impassiveness so unnatural as not to be touched.[1]

Good princes regard their unlimited power over human life as the heaviest burden of their crown. They know that they are men just like those whom they must judge. They know that wrongs, injustices, and injuries can be repaired in this world, but that a hasty death sentence is an irreparable evil. They opt for severity only to avoid a worse alternative, and they make these ghastly decisions only in desperate cases, like a man with a gangrened limb who would reluctantly resolve to have it amputated in order to save the rest of his body. It is thus only under the greatest necessity that a prince must extinguish the life of his subjects, and he must be extremely circumspect and scrupulous about it.

Machiavelli treats such grave, serious, and important things as trifles. Human life is nothing to him, and interest, his only god, is everything. He prefers cruelty to clemency, and he counsels those who have recently risen to sovereignty to be particularly indifferent to being reputed cruel.

It is executioners who place Machiavelli's heroes on the throne, and it is force and violence that maintains them there. Cesare Borgia is the refuge of this political thinker when he seeks for examples of cruelty just as *Telemachus* is for M. de Fénelon when he shows the way to virtue.

Machiavelli also cites some verses that Virgil puts into the mouth of Dido, but this citation is entirely out of context, for Virgil has Dido speak just as M. de Voltaire does with Jocasta in his *Oedipus*.[2] A poet has his personages speak in terms that are appropriate to their character. The authority of Dido and Jocasta has no bearing on a political treatise, which requires examples of great and virtuous men.

One reflection will suffice to answer the author in short. It is that crimes have such a ghastly interconnection that one necessarily leads to another. Thus usurpation is followed by banishment, proscription, confiscation, and murder. I ask if it is not being awfully harsh and execrably ambitious to aspire to sovereignty in view of the crimes that must be committed in order to maintain it. I ask if any man's personal interest justifies making the innocent who are opposed to his usurpation perish and what is the charm of a crown besmirched with blood. These reflections would perhaps make little impression on Machiavelli, but I am convinced that the whole world is not as corrupt as he is.

The political thinker recommends, above all, rigor towards the troops. He opposes the indulgence of Scipio to the severity of Hannibal. He prefers the Carthaginian to the Roman and immediately concludes that cruelty is the foundation of the order, discipline, and triumphs of an army. Machiavelli is not acting in good faith here, for he chooses Scipio, the softest and flabbiest of all disciplinarians, so as to oppose him to Hannibal in arguing for cruelty. The political thinker eloquently contrasts it to the weakness of Scipio, whom he himself confesses that Cato called the corrupter of the Roman army; and he presumes to use the differing success of these two generals in order to decry clemency, which he confuses as usual with the vice of excessive goodness.

I admit that order cannot subsist in an army without severity, for how can libertines, debauchees, scoundrels, poltroons, rash, crude, and mechanical animals be retained in their duty if the fear of punishments did not in part restrain them?

All that I ask of Machiavelli on this subject is moderation. Let him realize that if the clemency of an honest man leads him to goodness, his wisdom no less leads him to rigor. But he uses his rigor like an able pilot. He does not cut down the mast or the rigging of his vessel unless he is forced to do so by the imminent danger of storm and tempest.

But Machiavelli has not yet exhausted his subject. I am now at his most captious, subtle, and dazzling argument. He says that a prince finds it more to his advantage to be feared than loved since most people are ungrateful, fickle, dissimulating, cowardly, and avaricious; that love is made fragile by the malice and baseness of mankind, whereas fear of punishment gives much better assurance that people will do their duty; and that men are masters of their goodwill but not of their fear, so that a prudent prince will depend on it above all else.

I answer that I do not deny that there are ungrateful and dissimulating men in the world. I do not deny that fear is sometimes very powerful, but I claim that any king whose policy has no other goal than to be feared will reign over slaves, that he can expect no great actions from his subjects—for everything that is done out of fear or timidity always bears its imprint— that a prince who has the gift of being loved will reign over hearts since his subjects find it convenient to have him as a master, and that there are many examples in history of great and beautiful actions being performed out of love and fidelity. I may add that the fashion for seditions and revolutions seems to have entirely passed in our days, there being no kingdom except for England where the king has the least cause to fear his people; and even in England, the king has nothing to fear unless he himself rouses the tempest.

I thus conclude that a cruel prince is in more danger of treason than an easy going one; since cruelty is unbearable and one soon tires of fearing it, and goodness is always lovable and no one ever tires of loving it.

It would thus be desirable for the happiness of the world if princes were good without being too indulgent, so that their goodness would be a virtue and not a weakness.

NOTES

[1] Frederick's statement assumes greater poignancy in view of his witnessing the execution of Von Katte.

[2] "Difficult times and the newness of my reign compel me to act thusly and guard my boundaries on all sides." See Virgil's *Aeneid*, I:563–564.

How princes **Chapter XVIII**
should keep faith

It is in the nature of things that what is fundamentally bad will always remain that way. The Ciceros and the Demosthenes could exhaust their art before deceiving the world on this subject. Their eloquence would be praised, but their pitiful abuse of it would not. The goal of an orator must be to defend the innocent against the oppressor, to explain why men should make one decision in preference to another, to show the beauty of virtue in contrast to the deformity of vice, but eloquence must be abhorred when it is put to an opposite use.

Machiavelli, the meanest, the most scoundrelly of men, employs in this chapter every argument that he can imagine in order to glorify crime, but he stumbles and falls so often in this infamous effort that I could spend all my time just noting his lapses. The disordered and false reasoning in this chapter is staggering. It is perhaps the most malicious and feeble one in the entire work. Its logic is as bad as its morality is depraved. This sophist of crime assures us that princes can mislead the world by their dissimulation. This is where I must begin to confound him.

Everyone knows how curious the public is. It is an animal that sees, hears, and divulges everything. The public examines the conduct of private individuals for entertainment, but it judges the character of princes out of self-interest. Thus princes are more exposed than any other men to the reflections and judgments of the world. They are like stars upon which a nation of astronomers has trained its telescopes and astrolabes. The courtiers who observe them up close notice something each day—a gesture, a glance, a look betrays them—and the people approach them by conjectures. In short, the sun can no more hide its spots, the moon its phases, Saturn its rings, than can great princes hide their vices and the depths of their character from the eyes of so many observers.

Even if the mask of dissimulation covered the natural deformity of a prince for a while, he could not wear this mask continually. He would have to remove it, if only to breathe, and a single occasion suffices for the curious.

Thus artifice and dissimulation would live in vain on the lips of this prince. His wiliness in speech and actions would be useless to him. Men are not judged by their words—these are always misleading—but by their actions, so that falseness and dissimulation can never prevail.

One can only truly be himself and must actually possess the character he wants the world to attribute to him. Otherwise, whoever thinks he is fooling the public is his own dupe.

Sixtus V, Philip II, Cromwell passed in the world as subtle, wily, hypocritical, and ambitious men, but never as virtuous.[1] It is not possible to disguise oneself. No matter how able a prince is, he cannot, even if he were to follow all the maxims of Machiavelli, invest his crimes with the character of virtue.

Machiavelli, that corrupter of virtue, does not reason any better on the reasons that must lead princes to trickery and hypocrisy. The ingenious and faulty use of the fable of the centaur does not prove anything, for just because a centaur may be half human and half horse, does it follow that princes must be tricky and ferocious? It must take quite a desire to sanctify crime to employ such feeble and far-fetched arguments.

But here is some reasoning that is even more pitiful. The political thinker says that a prince must have the qualities of the lion and of the fox—of the lion to get rid of the wolves, of the fox to be wily—and he concludes, "which shows that a prince is not obliged to keep his word." This is a conclusion without premises. A student in the second form would be rigorously punished by his teacher if he argued in this manner.[2] Isn't the doctor of crime ashamed at thus stammering the lessons of impiety?

If one wanted to attribute integrity and good sense to the muddled thoughts of Machiavelli, here is approximately how they might be interpreted. The world is like a game in which there are both honest and dishonest players, so that a prince who plays in this game must learn how to cheat, not in order to do it, but in order not to be the dupe of others.

Let us return to the fall of our political thinker. "Because all men," he says, "are scoundrels and fail repeatedly to keep their word, you are not obliged to keep yours either." This is a direct contradiction to the author's statement a moment later that dissimulators always find simpletons to abuse. How does that follow? All men are scoundrels and you find simpletons to abuse? What a contradiction and, as to the reasoning, it is no better; for it is absolutely false that the world is composed only of scoundrels. It takes quite a misanthrope not to see that in every society there are many honest people, that the great number of persons is neither good nor bad, and that there are some rascals whom justice pursues and punishes severely if it catches them. But if Machiavelli had not supposed the world to be full of scoundrels, on what could he have based his abominable maxim? It is clear that he was honor bound by his engagement to sanctify trickery to act thusly and that he felt it permissible to fool men in teaching them to mislead. Even if we supposed that men were as bad as Machiavelli says, it would still not follow that we must imitate them. If Cartouche steals, pillages, and assassinates, I conclude that Cartouche is a miserable rascal and not that I must base my conduct upon his. If there were no more honor and virtue in the world, says a historian, one should look to princes for what was left of it.[3] In short, no consideration should be capable of engaging an honest man to depart from his duty.

After the author has proven the necessity of crime, he wants to encourage his disciples by the facility of committing it. "Those who are experts in the art of dissimulation," he says, "will always find simpletons to dupe," which comes down to this: your neighbor is a fool and you are smart, so you must dupe him because he is a fool. These are syllogisms for which the students of Machiavelli have been hung and broken at the wheel in the public square.

The political thinker, not satisfied with having demonstrated the facility of crime according to his way of reasoning, then emphasizes the happiness of perfidy, but the trouble is that

Cesare Borgia, the greatest scoundrel, the biggest traitor, the most perfidious of men, and the hero of Machiavelli, was actually very unfortunate. Machiavelli takes good care not to mention him on this occasion. He needed some examples, but where else could he have found them than in the records of criminal trials or in the history of the popes? It is on the latter that he settles, and he asserts that Alexander VI, the most false and impious man of his time always succeeded in his trickery because he was an expert in human credulity.

I dare say that it was not human credulity as much as certain events and circumstances which made the designs of this pope succeed. The conflict of French and Spanish ambitions, the disunion and hatred of the Italian families, the weakness of Louis XII, and the sums of money extorted by His Holiness, which rendered him very powerful, contributed no less to it.

If trickery is pushed too far, it is even a political fault. I cite the authority of a great statesman, Cardinal Mazarin, who said to Don Luis de Haro that his greatest political failing was that he was always tricky.[4] The same Mazarin wanting to employ [Marshal Fabert] in a shady negotiation [the marshal] told him, "Permit me, my lord, to refuse to mislead the Duke of Savoy over a mere trifle. I have a reputation for being an honest man. Save my integrity for an occasion when the safety of France is at stake."[5]

I am not even speaking now of honesty or virtue, but merely considering the interest of princes, I say that it is a very bad policy for them to be tricky and to dupe the world. They dupe only once and then lose the confidence of the other princes.

A certain power positively declared the reasons for its conduct in a manifesto and subsequently acted in a manner diametrically opposed to it.[6] I admit that such striking behavior entirely undermines confidence; for the closer the contradiction, the more blatant it is. The Roman church, to avoid a similar contradiction, has very wisely fixed for its saints a novitiate of one hundred years after their death, during which the memory of their faults and extravagances perishes with them. The witnesses to their life and those who might testify against them no longer exist, and nothing opposes the idea of holiness from being given to the public.

Please pardon me this digression. I admit, besides, that there are some disturbing necessities when a prince cannot avoid breaking his treaties and alliances. He must, however, do it properly, by warning his allies in time and not unless the welfare of his people and extreme necessity oblige him.

These sudden contradictions with which I have just reproached a certain power are very numerous in Machiavelli. He says in the same paragraph first: "It is necessary to appear kind, faithful, mild, religious, and upright; and to be so in fact," and later: "It is impossible for a prince to act like an upstanding man in everything. Thus he must bend with the wind and with the caprice of fortune and never depart from good if he can; but if necessity obliges him, he can sometimes appear to depart from it." These thoughts add up, it must be admitted, to a lot of balderdash. A man who reasons in this manner does not understand himself and does not merit our taking the trouble to resolve his enigma or unravel his chaos.

I shall finish this chapter with a single reflection. Please notice how quickly vices multiply in the hands of Machiavelli. It is not sufficient for his prince to have the misfortune of being irreligious. He wants to crown his irreligion with hypocrisy. He thinks that people will be more impressed by the preference that a prince gives to Polignac over Lucretius than by his bad treatment, and some people share this sentiment.[7] It seems to me that there must be some indulgence for the errors of speculation when they do not entail the corruption of the heart and that people would prefer an irreligious but honest prince who is their benefactor to an orthodox scoundrel and malefactor. It is not the thoughts of princes, but their actions that render men happy.

N.B. No mention of ends & means

NOTES

[1] See Gregorio Leti's scurrilous *Vita di Sisto V* (Lausanne, 1669) in the French translation (Amsterdam, 1693). See also the same author's *Histoire du Roi Philippe II*, (Amsterdam, 1734), 6 vols., and his *Historia di Olivero Cromvele* (Amsterdam, 1692) in the French translation (Amsterdam, 1694).

[2] Eighth grade.

³ A statement attributed to John the Good (1319–1364), King of France from 1350, who voluntarily returned to captivity in England after being unable to raise his ransom. The first authority for this attribution, however, is François de Mézeray in his *Historie de France* (Paris, 1643–1651), I, 851.

⁴ This statement, with Don Luis de Haro accusing Cardinal Mazarin, is found in Voltaire's *Age of Louis XIV*, Ch. VI. Voltaire seems to have derived it from Saint-Evremond's *Lettre sur la paix*. See Saint-Evremond's *Oeuvres méslees* (Amsterdam, 1699–1700), 6 vols.

⁵ This seems like a variation of the Vicomte de Orte's reply to King Charles IX following the massacre of St. Bartholomew when ordered to kill the Huguenots in Bayonne, "Sire, I have not found among the inhabitants a single executioner . . . we implore your Majesty to employ us for more feasible things." See Agrippa d'Aubigné's *Histoire universelle* (Paris, 1626–1620), Vol. II, Bk. I, Ch. V. Voltaire inserted the name of Marshal Fabert in both of his editions, thus compounding the fabrication.

⁶ The French declaration of March 17, 1733, which opposed the intervention of foreign powers in the choice of a Polish king at the same time that French diplomacy and resources were working for the election of Stanislas Leszczynski.

⁷ Melchior de Polignac (1661–1741), was a learned French ecclesiastic, diplomat, and ultimately cardinal, who had composed an eloquent Latin poem against Lucretius. Frederick probably knew of the *Anti-Lucretius*, which was not published until 1747, through Voltaire's *Temple du Goût*, in which the cardinal acts as Voltaire's guide through a temple of literary taste.

On avoiding contempt and hatred

Chapter XIX

The spirit of system has always been a fatal shoal to human reason. It has taken in those who believed that they had found some ingenious basis for truth, filled them with prejudices that have stymied their search for it, and led them to produce romances rather than demonstrations.

The planetary havens of the ancients, the vortices of Descartes, and the pre-established harmony of Leibnitz are all errors caused by the systematic spirit.[1] These philosophers have presumed to map out an unknown country without even taking the trouble to explore it. They learned the names of some cities and rivers and located them wherever they pleased. Subsequently, to the humiliation of these poor geographers, inquisitive men have traveled to these well-described countries with two guides, analogy and experiment, and found to their great astonishment that the cities, rivers, and distances were entirely different from what had been presumed.

The rage for systems is not just a folly limited to philosophers. It has also become the folly of political thinkers. Machiavelli is particularly infected by it. He wants to prove that a prince must be vicious and sly—these are the magic words of his pitiful system. Machiavelli has all the viciousness of the monsters crushed by Hercules but not their strength, so that it doesn't take a Hercules to bring him down;[2] for what is more simple, natural, and proper to princes than justice and goodness? There is no need to argue this at length—everyone is convinced of it. The political thinker must necessarily lose by maintaining the contrary; for if he maintains that a prince established on the throne must be cruel, sly, faithless, etc., he makes him vicious for nothing, and if he wants to invest a prince who rises to the throne with all these vices, they will rouse all the sovereigns and republics against him. For how can a private individual rise to sovereignty without dispossessing a sovereign prince of his states or usurping the authority in a republic? This is assuredly not to the liking of the princes of Europe, and Machiavelli could not have written a more reprehensible work if he had composed a collection of sly tricks for the use of highwaymen.

I must, however, recount the false reasonings and contradictions which are found in this chapter. Machiavelli claims that what renders a prince odious is if he unjustly appropriates the goods of his subjects and assails the chastity of their women. It is sure that a self-interested, unjust, violent, and cruel prince will come to be hated by his people, but it is not the same for gallantry. Julius Caesar, who was known in Rome as the husband of all the wives and the wife of all the husbands,[3] Louis XIV, who liked women very much, Augustus I, king of Poland, who shared them with his subjects—these princes were not hated because of their affairs; and if Caesar was assassinated, if Roman liberty drove a dagger into his side, this is because Caesar was an usurper, not because he was gallant.

One might advance in support of Machiavelli's sentiment the expulsion of the kings of Rome due to the assault against the chastity of Lucretia, but I answer that it was not the love of young Tarquin for Lucretia, but his violent way of making love, that occasioned the revolt of Rome; and since this violence revived in the people the memory of the other violences committed by the Tarquins, they thought seriously of vengeance.[4]

I don't mean to excuse the gallantry of princes. It may be morally bad. I have sought only to show here that it does not make sovereigns odious. Love is regarded as a weakness in good princes just as intelligent people regard the commentary on the *Apocalypse* as a weakness of Newton's.[5]

But what seems to merit some reflection is that this doctor who preaches abstinence from women to princes was a Florentine. Among Machiavelli's other good qualities, was he also a Jesuit?

Let us come now to the counsels that he gives to princes for avoiding contempt. He wants them to be neither capricious, nor vacillating, cowardly, effeminate, or indecisive—in which he is assuredly right—but he goes on to counsel them to display a great deal of grandeur, gravity, courage, and firmness. Courage is good, but why must princes merely display these virtues? Why can't they actually possess them? If princes did not actually possess these qualities, they would display them very badly, and it would be felt that they were putting on an act.

Machiavelli adds that a prince must not let himself be governed, so that no one is presumed to have enough ascendancy over him to make him change his mind. He is in fact right, but I maintain that there isn't a person in the world who doesn't let himself more or less be governed. They say that the city of Amsterdam was once governed by a cat. By a cat? How, you say, was a city governed by a cat? The mayor of the city had the first voice in the council and was highly esteemed there. This mayor had a wife whose counsels he followed blindly. A servant had an absolute ascendancy over this woman and a cat over the servant. It was thus a cat who governed the city.[6]

There are, however, occasions when it is even glorious for a prince to change his conduct, and he must do so whenever he notices his errors. If princes were as infallible as the pope believes himself to be, they would do well to be as firm as stoics; but since they are only human, they must constantly think about perfecting their conduct. Let it be recalled that the excessive firmness and obstinacy of Charles XII almost lost him at Bender and that it was his unshakable firmness which did more to ruin his affairs than the loss of some battles.[7]

Here are some other errors of Machiavelli. He says "that a prince will never lack for allies as long as he can rely on his armies;" and this is false unless you add *and on his word;* for the army depends on the prince, and it is on his honesty or dishonesty that the fulfillment of his alliances and the movements of his army depend.

But here is a pure contradiction. The political thinker wants "a prince to be loved by his subjects in order to avoid conspiracies;" and in chapter seventeen he says "that a prince must be feared, since he can count on something that depends on him, which is not the case with the love of the people." Which is the true sentiment of the author? He speaks the language of oracles—one can interpret him as one wishes—but this language of oracles, let it be said in passing, is the language of tricksters.

I must say in general on this occasion that conspiracies and assassinations are not too common any longer in the world. Princes can rest easy on that score. These crimes have passed out of fashion, and Machiavelli's reasons are very good. Only the fanaticism of some monks might make them commit such shocking crimes out of devotion or sanctity. Among the good things that Machiavelli says on the subject of conspiracies, there is a very good one which becomes bad in his mouth. Here it is: "A conspirator," he says, "is disturbed by the fear of the punishments that threaten him, and kings are maintained by the majesty of empire and the authority of the laws." It seems to me that an author who inspires only interest, cruelty, despotism, and usurpation is in no position to speak of laws. Machiavelli does as the Protestants, who use the arguments of the unbelievers to combat the transubstantiation of the Catholics and then use the arguments with which the Catholics support transubstantiation to oppose the unbelievers. What subtle minds!

Machiavelli thus counsels princes to be loved and to cultivate both the good will of the great and of the people. He is right to counsel them to discharge what might draw the hatred of these two estates upon others by establishing magistrates to judge between the people and the great. He advances the government of France as a model, and this great friend of despotism and usurpation approves of the power that the *parlement* once had in France. It seems to me that if there were a government which could be proposed as a model of wisdom today, it is that of England. There the parliament is arbiter between the people and the king, and the king has all the power to do good and none to do evil.[8]

Machiavelli then replies to the objections that could be raised against his assertions regarding the character of princes, and he goes into a long discussion on the lives of the Roman emperors from Marcus Aurelius down to the two Gordians. Let us follow

him and examine his reasoning. The political thinker attributes
the cause of these frequent changes to the sale of the Empire. It
is sure that from the time that the post of emperor was sold by
the praetorian guards, the emperors were no longer sure of
their lives. This post was at the disposal of the soldiers, and its
holder perished if he did not cater to their complaints or
minister to their violences, so that the good emperors were
massacred by the soldiers and the vicious ones by conspiracy or
by order of the senate. Let us add that the ease with which it was
then possible to rise to the empire contributed greatly to these
frequent changes and that it was just as fashionable then in
Rome to kill the emperors as it is in our days in some American
countries for sons to strangle their fathers when they are too
old. Such is the power of custom upon men that it even
overcomes natural sentiments. Here is a reflection on the life of
Pertinax which is hardly consistent with the precepts that the
author gives at the beginning of this chapter. He says "that a
sovereign who wants to be sure of conserving his crown is
sometimes obliged to depart from the bounds of justice and
goodness." I think I have shown that in those unhappy times
neither the goodness nor the crimes of the emperors saved
them from assassins. Commodus—unworthy successor of
Marcus Aurelius, held in contempt by the people and the
soldiers—was put to death. I shall save Severus for the end of
the chapter.   I therefore pass to Caracalla, who could not
maintain himself because of his cruelty and who lavished upon
the soldiers the sums amassed by his father in order to
obliterate the murder of his brother Geta. I pass over Macrinus
and Heliogabalus in silence—both put to death and unworthy of
the attention of posterity. Alexander, their successor, had good
qualities. Machiavelli believes that he lost his life because of his
effeminacy, but he actually lost it because he wanted to
reestablish the military discipline which the cowardice of his
predecessors had entirely neglected. When the unbridled troops
heard the sound of the word "order", they got rid of the prince.
Maximius followed Alexander. He was a great warrior, but he
could not preserve the throne. Machiavelli attributes this to his
low birth and great cruelty. He is right as to cruelty, but he is
mistaken as to the low birth. It may ordinarily be supposed that

a man needs exceptional merit to rise without support or ancestors, since he draws his luster only from his virtue; and it often happens that well-born persons are scorned when they do not measure up to the idea of nobility.

Let us now return to Severus, of whom Machiavelli says "that he was a ferocious lion and a wily fox." Severus had some great qualities. His falseness and perfidy can be approved only by Machiavelli. He would, besides, have been a great prince if he had been good. It should be noted on this occasion that Severus was governed by his favorite Plautian just as Tiberius was by Sejanus and that neither of these princes was scorned. Since the author often reasons badly, he also does so in regard to Severus, for he says that the reputation of this emperor "effaced the greatness of his extortions and kept him immune from the public hatred." It seems to me that it is present extortions and injustices which efface the greatness of a present reputation. It is for the reader to judge. If Severus maintained himself on the throne, he was somehow beholden for it to the emperor Hadrian, who established military discipline; and if the successors of Severus could not maintain themselves, the relaxation of discipline by Severus was the cause. Severus also committed a great political error. It was because of his proscriptions that many soldiers from the army of Pescennius Niger withdrew to the Parthians and taught them the art of war, to the great prejudice of the empire. A prudent prince must not only think of his own reign, but also of future ones.

Machiavelli is thus gravely mistaken when he believes that in the time of Severus it sufficed to coddle the soldiers in order to survive, for the history of these emperors contradicts him. In our own time, a prince must treat all the orders in his state equally, without making distinctions that will have ghastly consequences for his interests.

The model of Severus, proposed by Machiavelli to those who rise to empire is thus as bad as that of Marcus Aurelius is good. But how can one lump Severus, Cesare Borgia, and Marcus Aurelius together as models? This is combining the purest wisdom and virtue with the most awful scoundreliness.[9]

I cannot finish this chapter without one more remark. It is that Cesare Borgia, in spite of his cruelty and perfidy, ended very badly and that the crowned philosopher Marcus Aurelius, always good and virtuous, never experienced a reversal of fortune.

NOTES

¹ See Ch. I, note 1.

² Heracles, or Hercules, the mythical Graeco-Roman hero. See Ovid's *Metamorphoses*, IX: 182–198.

³ See Suetonius, *Lives of the Twelve Caesars*, "Julius Caesar", LII.

⁴ Sextus Tarquinius, the youngest son of Tarquin the Proud. See Livy's *History of Rome*, Bk. I, Chs. LVII–LVIX.

⁵ The great Isaac Newton's *Observations upon the Prophecies of Daniel and the Apocalypse of Saint John* was published posthumously in 1733. It was an old-fashioned attempt to prove the validity of these prophecies and caused a constant embarrassment among Newton's "enlightened" admirers.

⁶ This story, with the cat replaced by the devil, was told on Andries Bicker (1586–1652) by his enemies supporting the house of Orange in the pamphlet *'t Muyder Spoockje* (1650).

⁷ After his defeat at Poltava, Charles XII and his remaining forces set up headquarters at Bender in Bessarabia, where he continually intrigued and even came to armed confrontation with his Turkish hosts, who finally forced him to return to Sweden. See Voltaire's *Histoire de Charles XII*, Bks. V–VII.

⁸ This same statement is found in Fénelon's *Télémaque*, Bk. V and Voltaire's *Philosophical Letters*, VIII.

⁹ This entire discussion of the Roman Empire is largely inspired by Montesquieu's *Considerations on the Causes of the Greatness of the Romans and Their Decline*, Ch. XVI.

If fortresses and other things on which princes regularly rely are useful or not

Chapter XX

Paganism portrayed Janus with two faces to represent his perfect knowledge of past and future. This imagery is very well applicable to princes. They must, like Janus, look behind them to all past history for salutary lessons of conduct and duty. They must, like Janus, look ahead of them with penetrating judgment and read into present circumstances for what is to follow.

The study of the past is necessary to princes as a school of wisdom which furnishes them with examples of illustrious and virtuous men. The study of the future is useful to them as a school of prudence which makes them foresee the misfortunes they must try to avert. These two virtues are as necessary to princes as the magnet and the compass are to pilots.

The knowledge of history is also useful in that it adds to one's self-awareness. It enriches the mind and portrays the vicissitudes of fortune along with salutary examples of resourcefulness and expediency.

Penetration into the future is good in that it helps us somehow to decipher the mysteries of fate; and by considering everything that might happen to us, we can be prepared to react sensibly when the event happens.

Machiavelli in this chapter poses five questions to princes, both to those who have made new conquests and to those who need only to solidify their possessions. Let us see what prudence might counsel by combining the past with the future and by always deciding through reason and justice.

The first question is whether a prince must disarm a conquered people or not.

I answer that the manner of waging war has changed greatly since Machiavelli's time. Princes have armies to defend their countries, a troupe of armed peasants would be scorned, and the bourgeoisie only takes up arms during sieges, although the besiegers will ordinarily try to prevent this by threatening them with a bombardment and incendiary bullets. It appears, besides, that it is prudent to disarm the bourgeois of a conquered city initially, particularly if one has something to fear from them. The Romans who had conquered Great Britain, but could not pacify it due to the turbulent and bellicose temperament of the people, decided to moderate their instincts by effeminating them and succeeded in doing so. The Corsicans are a handful of men as brave and stubborn as the English.[1] They will not be subdued by courage; only by kindness. I think that to maintain one's sovereignty over this island, it would be absolutely necessary to disarm the inhabitants and to soften them. Let me say in passing in regard to the Corsicans that they are an example of how courage and virtue inspires a love for liberty and that it is dangerous and unjust to oppress it.

The political thinker's second question is whether a prince who has become master of a new state should give his confidence to those new subjects who have aided him to become master or to those who remained faithful to their legitimate prince and opposed him the most.

When one takes a city by connection and trickery, it would be very imprudent to trust the traitor, since what he has done for you he is always ready to do for someone else. On the contrary, those who display fidelity for their legitimate sovereign give examples of constancy which can be counted upon, and they will presumably act toward their new masters as they did toward their previous ones. Prudence requires, however, not to trust anyone without taking precautions.

But let us suppose for a moment that an oppressed people forced to overthrow the yoke of their tyrants call upon another prince to govern them without his having intervened. I believe that this prince must respond totally to the confidence shown him and that if he were lacking toward those who had entrusted him with their most precious possession, such flagrant ingratitude would not fail to blemish his memory. William of Orange always preserved the confidence of those who had placed the government of England into his hands, while his opponents abandoned their fatherland and followed King James.[2]

In elective kingdoms where, no matter what they say, most of the elections are fixed and the throne is sold, I believe that the new sovereign will find it easy, after his election, to bribe his opponents just as he has won the favor of his supporters. Poland furnishes us with some examples.[3] The throne is so blatantly on sale that it seems as if it is purchased in the public market, and the liberality of a king of Poland clears away all opposition by conferring the palatinates, starosties, and other offices upon the great families. But since the Poles have a very short memory on the subject of favors, he must keep returning to the attack. In short, the Polish Republic is like the Danaïdes barrel.[4] The most generous king will shower his favors vainly upon it without ever filling it up. Thus a king of Poland has to be sparing with his meager resources and pass out his liberality only when necessary.

Machiavelli's third question is whether it is better for a hereditary king to maintain unity or animosity between his subjects.

This question might have been valid in the time of Machiavelli's ancestors in Florence, but I don't think that any political thinker now would answer it without qualification. I need only cite the famous argument by which Menenius Agrippa reunited the Roman people.[5] Republics, however, must somehow maintain jealousy between their members; for if they unite, the form of government changes into a monarchy. This must not extend to private individuals, for whom disunion is prejudicial, but solely to those who might unite to wrest the supreme authority.

There are some princes who believe the disunion of their ministers to be in their interest. They think that they are less likely to be misled by men whose mutual hatred keeps on their guard against each other. But if these hatreds produce this effect, they also produce some others which are very prejudicial to the interests of the princes; for instead of the ministers each contributing his share, they will counter each other's best ideas and subordinate the advantage of the prince and the good of the people to their private quarrels.

Thus nothing contributes as much to the strength of a monarchy as the close knit union of all its members and the goal of a wise prince must be to establish it.

My answer to Machiavelli's third question can somehow serve as a solution to his fourth problem. Let us consider briefly if a prince must foment factions against himself or if he must gain the friendship of his subjects.

Creating enemies in order to defeat them is like forging monsters in order to fight them. It is more natural, reasonable, and human to make friends. Happy are the princes who know the delights of friendship! Even happier are the ones who merit the love and affection of their peoples!

Machiavelli's last question is whether a prince must have fortresses and citadels or if he must raze them.

I believe I have expressed in the tenth chapter my sentiment in regard to petty princes. Let me come now to the conduct of kings.

In Machiavelli's time, the world was in general ferment. The spirit of sedition and revolt reigned everywhere, there was nothing but rebellious cities—people stirring—and no end of trouble and war for sovereigns and their states. These frequent and continual revolutions obliged princes to build citadels overlooking cities so as to contain the restless spirit of the inhabitants and to settle them down.

Since that barbarous age, be in that men have gotten tired of murder and bloodshed or that they have become more reasonable, there isn't so much talk of seditions and revolts any more; and one might say that this spirit of restlessness has worked itself into a more tranquil disposition, so that there is no more need of citadels to insure the fidelity of town and country. It is not the same, however, for citadels and fortifications to guard against enemies and insure the safety of the state.

Armies and fortresses are equally useful to princes; for if they can use their armies to oppose their enemies, they can save their armies under the cannon of their fortresses in case of a lost battle; and the siege of a fortress by the enemy gives time to regroup and collect new forces with which to make the enemy raise the siege.

The recent wars in Brabant between the emperor and France hardly got anywhere because of the vast number of strongholds, and victorious battles between one hundred thousand men on each side were followed by the taking of only one or two cities.[6] The next campaign the other side would repair its losses and reappear to dispute the gains of the previous year. In countries where there are many strongholds, an army two miles long could wage war for thirty years and win twenty battles before gaining ten miles of land.

In open country, the outcome of a battle or of two campaigns settles the fortune of the victor and subjugates entire kingdoms. Alexander, Caesar, and Charles XII owed their glory to the scarcity of fortified strongholds in the countries they conquered. The conqueror of India undertook only two sieges in his glorious campaigns: the arbiter of Poland undertook no more.[7] Eugene, Villars, Marlborough, and Luxembourg were in a different class from Charles and Alexander, but fortresses somehow tarnished the brilliance of their successes, which, if one judges solidly, are superior to those of Alexander and Charles.[8] The French are well aware of the utility of fortresses, and, from the Brabant to Dauphiné, they have a double chain of fortified strongholds. France's German frontier is like the gaping mouth of a lion. It presents two tiers of menacing teeth and looks ready to swallow everything in sight.

This should show the value of fortified cities.

NOTES

[1] In the later first century, the Roman governor Gnaeus Julius Agricola pacified the Britons by "civilizing" them, according to Tacitus, *Agricola*, XXI, while in the early eighteenth century, the Corsicans were in revolt against the Genoese and arousing considerable sympathy in "enlightened" circles.

[2] William of Orange (1650–1702), King of England from 1688. James II (1633–1701), king from 1685 until deposed by William.

[3] Poland was the only elective monarchy left in Europe, if one discounts the Holy Roman Empire, which was more like an association of independent

princes who habitually elected a Hapsburg as "emperor". The indiscipline of
the Polish nobility had already made their country into the pawn of its
neighbors by the early eighteenth century and was leading Poland towards the
partitions of the second half of the century.

4 The Danaïdes, daughters of Danaus, were Argive water nymphs who
killed their husbands and were condemned to filling a bottomless barrel in
Hades. See Ovid's *Metamorphoses*, IV:462.

5 Agrippa got the seceding plebeians to reconsider by telling them about the
revolt of the human body against the belly and its fatal consequences for the
entire body. See Livy's *History of Rome*, Bk. II, Ch. XXXII.

6 The Nine Years' War (1689–1697) and the War of the Spanish Succession,
since the War of the Polish Succession saw no action in Flanders.

7 Tyre and Gaza, besieged by Alexander. See Quintus Curtius, *History of
Alexander*, Bk. IV, Chs. II–IV, VI. Thorn, Lvov, and Poltava were besieged by
Charles XII. See Voltaire's *Histoire de Charles XII*, Bks. II–IV.

8 On Eugene and Marlborough, see Ch. XIV, note 3. François-Henri de
Montmorency-Bouteville (1628–1695), Duke de Luxembourg, Marshal of
France from 1675 and Charles-Louis (1653–1734), Duke de Villars, Marshal
of France from 1702, were two of Louis XIV's most successful generals.

What a prince should do to be esteemed

Chapter XXI

There is a difference between causing a stir in the world and acquiring glory. The vulgar, who cannot evaluate reputations, are easily seduced by appearances, confusing good actions with extraordinary ones, wealth with merit, and brilliance with solidity. Enlightened people judge quite differently. They are hard to please. They dissect great men like cadavers. They examine if their intentions were honest, if they were just, if they contributed to the good of mankind, and if they tempered their courage with wisdom. They judge effects by causes rather than the other way around. They are not dazzled by brilliant vices and find that only merit and virtue are worthy of glory.

What Machiavelli finds great and worthy of reputation is the false brilliance which takes in the vulgar. He caters to the taste of the vilest and lowest people, but it is as hard for him as it is for Molière to combine a trivial manner of thinking with the nobility and taste of upstanding people. Those who appreciate the *Misanthrope* are all the more contemptuous of *Scapin*.[1]

This chapter of Machiavelli contains both good and bad things. I shall first evoke Machiavelli's errors, I shall confirm what he says that is good and praiseworthy, and I shall then venture my sentiments on some related subjects.

The author sets up Ferdinand of Aragon and Bernabò of Milan as models for those who would distinguish themselves through great undertakings and extraordinary actions.[2] Machiavelli finds their secret in boldness of undertaking and rapidity of execution. This is great, I agree, but it is not laudable unless the undertaking is just. "You who take pride in

131

exterminating thieves," said the Scythian ambassadors to Alexander, "you are the biggest thief on earth, for you have pillaged and sacked all the nations that you have conquered. If you are a god, you must do good to mortals and not despoil them. If you are a man, remember what you are."[3]

Ferdinand of Aragon did not merely wage war, but he used religion to veil his designs. If this king was religious, he committed an enormous sacrilege by using the cause of God as a pretext for his fury. If he was an unbeliever, he was a sly impostor and a hypocrite who made the credulity of the people serve his ambition.

It is dangerous for a prince to accustom his subjects to fight for quibbles. This renders the clergy indirect masters of war and peace. The Western Empire owed its fall in part to religious quarrels, and we have seen in France under the last Valois the ghastly consequences of the spirit of fanaticism and false zeal.[4] A sovereign, it seems to me, should not interfere in the religion of his people and should do his utmost to recall his clergy and subjects to a spirit of mildness and tolerance. This policy is not merely in accord with the spirit of the Gospel, which preaches only peace, humility, and charity, but it is also in conformity with the interest of princes; since by uprooting false zeal and fanaticism from their states, they remove the most dangerous stumbling block from their path and avoid the most fearful of shoals; for the fidelity and good will of the vulgar will not hold up against the furor of religion and the enthusiasm of fanaticism, which offers martyrdom and heaven itself to assassins as the reward of their crimes and punishments.

A sovereign could thus not display enough contempt for the frivolous disputes of priests, which are only disputes of words, and he cannot be too careful to suppress superstition and the religious fervor that results from it.

Machiavelli advances, in the second place, the example of Bernabò of Milan to suggest to princes that they must reward and punish in an exemplary manner, so that all their actions bear the imprint of grandeur. Generous princes will not lack for reputation, particularly when they are liberal from greatness of soul rather than from pride.

Kindness can make them greater than all the other virtues.

Cicero told Caesar, "There is nothing greater in your fortune than the power to save so many citizens, nor more worthy of your kindness than the will to do it."[5] Thus a prince should always underpunish offenses and overreward services.

But here is a contradiction. In this chapter the political doctor wants princes to honor their alliances, and in the eighteenth chapter he formally dispensed them from keeping their word. He is like a good story teller who tells everyone a different yarn.

If Machiavelli reasons badly on all of the above, he speaks well about princes not committing themselves lightly with more powerful princes who might ruin them.

This is what a great German prince, esteemed by friends and enemies alike, knew full well. The Swedes invaded his states while he had gone to the aid of the emperor against France on the lower Rhine. On receiving this news, his ministers counseled him to call the Tzar of Russia to his aid. But this penetrating prince answered that the Muscovites were like bears who, once they were unchained, would not be easy to rechain. He sought his own vengeance, and he had no reason to repent of it.[6]

Were I living in the next century, I would assuredly extend this article with some appropriate reflections, but it is not for me to judge the conduct of modern princes; and in this world one must know when to keep his mouth shut.[7]

The topic of neutrality is as well treated by Machiavelli as that of alliances. Experience has clearly demonstrated that a neutral prince exposes his country to injury from both belligerents, that his states become the theater of war, and that he has everything to lose and nothing to gain by neutrality.

There are two manners of self-aggrandizement for a sovereign. One is by conquest, as when a warrior prince extends the limits of his dominion by force of arms. The other is by activity, as when a hard working prince makes the arts and sciences flourish in his states, rendering them more powerful and civilized.

This whole book deals only with the first manner of self-aggrandizement. Let us say something for the second, which is more innocent, more just, and every bit as useful as the first.

The arts most necessary to life are agriculture, commerce,

and manufacturing. The sciences most uplifting to the human spirit are geometry, philosophy, astronomy, eloquence, poetry, and everything that goes under the name of fine arts.

Since every country is different, there are some whose strength lies in agriculture, others in vineyards, others in manufacturing, and others in commerce: these arts sometimes even prosper together in some countries.

The sovereigns who choose this mild and charming manner of becoming more powerful should study particularly the condition of their country, so as to see which arts would be most likely to flourish there with some encouragement. The French and Spanish have noticed that they were lacking in commerce and have sought for this reason to ruin that of the English. If France succeeds in ruining the commerce of England, this will increase its power more than the conquest of twenty cities and a thousand villages ever could; and England and Holland, the two most beautiful and richest countries in the world, would gradually perish, so to speak, of consumption.[8]

Countries rich in grains or vines must observe two things: one is to clear all lands carefully so as to put every inch of soil to good use; the other is to concentrate on finding new markets, cheaper means of transport, and ways to lower prices.

As to manufactures of all kinds, they may be what is most useful and profitable to a state; since they provide for the needs and luxuries of the inhabitants while neighbors are obliged to pay a tribute to your industry. On the one hand, they prevent money from leaving the country; and on the other, they bring it in.

I have always been convinced that the lack of manufactures was the cause in part of the great migrations from the northern countries by the Goths and Vandals who so often invaded the South. In those remote times, the only art known in Sweden, Denmark, and in most of Germany was agriculture. Cultivable lands were divided among as many proprietors as they could feed.

But since the human race has always been very fertile in cold countries, there came to be twice as many inhabitants in a country as could subsist by cultivation, so that the younger sons of good families got together and, making a virtue out of necessity, ravaged other countries and dispossessed their masters. Thus we see in the history of the Eastern and of the Western Empire, that the barbarians ordinarily asked only for fields to cultivate so as to obtain their subsistence. The northern countries are no less populous today, but since luxury has wisely multiplied our needs, it has given rise to manufacturing and to all those arts that provide subsistence to entire peoples who would otherwise be obliged to seek for it elsewhere.[9]

A wise sovereign must exploit these ways of making a state prosper to the fullest. The surest mark of a well governed and affluent country is if it gives birth to the fine arts and to the sciences. These are flowers which grow in rich soil and good weather, but die under adverse conditions.

Nothing makes a reign more illustrious than the arts that flourish under its wing.[10] The age of Pericles is as famous for Phidias, Praxiteles, and so many other great men who lived in Athens as for the battles won by the Athenians. That of Augustus is better known for Cicero, Ovid, Horace, and Virgil than for the proscriptions of this cruel emperor, who, after all, owes much of his reputation to Horace's lyre. That of Louis the Great is more famous for the Corneilles, the Racines, the Molières, the Boileaus, the Descartes, the Coypels, the Le Bruns, and the Ramondons than by that overblown passage of the Rhine, by that siege of Mons to which Louis came in person, and by the battle of Turin, which M. de Marsin lost for the Duke d'Orléans by official order.[11]

Kings honor humanity when they distinguish and reward those who honor it the most, and who may these be if not those superior minds who work at perfecting our knowledge, who devote themselves to the cult of truth, and who neglect material comforts in order to develop the art of thinking. These wise men who enlighten the world deserve to be its legislators.

Happy are the sovereigns who themselves cultivate the sciences, who think like Cicero, the Roman consul, liberator of his country, and father of eloquence: "Letters mold youth and constitute the charm of old age. They make our prosperity more brilliant, console us in adversity; and in our homes, in those of others, in voyages, in solitude, anytime, anywhere, they make for the mildness of life."[12]

Lorenzo de Medici, the greatest man of his nation, was the pacifier of Italy and the restorer of the sciences. His probity won him the general confidence of all the princes. Marcus Aurelius, one of the greatest Roman emperors, was a successful warrior no less than a wise philosopher. He practiced the most austere morality as well as preached it. Let us finish with his words: "A king who is conducted by justice has the universe for his temple. Upstanding people are its priests and worshippers."[13]

Stoic

NOTES

[1] Two comedies by the great Jean-Baptiste Molière (1622–1673). The *Misanthrope* is probably his most philosophical, whereas *Les fourberies de Scapin* is an undiluted farce.

[2] Ferdinand of Aragon (1452–1516), King of Aragon from 1479. Bernabò Visconti (1354–1385), Duke of Milan from 1378.

[3] See Quintus Curtius, *History of Alexander*, Bk. VII, Ch. VIII, 19, 26.

[4] See Montesquieu's *Considerations on the Causes of the Greatness of the Romans and Their Decline*, Ch. XIX and Voltaire's *Henriade*.

[5] In the oration *Pro Ligario*, XII:38.

[6] Frederick William (1620–1688), the "great" elector, who had come to the throne in 1640. Louis XIV, in the course of his war against the Dutch and their allies (1672–1678/9), had brought in the Swedes to draw off the Brandenburgers. Frederick William had sought Russian aid, in spite of Frederick's little story, but when he failed to obtain it, he turned upon the Swedes and, to the surprise of everyone, defeated them at Fehrbellin in 1675.

[7] Frederick is alluding to the fact that the emperor had called the Russians to his assistance in the War of the Polish Succession.

[8] Frederick has at this relatively early date put his finger on the great Franco-English conflict that was about to explode.

[9] Compare with Montesquieu, *loc. cit.*

[10] Compare with Voltaire's *Age of Louis XIV*, Ch. I (Introduction).

[11] Phidias (fl. 450 B.C.) and Praxiteles (fl. 364 B.C.), sculptors. Cicero (106–43 B.C.), orator and politician. Ovid (43 B.C.–17 A.D.), Horace (65–8 B.C.), and Virgil (70–19 B.C.), poets. Pierre Corneille (1606–1684) and Jean Racine (1639–1699), playwrights, Nicolas Boileau (1636–1711), poet and literary critic. René Descartes (1596–1650), philosopher. Noel Coypel (1628–1707) and Charles Le Brun (1619–1690), painters. Ramondon seems to be a contraction of Thomas Regnaudin (1622–1706) and François Girardon (1628–1715), sculptors. Louis XIV's memorable crossing of the Rhine had taken place in 1672, during his war against the Dutch, his siege of Mons in 1691, during

the Nine Years' War, and the battle of Turin in 1706, during the War of the Spanish Succession. See Voltaire, *op. cit.*, Chs. X, XVI, and XX.

[12] See the oration *Pro Archia Poeta*, VII:18.

[13] This would seem to refer to Pliny the Younger's statement in the *Panegyric of Trajan*, LV: 8–11, "Temples are demolished and fall into oblivion. A prince must not seek after lasting renown, which is his anyway, but good reputation, which is not perpetuated by images and statues, but by virtue and merit. Besides, gold and silver do not capture and preserve something as perishable as the physical appearance of a prince as does the affection of men." Certainly, the thought is most un-Marcus Aurelian and does not appear in that emperor's writings.

On the confidential councillors of princes

Chapter XXII

There are two kinds of princes in the world: those who see everything with their own eyes and govern their states by themselves; and those who rely on the good faith of their ministers and let themselves be governed by those who have gained an ascendancy over them.

The sovereigns of the first kind are the very soul of their states. They carry the weight of government on their shoulders like Atlas carried the world. They regulate internal as well as foreign affairs. All ordinances, all laws, all edicts flow from them, and they act at the same time as supreme judge, general of the armies, intendant of finance, and whatever else may relate to politics. Their minds—like God, who uses his supernatural intelligence to work his will—are sufficiently penetrating and active to execute their great designs and projects. Their ministers are but tools in the hand of a wise and able master.

Sovereigns of the second order are plunged into lethargy by a lack of intelligence or natural indolence, and just as fainting is revived with strong odors and pungent balsams, a state which is faltering because of the weakness of the sovereign must be sustained by the vivacity of a minister capable of supplementing the lackings of his master. In this case, the prince is but the organ of his minister and serves at the most to represent the empty shadow of royal majesty to the people, and his person is as useless to the state as the minister's is necessary. With the sovereigns of the first kind, the selection of good ministers may facilitate their work without affecting the happiness of the people. With those of the second kind, the happiness of the people depends on the selection of ministers.

It is not to easy for a sovereign to evaluate the character of his servants, for private individuals can just as easily disguise themselves before their masters as princes find it hard to dissimulate their inner being before the public.

The character of courtiers is like the face of a painted woman. Both carry artifice to perfection. Kings never see men in their natural state, but as they wish to appear. A man who is at mass during the consecration, a courtier who is at court in the presence of the prince is entirely different from what he is in the society of his friends. The Cato of the court is the Anacreon of the town, the wise man in public acts crazy at home, and the pompous displayer of virtue feels the disclaimer of his heart deep down inside.[1]

This description of ordinary dissimulation is nothing to what happens when interest and ambition are involved, when a vacant post is coveted as avidly as Penelope by her suite of lovers.[2] The avarice of the courtier augments his assiduity toward the prince and his mastery over himself. He uses every imaginable way of rendering himself agreeable. He flatters the prince, enters into his tastes, approves his passions, and changes his colors like a chameleon.

After all, if Sixtus V could fool seventy cardinals who should have known him, isn't it all the more easy for a private individual to catch his unwary sovereign by surprise?[3]

An intelligent prince can easily judge the intellect and capacity of those who serve him, but it is almost impossible for him to judge their disinterestedness and fidelity, since ministers ordinarily make it a policy to hide their evil practices from him.

Men have often appeared virtuous for lack of occasion to give themselves away, yet renounced honesty once their virtue was put to the test. Tiberius, Nero, and Caligula were not badly thought of in Rome before they attained the throne. Their scoundreliness might have remained inert had it not been activated by an occasion which, so to speak, fertilized the germ of their viciousness.

There are men who combine the blackest and most

ungrateful souls with a great deal of intelligence, subtlety, and talent. There are others who possess all the qualities of the heart, yet lack a lively and brilliant intellect.

Prudent princes have ordinarily given preference to those in whom the qualities of the heart prevail for employment in the interior of their country. They have preferred, on the other hand, the more vivacious and fiery for service in negotiations. Their reasons have no doubt been that honesty suffices within the state, where it is only a question of maintaining order and justice; whereas skill and intelligence are required in foreign affairs, where it is a question of seducing one's neighbors with specious arguments, intrigue, and corruption.

It seems to me that a prince could not reward his faithful and zealous servants enough. We all have sentiments of gratitude that we cannot help following. But it is, besides, in the interest of the great to reward with as much generosity as they punish with clemency, for ministers who notice that their virtue makes their fortune will prefer the favors of their master to the bribes of foreigners. [4]

The ways of justice and of worldly wisdom are thus in perfect agreement on this point, and it is both imprudent and harsh to put the attachment of ministers to a dangerous test for lack of rewards and generosity.

There are princes who commit a fault just as contrary to their true interests as this one. They change ministers flippantly and punish the least irregularity in their conduct vigorously.

After the ministers who work directly under a prince have been at their post for a while, they cannot entirely hide their faults from him. The more penetrating the prince, the more easily he detects them.

Sovereigns who are not philosophers are quick to get impatient. They react against the weaknesses of their servants by disgracing and ruining them.

Princes who reflect more deeply know that men are human, that no one is perfect in this world, that great qualities are, so to speak, balanced by great faults, and that the intellectual must take advantage of everything. This is why, short of prevarication, they hold on to their ministers with their good and bad qualities, and they prefer those who are familiar to those who are not, like able musicians who prefer to play on instruments that they have tested rather than on new ones.

NOTES

[1] Cato the Elder (234–149 B.C.), who held the Roman censorship in 184 and distinguished himself as an enemy of luxury and the spread of Hellenism. Anacreon (fl. 515 B.C.), Greek lyric poet, famous for his glorification of wine, women, and song.

[2] Penelope, the faithful wife of Ulysses. See Homer's *Odyssey*.

[3] Felice Peretti (1521–1590), who became Pope Sixtus V in 1585. A discreet and self-effacing cardinal, he became one of the most active "Counter-Reformation" popes and beautifiers of Rome. Frederick's impression of him comes from Leti's scurrilous *Vita di Sisto V* in French translation and from Voltaire's *Henriade*, IV:14.

[4] A subtle criticism of Frederick William I, who was so avaricious that he did not mind his ministers supporting themselves with foreign bribes.

How flatterers   **Chapter XXIII**
are to be avoided

There isn't a single book on morality or history in which the susceptibility of princes to flattery is not roundly castigated. Kings are expected to love truth, and be accustomed to hearing it; and this is right, except that men expect contradictory things. Since pride is the source of our virtues, and consequently of all the happiness in the world, princes are expected to have enough of it to seek after glory and at the same time be sufficiently self-effacing to give up the fruits of their labors. The same principle must push them towards meriting praise and scorning it. This is asking a lot of humanity. If, however, anything can encourage princes to resist the charm of flattery, it is the idea of being well regarded and of exercizing more control over themselves than over others.

The only princes insensitive to their reputation have been indolent voluptuaries abandoned to softness, blobs of vile and abject matter devoid of any virtues. It is true that some very cruel tyrants have loved praise as an adornment to vanity, or better still, as one more vice. They wanted the esteem of mankind, but neglected, at the same time, the only way of becoming worthy of it.

For vicious princes flattery is a fatal poison that merely compounds their corruption. For worthy princes flattery is a tarnish which corrodes their glory and diminishes its brilliance. An intelligent man is revulsed by blatant flattery. He rejects the clumsy adulator who waves the compliments right under his nose. It would take infinite conceit and superstition to accept this exaggerated sort of praise, and it is less to be feared by great men, since it does not speak with conviction. Another sort of flattery, the sophistry of faults and vices, rhetorically minimizes everything that is bad about its object and indirectly raises it to perfection. It furnishes arguments for the passions, gives cruelty the character of justice, makes profusion indistinguishable from liberality, and cloaks debauchery with the veil of amusement and pleasure. It emphasizes the vices of others and de-emphasizes those of its hero. It excuses and justifies everything. Most men surrender to whatever flattery justifies their tastes and inclinations. It takes a hard look into our weaknesses in order to know them well and the strength to admit our faults in order to resist the insinuating advocates of our passions and to control ourselves. There are, however, princes with sufficiently manly virtue to be contemptuous of this sort of flattery. They are sufficiently penetrating to notice the venomous serpent slinking under the flowers, and these born enemies of falsehood will not even tolerate it when it feeds their pride and caresses their vanity.

But if they hate falsehood, they love truth, and they cannot be so rigid toward those who speak well of them with conviction. Well-founded flattery is the most subtle of all. It takes extreme discernment to catch all of its nuances. It will not have a king accompanied to the trenches by poet-historians who are to witness his valor.[1] It will not compose hyperbolical prologues of operas, insipid prefaces, and flowery epistles; it will not dazzle a hero with the recital of his own victories, but will assume a sentimental air, be sparing in names, and have the qualities of an epigram. How can a great man, a hero, an intelligent prince be displeased at hearing the truth from the mouth of a lively friend? Modesty seems inappropriate when wit is the vehicle of praise.

Princes who were men before they became kings can remember what they were and are less susceptible to flattery. Those who have reigned their entire life have grown up smelling incense and would die of neglect if they were not praised.

It seems to me that it would be more fair to pity kings than to condemn them. It is the flatterers and, above all, the slanderers who merit the condemnation and hatred of the public, along with all those enemies of princes who hide the truth from them.

NOTES

¹ A criticism of Louis XIV, who appointed Jean Racine and Nicolas Boileau as his official historians in 1677 and had them accompany him on a number of his campaigns. Louis also encouraged Philippe de Quinault (1635–1688), who composed many operas with hyperbolical prologues. The insipid prefaces were legion, but probably the most famous flowery epistle was Boileau's *Au Roi* of 1672.

Why the princes of Italy have lost their states
Chapter XXIV

The fable of Cadmus, who sowed the earth with the teeth of a serpent he had vanquished, from which arose a people of warriors who destroyed each other, is very suitable to the subject of this chapter.[1] This ingenious fable symbolizes the ambition, cruelty, and perfidy of men, which is always fatal to them in the end. It was the unlimited ambition and cruelty of the princes of Italy which made them the horror of mankind. It was the perfidies and treacheries that they committed against each other that ruined their affairs. Just read the history of Italy from the end of the fourteenth to the beginning of the fifteenth centuries.[2] It is nothing but cruelties, seditions, violences, leagues to destroy each other, usurpations, assassinations—in short—an enormous collection of crimes the very idea of which inspires horror.

If, following Machiavelli's example, justice and humanity were overthrown, this would overturn the world. No one would be content with his own possessions, everyone would envy those of others; and since nothing could stop them, they would go to any extent to satisfy their cupidity. One would swallow up the goods of his neighbors; another would come along and dispossess him in turn. The right of the stronger would reign supreme, and this flood of crimes would soon reduce our continent to a vast desert. It was thus the iniquity and barbarism of the princes of Italy which made them lose their states, just as the false principles of Machiavelli would be sure to ruin those who are foolish enough to follow them.

I am not mincing words. The cowardliness of some Italian princes may have contributed to their ruin just as much as their viciousness. It is sure that the weakness of the kings of Naples ruined their affairs. But say all you want about politics, argue, build systems, advance examples, use all the subtlety of the sophists, you will have to come back to justice in spite of yourself unless you choose to part with good sense. Machiavelli himself is only talking pitiful gibberish in teaching other maxims, and, try as he may, he has not been able to bend the truth to his principles. The beginning of this chapter is a disturbing spot to this political thinker. He has stumbled into a maze and he looks vainly for Ariadne's thread in order to escape.

I humbly ask Machiavelli what he meant by these words, "If prudence and merit are noted in a sovereign recently raised to a throne, that is in an usurper, men will be more attached to him than to those who owe their greatness only to their birth. The reason for this is that the present is more striking than the past, and when one is satisfied with it he goes no further."

Does Machiavelli suppose that between two men of equal valor and intelligence the people will prefer an usurper to the legitimate prince, or is he referring to a sovereign without virtue as opposed to a valiant and capable one? The author cannot possibly maintain the first supposition. It is opposed to the most ordinary common sense. The preference of a people for a man who engaged in violence in order to become their master and who, besides, was in no way superior to their legitimate sovereign is an effect without a cause. Machiavelli, reinforced by all the sorites of the sophists and by Buridan's ass itself could not resolve this problem.[3]

The second proposition is as frivolous as the first. Whatever qualities an usurper may have, it must be admitted that the violent action by which he rises to power is an injustice. Now what else can be expected from a man who begins with crime other than a violent and tyrannical government? It is as if a man were changed into Actaeon by his wife on his wedding day.[4] I don't think that this token of her inconstancy would augur well for the fidelity of his new spouse.

Machiavelli condemns his own principles in this chapter, for he clearly states that without the love of his people, the affection of the great, and a disciplined army, it is impossible for a prince to maintain himself upon the throne. Truth seems to force him to render it this homage, almost like the fallen angels who, according to the theologians, recognize God while raging against him.

Here is the contradiction. In order to gain the affection of the people and the great, it is necessary for the prince to have a fund of probity and virtue, to be humane and gracious, and to inspire confidence through his wisdom. What a difference between these qualities and those that Machiavelli gives to his prince! In order to gain hearts, it is necessary to be what I have just described and not, as Machiavelli teaches in the course of this work, unjust, cruel, ambitious, and preoccupied solely with self-aggrandizement.

Thus stands unmasked this political thinker who was considered a great man in his own age, who has been recognized as dangerous and yet followed by many ministers, whose abominable maxims princes have been made to study, who has never yet been formally refuted, and who is still followed privately by many political thinkers.

Happy would be he who could entirely destroy Machiavellism in the world! I have shown its incoherence. It is for those who govern to set an example of virtue. I dare say that they are obliged to correct the bad impression that the public has of politics, which is properly only the system by which princes exercise wisdom, but is commonly suspected of being the breeding ground of slyness and injustice. It is for them to banish subtleties and bad faith from treaties and to restore the vigor, honesty, and candor which, to tell the truth, is no longer found among sovereigns. It is for them to show that they are as little envious of the provinces of their neighbors as they are jealous for the preservation of their own states. Sovereigns are respected—this is a duty as well as a necessity—but they would be loved if they thought less about extending their domination and more about governing well. The first is an effect of an unsettled imagination, the second is the mark of a judicious mind which grasps the truth and prefers duty to vanity. The prince who wants to possess everything is like a glutton who stuffs down more food than he can digest. The prince who limits himself to governing well is like a man who eats sensibly and enjoys a good digestion.

NOTES

1 See Ovid's *Metamorphoses*, III: 31–98, IV: 570–572.

2 Frederick probably meant to say, "end of the *fifteenth* to the beginning of the *sixteenth* centuries," the period covered by Guicciardini's *History of Italy*.

3 A sorite is a sequence of connected syllogisms leading to a general conclusion, a kind of verbal demonstration, while Jean Buridan (c. 1297–c. 1358) was a late scholastic French philosopher. His theory that the disposition of the will depended on the relative strength of conflicting motives came to be identified with the story of an ass which died of hunger from inability to decide between two equidistant bales of hay.

4 Actaeon, mythical Greek hero and hunter, having accidentally come upon the chaste goddess Artemis while she was bathing, was changed by her into a stag and killed by his own hounds. See Ovid's *Metamorphoses*, III: 131–252. It seems hard to imagine a more far fetched analogy.

How much fortune **Chapter XXV**
can do in human
affairs and how to
cope with it

The question of man's liberty is one of those problems which pushes the reasoning of philosophers to the limit and which has often drawn anathemas from the sacred mouth of theologians. The partisans of liberty say that if men are not free, then it is God who acts in them and who, through their agency, commits murders, thefts, and all sorts of crimes manifestly opposed to his holiness; aside from the fact that if the Supreme Being is the father of the vices and the author of iniquity, one can no longer punish the guilty, and there will be neither crimes nor virtues in the world. Now since this awful dogma cannot be conceived without seeing its contradictions, the best thing to do is to support the liberty of man.

The partisans of absolute necessity say, on the contrary, that God would be worse than a blind artificer if, after having created the world, he had ignored the result. A watchmaker, they say, knows the action of the smallest wheel of a watch, since he knows what movement he has imparted on it and for what purpose he has made it. Would God, this infinitely wise being, remain an interested and helpless spectator of men's actions? How can this same God, whose works are all characterized by order and subject to certain immutable and constant laws, have left for man alone to enjoy independence and liberty? It would no longer be Providence, but the caprice of men that governed the world. If it comes to a choice between the Creator and the creature, which of the two should be mechanical? It is more

149

reasonable to believe that the being is weak rather than powerful. Thus reason and the passions are like invisible chains by which the hand of Providence, in its infinite wisdom, leads the human race to concur in the events that are to happen so that each individual can fulfill his destiny in the world.

Thus to avoid Charybdis one approaches Scylla, and philosophers push each other into the abyss of absurdity while theologians clash in obscurity and devoutly damn each other out of charity and zeal. These parties wage war upon each other almost like the Carthaginians and Romans used to do. When it was feared to see Roman troops in Africa, the flame of war was carried into Italy; and when Rome wanted to rid itself of the fearful Hannibal, it sent Scipio at the head of the legions to besiege Carthage. Philosophers, theologians, and most of the heroes of debate share the spirit of the French nation: they attack vigorously, but they are lost if reduced to a defensive war. This is what led a wit to say that God was the father of all the sects since He had given them all equal weapons, a good side and a reverse.[1] This question of the liberty and predestination of men is transferred by Machiavelli from metaphysics to politics. It is, however, a terrain which is both foreign and unproductive for him; for in politics, instead of wondering whether we are free or whether we are not, if fortune and chance can do something or if they can do nothing, one should think only of perfecting his penetration and nourishing his prudence.

Fortune and chance are words devoid of meaning, born in the minds of poets, and which, from all appearance, owe their origin to the profound ignorance in which the world wallowed when vague names were given to effects whose causes were unknown.

What is vulgarly called the fortune of Caesar properly means all the circumstances which favored the designs of this ambitious man. What is meant by the bad fortune of Cato are the unpredictable misfortunes which happened to him, those setbacks in which effects follow causes so immediately that his prudence could neither foresee nor counteract them.

What is meant by chance can best be explained by the game of dice. Chance, it is said, made my dice come out twelve rather than seven. In order to dissect this phenomenon, one should pay attention to a great many things, like how the dice were inserted into the cup, the strength and repetition of the shaking they receive, and how they are thrown upon the table. These causes, when combined, are called chance. An analysis of this nature needs a great deal of discussion and requires an attentive and philosophical spirit, but since everybody is not made for delving into matters, most prefer to spare themselves the trouble. I admit that it is much easier to be contented with a name which has no reality, so that of all the gods of paganism fortune and chance are the only ones which have remained. This is not so bad, for the imprudent ascribe the cause of their misery to the opposition of fortune, while those who succeed in the world without eminent merit erect blind destiny into a wise, admirable, and just divinity.

As long as we are but men, that is to say very limited beings, we will never be entirely superior to what are called the blows of fortune. We must wrest what we can by wisdom and prudence from chance events, but our view is too short and our mind too narrow to notice everything. Although we may be weak, however, this is no reason to neglect the limited forces that we have. On the contrary, we must make the best use of them that we can and not degrade our being by descending to the level of brutes just because we are not gods. Indeed, men would need a divine omniscience in order to combine an infinity of hidden causes and understand the minutest springs behind events well enough to draw the right conjectures for the future.

Here are two events which will show clearly that it is impossible for human wisdom to foresee everything. The first is the surprise of Cremona by Prince Eugene, an undertaking conceived with all imaginable prudence and executed with infinite valor. Here is how the plan failed: the prince penetrated into the city in the morning through a sewage canal opened for him by a priest with whom he was in contact; he would infallibly have become master of the stronghold if two unimaginable things had not happened. First, a Swiss regiment which was to drill that very morning happened to be under arms and offered resistance until the rest of the garrison could assemble. In the second place, the guide who was to lead the Prince de

Vaudemont to seize another gate of the city took the wrong road so that this detachment arrived too late. I don't think that the priestess of Delphi foaming at the mouth on her sacred tripod could have foreseen this accident by any secret of her art.[2]

The second event that I want to describe is the separate peace that the English made with France toward the end of the war of succession. Neither the ministers of the Emperor Joseph, nor the greatest philosophers, nor the most able statesmen could have suspected that a pair of gloves would change the fate of Europe, but that is precisely what happened, as can be seen.

Lady Marlborough filled the post of grand mistress of Queen Anne in London while her husband reaped a double harvest of laurels and riches in the fields of Brabant. The duchess sustained through her favor the party of the hero, and the hero sustained the influence of his spouse by his victories. The Tory party, which was opposed to them and which favored peace, could do nothing as long as the duchess was all powerful with the queen. She lost this favor for a rather flimsy cause: the queen had ordered some gloves from her glovemaker, and the duchess had ordered some at the same time; her impatience to have them made her press the glovemaker to serve her before the queen. Meanwhile, Anne wanted to have her gloves. A lady of the palace who was an enemy of Lady Marlborough informed the queen of everything that had happened and took such malicious advantage of it that the queen from that moment on considered that she could no longer bear the insolence of her favorite. The glovemaker finished embittering this princess by relating the story of the gloves to her with all possible malice. This yeast, though light, was sufficient to put all spirits in ferment and to provide all the ingredients for a disgrace. The Tories, with Marshal de Tallard at their head, took advantage of this affair to strike their first blow. The Duchess of Marlborough was disgraced soon thereafter, and with her fell the Whig party along with that of the allies and the emperor. So it goes with the most serious things in the world! Providence laughs at human wisdom and greatness. Frivolous and sometimes ridiculous causes often change the fortune of states and of entire monarchies. On this occasion, the petty intrigues of women saved Louis XIV from a predicament from which all of his wisdom, forces, and power might not have been able to extricate him, and obliged the allies to make peace in spite of themselves.[3]

These sorts of events happen, but I admit that they are rare and that their authority is not entirely sufficient to discredit prudence and penetration. It is like those maladies that temporarily alter men's health, but do not normally prevent them from enjoying the advantages of a robust constitution.

It is thus necessary for those who govern the world to cultivate their penetration and prudence, but this is not everything; for if they want to master fortune, they must learn to adapt their temperament to circumstances, which is very difficult.

I speak, in general, only of two sorts of temperaments, daring vivacity and slow caution; and since moral causes have a physical cause, it is almost impossible for a prince to have such self control as to change colors like a chameleon. There are ages that favor the glory of conquerors and those daring and enterprising men who seem born for action and for operating extraordinary changes in the world. Revolutions, wars, and particularly that spirit of giddiness which embroils sovereigns against each other furnish these men with occasions to display their dangerous talents. In short, all the circumstances which are favorable to their turbulent and active nature facilitate their success.

There are other times when a less agitated world appears to respond only to mildness, prudence, and caution. It is a kind of happy political calm that ordinarily follows the storm. It is then that negotiations are more effective than battles and that the pen is mightier than the sword.

In order for a sovereign to profit from all circumstances, he should adapt to the weather like an able pilot—who unfurls all his sails when the winds are favorable, but trims or even strikes them when the tempest obliges it—is concerned solely with getting his vessel to the port of destination regardless of how it gets there.

If a general were cautious and rash opportunely, he would be almost indomitable. There would be occasions when he would drag out the war, as when he was dealing with an enemy who lacked the resources to afford a long one, or when the opposing army was short of provisions or forage. Fabius checked Hannibal by his delays. The Romans did not ignore that the Carthaginians were lacking in money and recruits and that, without fighting, it sufficed to watch their army quietly melt away and perish, so to speak, from inactivity. The policy of Hannibal was, on the contrary, to fight. His was only an accidental force, from which he had to draw every possible advantage promptly and solidify it through the terror inspired by brilliant and heroic actions and by resources drawn from conquests.[4]

In the year 1704, if the Elector of Bavaria and Marshal de Tallard had not left Bavaria so as to advance upon Blenheim and Höchstadt, they would have remained masters of all Swabia; for the allied army, unable to subsist in Bavaria from lack of victuals, would have been obliged to retire toward the Main and separate. It was thus a lack of timely caution for the elector to trust to the fate of a battle—eternally glorious and memorable for the German nation—what it was purely up to him to preserve. This imprudence was punished by the total defeat of the French and the Bavarians, and by the loss of Bavaria and the entire country between the Upper Palatinate and the Rhine.[5] Temerity is brilliant, I admit, it strikes and dazzles; but its beauty is skin deep and it is fraught with danger. Prudence is less lively and less brilliant, but it marches at a steady pace without wavering.

One never hears of the rash who have perished. One hears only of those who have been favored by fortune. It is like dreams and prophecies. For a thousand which have proven false and are forgotten, only the small number which has come true is remembered. The world should judge events by their causes, and not causes by events.

I conclude thus that a people risks a great deal with a rash prince, that they are menaced by a continual danger, and that if the cautious sovereign may not be born for great exploits, he seems to be more suitable for rendering his people happy. The rash are good at conquests. The prudent are good at preserving them.

In order for either one to be great men, they must come into the world opportunely. Otherwise, their talents would be more pernicious than profitable. Every reasonable man, and particularly those whom heaven has destined to govern others, should formulate a plan of conduct as tightly reasoned as a geometric demonstration. Following such a system faithfully would provide a means of acting consistently and of never straying from one's goal. One could thereby channel all circumstances and events toward the advancement of his designs. Everything would combine for the execution of one's projects.

But who are these princes from whom we expect such rare talents? They are only men, and it would be true to say that it is by nature impossible for them to fulfill all their duties. It would be easier to find the phoenix of the poets and the unities of the metaphysicians than the Platonic man. It is just that the people should content themselves with the efforts of sovereigns to attain perfection. The most accomplished among them would be the most remote from Machiavelli's prince. It is also just that their faults should be endured when they are outweighed by qualities of the heart and by good intentions. We must always remember that nothing is perfect in the world and that error and weakness are the lot of all men. The happiest country is the one where a mutual toleration between sovereign and subject spreads an agreeable mildness over society, without which life becomes a heavy load and the world a vale of tears instead of a pageant of pleasure.

NOTES

[1] This seems to be a variation of the Italian saying, "Every medal has its reverse".

[2] This incident took place on the night of January 31/February 1, 1702, during the War of the Spanish Succession, but it was the Régiment des Vaisseaux which first attacked the enemy, and two Irish regiments also distinguished themselves. Feuquières in his *Mémoires* (London, 1736), Ch. LXV and Voltaire in his *Age of Louis XIV*, Ch. XVIII give a fairly accurate account of the event, but Frederick jumbles the Régiment des Vaisseaux and the Irish together, turning them into Swiss, although there were no Swiss at Cremona. It will be remembered that Frederick had a special affection for the Swiss (see above, p. 91).

[3] Sarah Churchill (1660–1744). See Voltaire, *op. cit.*, Ch. XXII, although Frederick seems to add more than his usual embellishments to the story.

[4] Fabius Maximus (d. 203 B.C.) "the delayer" and Hannibal (247–183 B.C.), the two great antagonists of the Second Punic War.

[5] Frederick accepts the argument of Feuquières, *op. cit.*, Ch. LXXX, which was rejected by Voltaire, *op. cit.*, Ch. XIX. Voltaire maintained that the Elector of Bavaria and Marshal Tallard should have advanced, but taken a different position.

On different sorts of **Chapter XXVI** negotiations and on just reasons for waging war

We have seen in this work all the false reasoning by which Machiavelli presumes to sell us a bill of goods and make us take scoundrels for great men.

I have done my best to prove the contrary and to disabuse people of their errors regarding the policy of princes. I have shown them that the true wisdom of sovereigns is to do good and to be the most accomplished at it in their states; that their true interest requires them to be just, so that necessity does not oblige them to condemn in others what they authorize in themselves; that it is not enough for them to perform brilliant actions and satisfy their ambition and glory, but that they must prefer the happiness of the human race to contributing to its ruin. I have said that this is the only means of establishing their reputation on a solid foundation and of meriting that their glory should pass without blemish to the most remote posterity.

I shall also consider two other matters: one regards the manner of negotiating, and the other concerns the valid reasons for a sovereign to engage in an open war.

The ministers maintained by princes in foreign courts are privileged spies who watch over the conduct of the kings with whom they reside. They must penetrate the designs of these princes, clarify their moves, and delve into their actions so as to keep their masters informed of anything contrary to their interests. One of the principal objects of their mission is to tighten the bonds of friendship between sovereigns, but instead of being the artisans of peace, they are often the organs of war. They can loosen the most sacred bonds of secrecy by means of corruption, they are supple, accommodating, skillful, and wily; and since their pride goes hand in hand with their duty, they are entirely devoted to the service of their master.

Princes have cause to be on guard against the corruptions and artifices of these spies. The government must watch their moves and be informed of them in time to prevent their dangerous consequences and to hide from the eyes of these lynxes the secrets that prudence forbids from disclosing. But if they are dangerous ordinarily, they are all the more so in proportion to the importance of their negotiation; and princes cannot examine the conduct of their ministers too rigorously, so as to determine if some shower of Danaë might not have mollified their virtue.[1]

During the critical times when treaties and alliances are being negotiated, sovereigns must be more prudent and vigorous than ever. They must be careful to make no promises that they cannot fulfill and must consider treaties from all sides so as to judge whether they are advantageous to the people or just a ploy of other sovereigns. They must, moreover, take the additional precaution of making the terms quite clear. The punctilious grammarian must precede the able politician, so that a fraudulent interpretation of the spirit and wording of the treaty cannot take place. It is sure that great men have never regretted the time that they have given to reflection before entering into any engagement, since they have no cause to repent of it later, or at least have less with which to reproach themselves than if they had made a hasty decision.

Not all negotiations are conducted by accredited ministers. Unofficial persons are often sent to neutral places where they can make proposals without arousing suspicion. The preliminaries of the last peace were concluded in this manner between the emperor and France unbeknownst to the Empire and to the maritime powers. This settlement was made at a count of the Empire's whose lands are on the Rhine.[2]

Victor Amadeus, the most able and cunning prince of his time, had no match anywhere in the art of dissimulating his designs. He misled the world repeatedly with his wiles, such as when Marshal Catinat, in the habit of a monk and under the pretext of working for the salvation of this prince's soul, detached him from the emperor's party and made him a French proselyte. This negotiation, which occurred between them alone, was conducted with so much dexterity that the new alliance between France and Sardinia appeared at that time as an unpredictable and extraordinary event.[3]

I am not advancing this example in order to justify the conduct of Victor Amadeus. My pen is as uncharitable to the trickery of kings as to the disloyalty of private individuals. I simply want to show the advantages of discretion and the profit which may be gained from skill as long as it is not used for anything unworthy and dishonest.

It is thus a general rule that princes must employ the most transcendent minds for these difficult negotiations—men who are not only wily and supple enough to ingratiate themselves, but who can read into eyes for the secret of hearts and judge by the slightest of gestures the secret intentions of others, so that nothing escapes their penetration and the force of their reasoning.

Sovereigns should use wiles and shrewdness only in the manner that a newly invested city uses fireworks: simply to discover the intentions of their enemies. Besides, if they make a sincere profession of integrity, they will infallibly gain the confidence of Europe, they will be happy without trickery, and powerful through their virtue. The peace and happiness of a country is the natural goal of negotiations. It is the center to which all the different political paths must lead.

The tranquillity of Europe is founded primarily upon the maintenance of that wise equilibrium by which the superior force of some sovereigns is counterbalanced by the united forces of other powers. If this equilibrium should fail, it is to be feared that a general revolution would take place and that a new monarchy would be established over the feeble and powerless remains of the disunited princes.

The policy of the princes of Europe thus seems to require them never to lose sight of the negotiations, treaties, and alliances by which they can establish equality between the most

formidable princes and to avoid carefully anything which might
sow vacillation and disunion amongst themselves, which would
sooner or later be mortal. A certain predilection for one nation,
an aversion for another, women's prejudices, private quarrels,
petty interests, minutiae, must never dazzle those who govern
entire peoples. They must aim broadly and sacrifice trifles to
principle without hesitating. Great princes have always
forgotten themselves for the common good, meaning that they
have carefully overcome their preconceptions in order to
embrace their true interests better. The reluctance of Alexander's successors to unite against the Romans is similar to
some people's aversion to being bled, which omission can lead to
a high fever or to vomiting blood, after which most remedies are
no longer effective. Thus impartiality and an unprejudiced spirit
are as necessary in politics as in justice: in the former for
conducting oneself constantly according to the dictates of
wisdom; in the latter for never violating equity.

The world would be a happy place if there were no other
means than negotiation for maintaining justice and for re-
establishing peace among nations. Arguments would be
substituted for arms, and people would debate instead of
slaughter each other. A disturbing necessity obliges princes to
have recourse to a more cruel, ghastly, and odious way. There
are occasions when it is necessary to defend the liberty of a
people by arms against its unjust oppressors, when it is
necessary to obtain by violence what the iniquity of men refuses
to mildness, and when sovereigns—born arbiters of their own
squabbles—can settle them only by matching their forces and
committing their cause to the fate of battle. In such cases the
paradox becomes true that a good war produces a good peace.

Let us examine now on what occasion sovereigns can
undertake wars without having to reproach themselves for
unnecessarily spilling the blood of their subjects out of vanity
and pride.

Of all wars, the most just and indispensable are the defensive
ones, when sovereigns are obliged by the hostility of their
enemies to defend themselves and to resist violence with
violence. The strength of their arms sustains them against the
cupidity of their neighbors and the valor of their troops

guarantees the tranquillity of their subjects; and just as one chases off a thief who is about to rob his house, kings and the great use force in order to compel usurpers to withdraw from their states. The wars of sovereigns for the maintenance of certain disputed rights or pretensions are no less just than the aforementioned ones. Since there is no tribunal superior to kings and no magistrate in the world to judge their disputes, combat decides their rights and judges the validity of their reasons. Sovereigns litigate arms in hand and they oblige, if they can, the envious to give free course to the justice of their cause. It is thus in order to maintain equity and to avoid slavery that such wars are waged, rendering their use sacred and indispensable.

There are some offensive wars which are as just as those that we have just mentioned. These are preventive wars, which princes are wise to undertake when the excessive greatness of the greatest powers of Europe seems about to overflow its banks and engulf the world. One sees a storm brewing which he cannot dispel alone: thus he joins with those who are united by a common danger into a single interest. If the other peoples had united against the Roman power, it could never have overturned so many great empires. A wisely planned alliance and a strenuously undertaken war would have stymied the ambitious designs which enslaved the universe.

Prudence requires that small evils be preferred to greater ones and that one act while he is master. It is thus better to engage in an offensive war when one is free to opt between the olive branch and the laurel wreath than to wait until those desperate times when a declaration of war can only momentarily postpone slavery and ruin. Although this situation may be disturbing for a sovereign, he could do no better than to use his forces before his enemies take the matter out of his hands. Since there are few if any princes who can sustain themselves with their own forces, sovereigns also engage to give each other mutual aid in case of need and to assist each other reciprocally with a stipulated number of troops. It is thus events which determine which of the allies will gather the fruits of the alliance. But since the occasion which favors one of the contracting parties at one time can favor the other in other circumstances, it is wise for princes to observe their treaties scrupulously. This is even in the interest of their peoples, since such alliances render the protection of the sovereigns more efficacious by rendering their power more redoubtable to their enemies.

Thus all wars which are, after rigorous examination, undertaken in order to repulse usurpers, to maintain legitimate rights, to guarantee the liberty of the world, and to avoid the oppression and violence of the ambitious, are in conformity with justice and equity. The sovereigns who undertake them are innocent of any bloodshed, since they are obliged to act and since, under the circumstances, war is less of a misfortune than peace.

This subject leads me naturally to speak of those princes who carry out an infamous traffic in the blood of their peoples. Their troops go to the highest bidder. It is a kind of auction in which whoever offers the highest subsidies to these unworthy sovereigns gets to take their soldiers to the slaughter. These princes should blush at the cowardice with which they sell the lives of men whom they, as fathers of their people, should be protecting. These petty tyrants should listen to the voice of humanity, which detests their cruel abuse of power and judges them unworthy of greater fortune or higher rank.

I have explained myself sufficiently in chapter twenty-one on wars of religion. I merely add here that a sovereign must do what he can to avoid them, or at least that he must prudently change the state of the question so as to diminish the venom, savagery, and cruelty which have always been inseparable from party quarrels and religious squabbles. One could not condemn enough, besides, those criminals who, under the guise of justice and equity, sacrilegiously use the Supreme Being as the instrument of their abominable ambition. It takes an infinite scoundreliness to mislead the public with such flimsy pretexts, and princes should be sufficiently skimpy with the blood of their people not to misuse their valor.

War is so full of misfortune, its outcome is so uncertain, and its consequences so ruinous for a country that sovereigns should think twice before undertaking it. I do not speak of the injustice and violence that they commit against their neighbors, but merely of the misfortunes which redound directly upon their subjects.

I am persuaded that if kings and monarchs could see a true picture of popular misery, they would not be insensitive to it. But they are simply not capable of imagining misfortunes from which they are sheltered by their condition. A sovereign pushed into war by his fiery ambition should be made to see all of the ghastly consequences for his subjects—the taxes which crush the people of a country, the levies which carry away its youth, the contagious diseases of which so many soldiers die miserably, the murderous sieges, the even more cruel battles, the maimed deprived of their sole means of subsistence, and the orphans from whom the enemy has wrested their very flesh and blood, so many useful men to the state cut down before their time! Princes who wage unjust wars are more cruel and cold blooded than any tyrant ever was. They sacrifice to their impetuous passions the well being of an infinity of men whom they are duty bound to protect instead of exposing them so flightily to everything that humanity has most to fear. It is thus certain that princes cannot be too miserly with the lives of their subjects, whom they must view not as their slaves, but as their equals and in some regards as their masters.

I beg of sovereigns, in finishing this work, not to be offended by the liberty with which I speak. My goal is to render homage to truth rather than to flatter, and my good opinion of the princes who now reign in the world makes me judge them worthy to hear it. It is from the Tiberiuses, the Borgias, from monsters and tyrants that it must be hidden because it would shock their crimes and scoundreliness too directly. Thank heaven, we have none among the sovereigns of Europe, but they would be the first to admit that they are not above human weakness, and one can pay them no greater compliment than to be able to condemn before them all the crimes of kings and all that is contrary to justice and humanity.

NOTES

[1] Zeus, in Greek mythology, seduced Danaë by coming to her in a golden shower. See Ovid's *Metamorphoses*, IV: 609–610, 696–697.

² The preliminaries of the Treaty of Vienna, which ended the War of the Polish Succession in 1735. They were negotiated on the estates of the Count von Neuwied.

³ It was the Count de Tessé who traveled in various disguises between Pignerolo and Turin, finally detaching Victor Amadeus from the emperor's party in 1696, but the monk would seem to have been Father Saluzzo, whom Victor Amadeus dispatched secretly to various Italian princes to inform them of his volte-face. Victor Amadeus' reputation for deviousness and the aura of secrecy surrounding this negotiation even in the early eighteenth century are reflected in both Voltaire's (see the *Age of Louis XIV*, Ch. XVII) and Frederick's confusion about it.

Index

165